THE SOCIAL SETTING OF PAULINE CHRISTIANITY

BY THE SAME AUTHOR

Sociology of Early Palestinian Christianity
A Critical Faith: A Case for Religion

Essays on Corinth

THE SOCIAL SETTING OF PAULINE CHRISTIANITY

by

GERD THEISSEN

edited and translated
and with an Introduction by
JOHN H. SCHÜTZ

T&T CLARK
EDINBURGH

Originally published in the USA by
Augsburg Fortresss, 426 S. Fifth St., Box 1209, Minneapolis, MN 55440

This edition published under licence from Augsburg Fortress by
T&T CLARK LTD
59 GEORGE STREET
EDINBURGH EH2 2LQ
SCOTLAND

This book is a translation, with an introduction by John H. Schütz,
of the following essays:

"Legitimation und Lebensunterhalt: Ein Beitrag zur Soziologie urchristlicher Missionaire," in *New Testament Studies* 21 (1975): 192–221,
copyright © by Gerd Theissen.

"Soziale Schichtung in der korinthischen Gemeinde: Ein Beitrag zur Soziologie des hellenistischen Urchristentums," in *Zeitschrift für die neutestamentliche Wissenschaft und die Kunde der älteren Kirche* 65 (1974): 232–72,
copyright © by Gerd Theissen.

"Die Starken und Schwachen in Korinth: Soziologische Analyse eines theologischen Streites," in *Evangelische Theologie* 35 (1975): 155–72,
copyright © by Gerd Theissen.

"Soziale Integration und sakramentales Handeln: Eine Analyse von 1 Cor. 11:17–34," in *Novum Testamentum* 16 (1974): 179–206,
copyright © by Gerd Theissen.

"Die soziologische Auswertung religiöser Überlieferungen: Ihre methodologischen Probleme am Beispiel des Urchristentums," in *Kairos* 17 (1975): 284–99,
copyright © by Gerd Theissen.

First published 1982
Latest impression 1996

ISBN 0 567 29183 9

British Library Cataloguing-in-Publication Data
Theissen, Gerd
The social setting of Pauline Christianity.
1. Christian church, to ca 200 – Sociological perspectives
I. Title II. Schütz, John H., John Howard
306.6

Printed and bound in Great Britain by the Cromwell Press, Melksham

Contents

Editor's Preface ix

Abbreviations xi

Introduction 1
John H. Schütz

A Bibliography of the Major Works of Gerd Theissen 25

1. Legitimation and Subsistence: An Essay on the Sociology of Early Christian Missionaries 27

Itinerant Charismatics 28

Socio-political Factors 29
Socio-economic Factors 30
Socio-ecological Factors 31
Socio-cultural Factors 32

The Community Organizers 35

Socio-political Factors 36
Socio-economic Factors 36
Socio-ecological Factors 38
Socio-cultural Factors 39

The Conflict Between Itinerant Charismatics and Community Organizers 40

Charismatic Legitimation 42
Traditional Legitimation 49
Functional Legitimation 51

EXCURSUS: On the Sociological Structure of the Corinthian Parties 54

2. Social Stratification in the Corinthian Community: A Contribution to the Sociology of Early Hellenistic Christianity 69

The Sociological Evaluation of Evidence for the Corinthian Congregation 70

Statements About the Community as a Whole 70
Statements About Individual Members of the Congregation 73
References to Offices 73
References to Houses 83
References to Services Rendered 87
References to Travel 91
Statements About Divisions Within Corinth 96

The Sociological Interpretation of the Evidence 99
The Social Structure of the City of Corinth 99
Social Conditions of the Pauline Mission 102

3. The Strong and the Weak in Corinth: A Sociological Analysis of a Theological Quarrel 121

Socio-cultural Factors 123

Socio-economic Factors 124

Class-specific Characteristics in Eating Habits 125
Signs of Stratification Within Patterns of Sociability 129
Class-specific Traits in the Forms of Legitimation 132
Class-specific Traits in the Forms of Communication 137

4. Social Integration and Sacramental Activity: An Analysis of 1 Cor. 11:17–34 145

The Social Conditions of the Conflict in 1 Cor. 11:17–34 147

Different Groups at the Lord's Supper 147
Variable Beginnings for the Meal 151
Different Amounts of Food and Drink 153
Meals of Different Quality 155

The Social Intentions of 1 Cor. 11:17–34 163

5. The Sociological Interpretation of Religious Traditions: Its Methodological Problems as Exemplified in Early Christianity 175

Constructive Methods 177

The Problem of Reliability 178
The Problem of Validity 179
The Problem of Representativeness 179

Analytic Methods 180

Inferences from Events 181
Inferences from Norms 182
Inferences from Symbols 187

Comparative Procedures 192

Bibliography 201

Editor's Preface

The decision to translate these essays grew out of the Seminar on the Social World of Early Christianity, a joint venture of the Society of Biblical Literature and the American Academy of Religion. I am happy to offer the translations as an expression of thanks to both learned societies for making available such a forum in recent years.

Among Gerd Theissen's many essays dealing with the social world of early Christianity, those on Corinth make a natural grouping. They comprise an internally coherent effort to understand the Pauline community in that city, while also representing concerns and perspectives to be found in his other writings as well. I have taken the liberty of arranging the four essays on Corinth in what seems to me their most logical sequence rather than in the order of their original publication. Internal cross-references, largely confined to the notes, have been retained as originally written. My reasons for including the final essay, with its attention to procedural and methodological matters, are stated briefly in the Introduction.

Quotations from ancient authors are rendered in accordance with standard English translations wherever these are available, and with the Loeb Classical Library whenever possible. If no standard translation lies at hand, then I have provided my own. Except where noted, quotations from the Bible are in the Revised Standard Version.

The University of North Carolina at Chapel Hill supported this project in a variety of ways. I am grateful for a Kenan leave of absence in 1979, some of which I used for this translation. I have also used a portion of a subsequent grant from the University Research Council to defray some expenses connected with the project. I would like to thank the council, and also the Institute for Research in the Social Sciences which, as always, generously made available its facilities. My thanks also to Professor Ruel W. Tyson, Jr., then chairman of the Department of Religion, for providing research assistants whose duties included this project. Dale Allison rendered both the notes and bibliography appropriate for English readers; Teresa Smith provided editorial consistency to the whole book; and Greg Robbins attended to the final details of a finished manuscript. They have my gratitude for that, and for all their typing through successive drafts. I am also grateful to my colleague Peter Kaufman for reading and commenting on an earlier version of the introductory essay, and to William C. West III, for improving considerably my translation of Aristides.

Finally, a word of thanks to Wayne Meeks for his enthusiastic support of the project from its inception, and to Professor Theissen himself, who has been prompt and courteous in responding to my queries and very patient in the face of delays neither of us anticipated.

Chapel Hill, N.C.

JOHN H. SCHÜTZ

Abbreviations

(All abbreviations in this book correspond with or are modeled on those in Siegfried Schwertner, *Internationales Abkürzungsverzeichnis für Theologie und Grenzgebiete = IATG.)*

AAWG.PH	Abhandlungen der Akademie der Wissenschaften in Göttingen—Philologisch-historische Klasse
AAWLM.G	Abhandlungen der Akademie der Wissenschaften und der Literatur in Mainz—Geistes- und sozialwissenschaftliche Klasse.
BA	*Biblical Archaeologist*
BCH	*Bulletin de correspondance hellénique*
BEvTh	Beiträge zur evangelischen Theologie
BHTh	Beiträge zur historischen Theologie
Bib.	*Biblica*
BJRL	*Bulletin of the John Rylands Library*
BrM	*The Collection of Ancient Greek Inscriptions in the British Museum*
BSt (F)	Biblische Studien. Freiburg
CIG	*Corpus inscriptionum Graecarum*
CIJ	*Corpus inscriptionum Judaicarum*
CIL	*Corpus inscriptionum Latinarum*
CSRB	*Council on the Study of Religion. Bulletin*

EvTh	*Evangelische Theologie*
ET	*Expository Times*
FGH	*Fragmente der griechischen Historiker*
Gn.	*Gnomon*
HAW	Handbuch der Altertumswissenschaft
HNT	Handbuch zum Neuen Testament
HR	*History of Religions*
HThR	*Harvard Theological Review*
HZ	*Historische Zeitschrift*
IEJ	*Israel Exploration Journal*
IG	*Inscriptiones Graecae*
IGRR	*Inscriptiones Graecae ad res Romanas pertinentes*
ILS	*Inscriptiones Latinae selectae*
JAC	Jahrbuch für Antike und Christentum
JAAR	*Journal of the American Academy of Religion*
JBL	*Journal of Biblical Literature*
JRH	*Journal of Religious History*
JRS	*Journal of Roman Studies*
JThS	*Journal of Theological Studies*
Jud.	*Judaica*
Kont.	*Kontexte*
KuD	*Kerygma und Dogma*
MAMA	Monumenta Asiae minoris antiqua
Mn.	*Mnemosyne*
NT	*Novum Testamentum*
NTS	*New Testament Studies*
Numen	*Numen*
NZSTh	*Neue Zeitschrift für systematische Theologie (1963 ff.:) und Religionsphilosophie*
OGIS	*Orientis Graecae inscriptiones selectae*
P.Oxy.	*The Oxyrhynchus Papyri*
Ph.	*Philologus*

Ph.S	*Philologus—Suppl.Bd.*
PRE	Paulys *Real-Encyclopädie der classischen Alterthumswissenschaft*
PRE. Suppl.	Paulys *Real-Encyclopädie der classischen Alterthumswissenschaft*—Supplement
RGG	*Die Religion in Geschichte und Gegenwart*
RelStR	*Religious Studies Review*
RHPhR	*Revue d'histoire et de philosophie religieuses*
RSR	*Recherches de science religieuse*
SBT	Studies in Biblical Theology
SHAW.PH	Sitzungsberichte der Heidelberger Akademie der Wissenschaften—Philosophisch-historische Klasse
SHT	Studies in Historical Theology
SIG	*Sylloge Inscriptionum Graecarum*
SJ	Studia Judaica
StANT	Studien zum Alten und Neuen Testament
StNT	Studien zum Neuen Testament
TEH	Theologische Existenz heute
ThLZ	*Theologische Literaturzeitung*
ThR	*Theologische Rundschau*
ThStKr	*Theologische Studien und Kritiken*
ThZ	*Theologische Zeitschrift*
TU	Texte und Untersuchungen zur Geschichte der altchristlichen Literatur
WMANT	Wissenschaftliche Monographien zum Alten und Neuen Testament
WPKG	*Wissenschaft und Praxis in Kirche und Gesellschaft*
WUNT	Wissenschaftliche Untersuchungen zum Neuen Testament
ZNW	*Zeitschrift für die neutestamentliche Wissenschaft* (21, 1922ff.:) *und die Kunde der älteren Kirche*
ZThK	*Zeitschrift für Theologie und Kirche*
ZWTh	*Zeitschrift für wissenschaftliche Theologie*

Introduction

JOHN H. SCHÜTZ

Recent investigation of the documents of the New Testament has stressed the social matrix out of which these documents arose. This is not without precedent, but the varied perspectives now being pursued constitute a new emphasis in the critical interpretation of the New Testament. The emphasis is not viewed everywhere with unrestrained enthusiasm, nor does it appear thus far to have developed a controlling orthodoxy of method or intent.

One sign of the fluid situation in such studies is the varied terminology used to describe what is being attempted. Some scholars conceive of the ultimate goal as nothing less than the "sociology of early Christianity." Others speak instead of achieving a clearer "social description" of primitive Christianity, with the accent falling on new insights into the social realities which helped shape it. In other instances the preferred term is "social world," a more specialized concept which is drawn from the sociology of knowledge and refers to the construction of a symbolic communal perception of reality. There is a similar lack of agreement about basic procedures. Some scholars are eager to exploit the theoretical views of sociology and interpretive models from across the range of social sciences, particularly as these have been developed by people working in cross-cultural studies. Others appear to have the appetite of more traditional historians. Their interest in the social and economic data within the texts parallels the interest of many contemporary historians working in diverse fields.

Clearly, it is early to attempt a critical sorting out of the various issues and approaches reflected in this emerging scholarly concern with the "social world of early Christianity." Nevertheless, several useful statements are available which help focus the discussion to date, review the scope of various efforts, or make suggestions about procedures and terminology.[1]

In the meantime, as the serious body of interesting and innovative work accumulates, much of it comes from the hand of Gerd Theissen. A young scholar who studied with Philip Vielhauer, Theissen writes prolifically and perceptively about the social world of early Christianity.[2] His work is marked by bold hypothesis balanced with exegetical insight and patience for detail. Some of these qualities have already become evident to readers of English through an earlier translation, *Sociology of Early Palestinian Christianity*.[3] Yet his most formidable and sustained contributions to the study of the social background of earliest Christianity are to be found in other essays. Four of these dealing with Corinth and Paul's correspondence with that Christian community are offered here. When taken together they provide a composite picture of social stratification in one Pauline community and the concrete organizational and ethical problems it engendered for the common life of Christians in an urban center.

Brought together in a book, these essays comprise a coherent exegetical selection and offer a detailed view of Theissen's innovative interpretation of the New Testament. To them has been added a fifth essay, "The Sociological Interpretation of Religious Traditions: Its Methodological Problems as Exemplified in Early Christianity." One of two major statements Theissen has made on basic methodological matters,[4] it addresses in systematic fashion the key interpretive issue raised by the other four essays: How does one read ancient religious texts for information on issues which are, by standards internal to the texts, of peripheral concern at best? Theissen's observations are centered on the specific difficulties posed by *religious* texts, but they are no less appropriate for any ancient historian who seeks to understand social background on the basis of textual evidence. This more theoretical statement also allows the reader to compare Theissen's professed notions of procedure with his own practice. Tracing out the relationship between prescriptions and exegesis adds an element of vitality to both.

I

Whether one should stress the continuity or the discontinuity between current interest in the social world of early Christianity and the work of earlier scholarship may be but a matter of choice. A case can be made that the issue was posed by Paul himself in 1 Cor. 1:26, to be picked up by Celsus' remarks about the scruffy background of the Christians and by Origen's reply, which was based on that Pauline text. Others would argue to the contrary, that the current coalescence of so much interest in the "sociology of early Christianity" is fundamentally different from anything in the past. Either way, a brief look at the recent past would seem helpful.

The "social factor" of history, to use a term against which J. H. Hexter has amply warned us, has always been, as Hexter points out, an ingredient in the stuff of history. For that reason historical method and research will often entail social data and questions. This is true whatever the larger differences, even antitheses, between history and sociology. Theissen's concluding essay grapples with these similarities and differences. Among the latter would have to be mentioned the sociologist's primary interest in groups and collectivities, in the normal pattern of behavior, in structural homologies. All of these stand in contrast to the historian's interest in the unique, the individual, the element of change and difference. Yet the dividing line is not clear and unequivocal. Theoretical literature on the problem[5] demonstrates this fact; so does the record of earlier efforts to thrust to the foreground the social dimension of early Christianity.

A number of these attempts have drawn only imperceptibly, if at all, on explicit social theory, remaining instead well within the province of the historian's traditional concerns. Nevertheless, they have had a significant impact on the way this social setting is perceived. Adolf Deissmann offers one clear example.[6] A lexicographer, Deissmann seized upon the flood of papyri discoveries made at the turn of the century to help clarify two difficult problems. The first of these concerned the nature of the Greek which is used in the New Testament. That it had a certain distinctive cast was evident, leading some interpreters to assume that the Holy Spirit used a special Greek otherwise unknown. Armed with abundant evidence from the papyri, Deissmann could declare that "the New Testament has been proved to be, as a whole, a monument of late colloquial Greek, and in the great majority of its component parts the monument of a more or less *popular* colloquial language."[7] This would mean that in its creative period Christianity was a nonliterary movement. More than that, it suggests that we can speak confidently, if only generally, about the social classes from which were drawn the earliest recruits to Christianity. The vast bulk of the papyri and ostraca provide "evidence of the middle and lower classes, in countless depositions made by themselves, and in most cases recognisable at once as such by their contents or the peculiarity of their language. These are records of the people's speech, records of the insignificant affairs of insignificant persons. Peasants and artisans, soldiers and slaves and mothers belonging to the common people speak to us of their cares and labours." Such records "place us in the midst of the classes in which we have to think of the apostle Paul and the early Christians gathering recruits."[8]

Neither of Deissmann's two propositions has gone unchallenged, and his somewhat romantic vision of the lower social origins of most early Christians has yielded to further investigation. From the linguistic side it has been rendered problematic by more recent analysis of the role played in the New Testament by professional prose. This nonliterary and nonclassical style of expository writing was used by professional people who learned their Greek in schools and wished to communicate facts. The presence of such a prose style in the New Testament, in contrast to Deissmann's emphasis on a vernacular style, suggests a correspondingly higher social and economic status for at least some New Testament authors.[9]

Such a view agrees with other recent studies which do not focus on the problem of language but instead confront the problem of social classes. E. A. Judge has canvassed the evidence for early Christians in such diverse locations as Jerusalem, Antioch, and Corinth, concluding that they represent a diverse mixture with clear contributions from those who are relatively well off.[10] His judgment about Corinth could even be taken as the text which Theissen, in the essays in this volume, unfolds in greater detail: "Far from being a socially depressed group, then, if the Corinthians are at all typical, the Christians were dominated by a socially pretentious section of the population of the big cities. Beyond that, they seem to have drawn on a broad constituency, probably representing the household dependents of the leading members."[11] Elsewhere Judge has extended the implications of this reassessment which places early Christianity more clearly in the mainstream of its culture,[12] while A. J. Malherbe has carried parallel studies even further.[13]

Deissmann's *Light from the Ancient East* seems entirely innocent of formal commitments to social theory or ideology. Nevertheless, it is amply furnished with casual asides about mistaken fashions in biblical scholarship, directed particularly to the scholarly presumption that learned theological discourse was the central concern of biblical writers, as it was, of course, of the scholars themselves. A similar disdain for the primacy of theology was expressed somewhat later by Shirley Jackson Case, whose name is permanently linked with the "Chicago school," sometimes described as the only truly indigenous strand of American New Testament scholarship. His view, that theological concerns represented an unfortunate bias which masked the evidence for "religion" in the New Testament, was not the only similarity between the two men. Like Deissmann, Case worked with no very clearly articulated notions of social theory, groups, institutions, roles, or functions. In Deissmann's case this lacuna mattered little since he could claim that his conclusions followed from the linguistic evidence he set out to examine. In the instance of Case, the problem was greater, for he began with nothing other than the express intent of determining Christianity's social origins.

Case began his *Social Origins of Christianity* with reflections on why it had taken New Testament scholars so long to come to terms with the "comprehensive and fundamental matter of social experience as a key to the understanding of the genesis and early history of the Christian Movement."[14] In his opening chapter, entitled

"The 'New' New Testament Study," he sought to locate his interests within the larger history of scholarship, suggesting what he considered the difficulties to be. First, interest in the early Christian movement and the whole of its literature had always been subordinated to narrower interest in the New Testament as such. Furthermore, this focus had been dominated by a Protestant biblicism inherited from the Reformers and perfected through centuries to the point that it had become a "machine . . . mechanically perfect in its structure." Case felt that the development of an alternative historical-critical approach, as impressive as it was when it finally came, nevertheless failed to shift focus sufficiently to the central point. "Back of the literature stand the persons who were responsible for its rise, and these individuals in turn were members of Christian groups closely bound up with the interests of the Christian society. The various New Testament books were written to serve the Christian cause, and it was amid the activities of the communities as going concerns that the documents were preserved and finally assembled into a canon. . . . Instead of concentrating exclusively upon the New Testament documents, one presses inquiry on to the more remote Christian society within which the writings arose and were finally assembled into a collection to be used for purposes of propaganda and control. The attempt to reexamine the New Testament in the light of this social setting carries interpretation on to the most recent phase in its history."[15]

In retrospect Case's program seems more impressive for its intentions than for its accomplishments. Like Deissmann, he played "religion" off against "theology" without offering any very clear idea of what constituted the difference. Theological ideas were out, but religious ideas, of a very general sort, were often taken to be the motivating forces in Christian behavior. The chief difference was that religious ideas were expressions of response to felt need, while theological ideas were regarded as mere abstractions. This reveals a sturdy reliance on a general functionalist approach to religious behavior which stresses the momentary value of any action or thought. To this was wed an implicit evolutionism and an oft-stated preference for empirical fact over theoretical speculation. Case offered New Testament scholarship a clear and interesting point for departure into new areas. Yet a recent judgment also seems appropriate: "Case did not really analyze sociologically the groups and communities which composed early Christianity, but, relying on his functional view of religion, was apparently content to generalize on the basis of ideas and social aspects of the Graeco-Roman world."[16]

It is a curious feature of Case's work that he did not perceive the implications of his one suggestion about a close connection between social experience within communities and the literary products which make up the New Testament and later Christian literature. This is all the more surprising since he published *Social Origins* after Martin Dibelius and Rudolf Bultmann had set forth their pioneering studies in form criticism. One searches in vain for any evidence of contact with that new formal procedure which was, at least in theory, to emphasize the social setting of New Testament literary forms.

Others, however, quickly saw the unusual dimension offered by form criticism's sociological orientation. Oscar Cullmann went so far as to say that one's attitude toward this element determined whether the method was viewed negatively or positively, since this new sociological interest entailed a shift away from the more traditional concern with individual authors. Cullmann was skeptical that the sociological underpinnings were secure and called for the development of a kind of sociology capable of studying the norms governing the growth of popular traditions.[17]

What Cullmann called for never quite materialized, and to that extent form criticism failed to fulfill its own promise. Dibelius' work displays a strong interest in the social setting out of which arise specific patterns of tradition.[18] Yet that interest remains very general. Most examples are traced to a putative setting in worship without further specification or differentiation. Bultmann's contribution paid even less attention to the social setting of traditions, yet because of his greater analytical rigor, Bultmann emerged as the primary form-critical authority.[19] Thus the statement of G. Iber that "the viewpoint of so-called form criticism, unlike literary criticism, does not inquire after the personalities which have written this or that document, but speaks instead of the congregation from the total life of which is shaped the early Christian literature, and especially the gospel literature," is more appropriate as an expression of intent than as an assessment of accomplishment.[20]

There are at least three reasons for this failure to carry through on a crucial matter. First, form criticism came upon the horizon almost simultaneously with the new wave of dialectical theology inaugurated by Barth. That theological stance proved an irresistible challenge and invitation to New Testament criticism to let theological matters set the examination questions to which it would respond. Second, one of the most powerful voices in form criticism, Bultmann, insisted that kerygma as a theological category was not to be identified with kerygma as literary tradition. This surely dampened the potential enthusiasm for pursuing rigorous historical questions of setting (as distinct from literary questions) in tracing the earliest traditions. In a climate dominated by questions of the theological intent of kerygma, the matter of its origins turns out to have little to do with its theological significance.

The third and most significant reason has to do with the intellectual roots of form criticism and its prior development within Old Testament studies. At the heart of form criticism as Hermann Gunkel conceived and explicated it was an understanding of the relationship of a *Gattung* to some element within the structure of life of a people. This notion of the life of a *Volk*, with its antecedents in J. G. Herder and its emphasis on an implicit contrast between what is literary and what is *volkstümlich*, could be applied rather easily to the people of the Old Testament. Here too was an organized community with observable ethnic and geographic boundaries spanning a long history throughout which it gradually developed institutions of various sorts—not just religious institutions, but those of a social and economic nature as well. Old Testament form criticism could presuppose what the idea of *volkstümlich* demanded, an entire cultural world stretched over a long period of time.

The transfer of this assumption, along with the critical method, to the world of the New Testament was bound to be problematic. The New Testament world was not a total culture but represented the rise of a new religion within an existing cultural setting. The setting was a mixture of a religious base in Judaism, a political base in the Roman Empire, and an ethnic base in whatever variety of ethnic customs persisted within the rather elastic framework of Roman provincial life. The setting was independent in the sense that not one of the institutions from this cultural potpourri was the creation of the Christian community which lived in such a world. Instead, that community had to meet each such institution and adjust to it in whatever way seemed proper. Some of these institutions could be exploited, up to a point. From the perspective of Acts and Paul, that seems to be the case with the Jewish synagogue and the Roman citizenship. Others seemed to offer no promise, or even appeared useless. Paul's attitude toward litigation comes to mind. Yet others were thought useful if not theologically significant. Again, Paul provides an example in his attitude toward marriage. In all these cases, however, the institutions are there regardless of the Christian response to them, whether that be positive or negative. Such institutions may shape early Christian tradition, but they do not generate it.

As for the passage of time, the disparity between the centuries available as a presupposition for Old Testament form criticism and the few decades available to New Testament form criticism presents obvious problems. Consequently, New Testament form criticism has not really been able to take seriously the idea of the development of forms or their persistence through change within the boundaries of a single community. Instead, it has substituted content for form often enough, or it has substituted the discontinuities of discrete cultural settings for the discontinuity of long historical periods of change: Jesus versus the early church, Galilee versus Jerusalem, Syria versus Asia Minor or Greece, Hellenistic Christian versus Jewish Christian, and so on. But that terminology brings us back to the first point: Christianity did not have many institutions in its earliest phase which were of its own devising. Like the cuckoo, it deposited its eggs in a nest of another's making.

These and other efforts[21] to shed light on the social and economic elements within early Christianity come from within biblical scholarship, where they have had to jostle for a place at the table with older and stronger siblings, especially the interpretive interests of theology.[22] This fact may explain the trace of a combative tone by which a Deissmann or Case seeks to set his work apart, but it also means that concern for the social background of New Testament Christianity is not simply a recent interest. Indeed, the sociological interest latent in form criticism makes it apparent that current attention to social questions is but continuous with the recent past of biblical scholarship.

When we turn outside the scholarly guild of biblical study we find only one more or less persistent impetus to the study of earliest Christianity as a social phenomenon, and that is Marxism. Its best-known representative was Karl Kautsky, whose book *The Foundations of Christianity*[23] began with the assumption that the modern proletarian mind would recognize truths in the history of the Christian movement masked to its bourgeois interpreters.[24] Kautsky regarded the earliest Christian movement as something rooted in the revolutionary messianism of Jesus and capable of exciting an anti-Roman proletarian following. There is little direct evidence for such a view within the New Testament. Kautsky explained this by appealing to the rapid development of the movement. Thrusting itself quickly into a vastly different world, Christianity soon betrayed its true beginnings. Kautsky still found some traces of proletarian origins in the New Testament, as in references to the early practice of communal goods in Acts, but that testimony grew fainter as the community spread its gospel to the educated of the middle and higher classes. This shift, Kautsky maintained, was accompanied by a parallel shift from parochial and closed oral traditions to written records which were themselves a product of the newfound class orientation. Thus, one must look behind the written New Testament to find its actual birth in a rural society marked by oppression, class conflict, and political resentment, all of which motivated the original teaching of Jesus as well as its earliest acceptance.

What is perhaps most curious about this and other efforts to read the New Testament through the lens of historical materialism[25] is the emphasis placed on the *nonproletarian* origin of so much of the New Testament. This observation laid the groundwork for taking seriously the variety of social classes and economic interests involved with the early church. Summarizing his reading of Paul's letters, Archibald Robertson states the matter clearly:

> Enough has been said to show that Pauline Christianity as reflected in the epistles was not a movement of the disinherited classes. Paul himself was a master-craftsman and a Roman citizen, and explicitly repudiated resistance to the Roman Empire. Though most of his converts were poor, the live wires of the Pauline churches were householders like Gaius and Stephanas of Corinth, Erastus "the treasurer of the city," Paul's fellow craftsman Aquila and the slave-owner Philemon—men perhaps not "wise after the flesh" or "mighty" or "noble," but at least of the middle class and middling education, ranging from small propertyowners to artisans in direct contact with the masses. We shall find, so far as the evidence goes, that the same is true of those who continued Paul's work.[26]

II

What Robertson gleaned from the surface of Paul's letters Theissen has now grounded in a wealth of detailed exegesis. More than that, Theissen conceives of this world of the Pauline mission as one coherent movement within early Christianity which contrasts sharply with the world of the Palestinian followers of Jesus. Paul's missionary arena is dominated by this economically self-sufficient figure whose primary role is that of the community organizer. His dominant ethic is "love-patriarchalism" (*Liebespatriarchalismus*), an integrative ethic which does not champion a particular social or economic status and does not seek to challenge the forces which lead to economic or social stratification. Love-patriarchalism advocates transcending such distinctions within the framework of a religious community which generates mutual respect and love.

In his *Sociology of Early Palestinian Christianity* and elsewhere,[27] Theissen has described another wing of earliest Christianity, the Jesus movement, which comes from a vastly different social world. This is the world of the "itinerant charismatic" beggar whose voluntary acceptance of poverty is rooted in the Jesus tradition and suited to his social, economic, and cultural surroundings.

The setting for the Jesus movement is rural Palestine, an area which in this period spawned so many efforts at Jewish reform. The politics of Palestine at the time of Jesus reveal stresses between

Western, Roman influences and indigenous political forces, between Hellenistic urban civilization and theocratic movements arranging themselves on a scale from the most politically active (the Zealots) to the most quietistic (the Jesus movement). All share a passionate hope for the establishment of God's sovereignty. They also share a sense of economic repression and show hostility to the economic status quo in one way or another. In the Jesus movement of itinerant radicals this hostility is expressed as a sharp criticism of property and riches, but according to Theissen it would be wrong to assume that this message was attractive only to those who were materially dispossessed. "Among the desperadoes of every age can be found the sons of 'better' families," evident in this instance from the fact that Zebedee, the father of James and John, can hire day labor (Mk. 1:20).

The Christian radical movement which arises in response to Jesus' ministry sends out beggar-missionaries who offer preaching in return for food and lodging. These are the curators of the Jesus movement. Their world is the settled village area of Palestine, just as Qumran is the world of the Essenes and the mountain hideouts the world of the Zealots. Jesus' parables describe this world, with its small villages so close together that if one "city" rejects the missionaries they can still go to another before day ends (Lk. 10:8–9).

Expressed culturally, the goal of Palestinian movements born of these circumstances—the Pharisees, the Zealots, the Essenes, the Jesus movement—was to provide a suitable identity for Judea under political restraints and in the face of powerful alien influences. At the heart of this common effort lies the "law," a central motif shared by various groups which differ greatly among themselves on the issue of its scope and interpretation. Such an emphasis on law leads to its being conceptually sharpened, now one way and now another. Such different views of the law come to differentiate the groups themselves, leading to further fragmentation and division on the socio-religious scene.

Unlike other groups, the Jesus movement sharpens the idea of law by stressing the solidarity of all those who find themselves excluded by the legal ideology of the other groups. By doing so it opposes all of them and is opposed by them. The Jesus movement puts forward a radical notion of trust in God. This is reflected in the trust shown by its missionaries who survive on the voluntary support offered by their hearers in return for the message. In this way they emulate Jesus and his disciples. What emerges is not the community organizer but the quite different figure of the charismatic beggar, one who appeals to popular piety about the poor as those who are religiously favored.

Seen through the work of these itinerant, economically "irrational" preachers, the message of this movement may be summarized as reflecting an ethos of homelessness, alienation from family and social units, and criticism of wealth and property. Its christology follows the pattern not of the Messiah or Son of God, but of the Son of man—suffering, homeless, but finally ascendent. Between the Son of man and his missionaries there is a dependent-independent relationship in which the Holy Spirit provides a crucial link. The Spirit brings prophetic insight to the charismatics, making it possible for them to distinguish their role from the Son of man's and even place theirs above his (cf. Mt. 12:32 and on it Didache 11:7). Theissen's reading obviously does not settle the issue of the authenticity of the synoptic sayings of Jesus, but he does declare himself opposed to the critical notion that a saying at home in some post-Easter setting must, on principle, be excluded from what may be regarded as authentic.[28]

By comparison with this Palestinian Jesus movement, Paul's world is vastly different. Here the sayings of Jesus matter little and the kingdom of God is not a central metaphor. The direction of christology is not from the bottom up (the ascending Son of man) but from the top down (the willing humiliation of the heavenly Redeemer). Politically, this is a world of cities, integrated urban centers benefiting sufficiently from their status to offer little encouragement to the growth of true political dissension.

In this more integrated world Paul is the "integrated" and "rational" man. He understand these large cultural centers among which he travels. He can use Greek, the tool which makes them accessible. From our information it appears that he avoids the more rural areas along the way where language barriers would present a greater problem. His ability to support himself as an artisan in various settings renders him mobile in a way that fishermen and farmers are not. Moreover, he is capable of the planning and organization required by this social setting, where one cannot live from day to day on the generosity of alms or by gleaning a handful of wheat while passing through a field. The distances involved require money, travel, and communication on a scale hardly compatible with the background of poor Galileans.

In four of the essays presented in this book Theissen focuses on Corinth as an example of this urban, Roman world as it lends social configuration to a Christian community. The Corinthian church is diverse, stratified, and divided at a number of points. Those divisions which Theissen singles out for particular scrutiny—the Lord's Supper, eating meat sacrificed to idols, the support of itinerant missionaries and of Paul himself—are not simply the result of theological differences. They point back to the different social and economic worlds from which the members of the Corinthian church come. There is no equivalent to this pluralism and diversity evident within the Jesus movement, and so it comes as no surprise that the radical ethic of that movement is ill-suited to the Pauline situation.

The way Paul deals with the social and economic differences in Corinth suggests that his goal is not a simple reformation of the existing social order. Instead, he offers the vision of transcending it, the prospect of transposing social and economic diversity to a new and more fundamental plane. This may in part be due simply to the fact that in a church comprised of both wealthy and poor, Paul must champion the view of the poor while also relying on the resources of the wealthy. Theissen, however, suggests that beyond this is a characteristic Pauline ethic of love-patriarchalism. The term is adapted from Troeltsch's "patriarchalism" and for Theissen stands in contrast with the ethical radicalism he finds more characteristic of the Palestinian setting. Troeltsch found the model of this patriarchal vision in the "family," that is, the structured form of differentiated roles and status. The religious ingredient in patriarchalism is "love," which reduces friction within the differentiated structure. According to Troeltsch, patriarchalism's

> basic idea of the willing acceptance of given inequalities, and of making them fruitful for the ethical values of personal relationships, is given. All action is the service of God and is a responsible office, authority as well as obedience. As stewards of God the great must care for the small, and as servants of God the little ones must submit to those who bear authority; and since in so doing both meet in the service of God, inner religious equality is affirmed and the ethical possession is enlarged by the exercise of the tender virtues of responsibility for and of trustful surrender to each other. It is undeniable that this ideal is perceived dimly by Paul, and only by means of this ideal does he desire to alter given conditions from within outwards, without touching their external aspect at all.[29]

Love-patriarchalism is a fundamental Pauline ethical stance which seeks integration at the level of the religious sphere when the apostle faces divisions arising from the social order.

III

The themes of conflict at Corinth and Paul's attempts at integration sound familiar enough to the student of the New Testament. Identification of the Corinthian "opponents" of Paul, and their own internal "divisions," have long been on the list of problems requiring an explanation. To a student of sociology, however, terms like "conflict" and "integration" have a more specialized meaning and carry theoretical or methodological connotations. Since Theissen himself sees the Corinthian conflicts as rooted in social and economic realities, it is fair to ask to what extent his work is informed by sociological theory or is indebted to particular views of the nature of social reality.

There is nothing elaborate or studied about the role of sociological theory or conceptual models in the following essays, or in most of Theissen's work.[30] Matters of that sort are kept to a minimum. It would seem fair to characterize his interests as more those of the social historian than those of the sociologist. More specifically, the value of theory is measured for Theissen by its capacity to contribute to the analysis of early Christianity, "to bring discrete data which are sociologically relevant into a systematic relationship or to construct relationships which can be tested by such data."[31]

Just beneath the surface of these studies, however, lies a basic concern for a general critical theory of religion which will also be responsive to the historian's perception of religious data,[32] a continuing quest toward which all of his studies make some contribution. Among three very basic forms of critical theory—phenomenological analysis, reductionistic analysis, and functional analysis—he chooses the third. A phenomenological analysis of religion proceeds from the self-understanding or "intention" of religious phenomena. Because it assumes that the reality of religion is distinctive, the tie between such reality and the social matrix in which it lives is cut, and despite the institutional forms of religious life, religion "at its core is inaccessible to sociological analysis." At the other extreme is the causal-genetic approach, which denies the distinctive intentionality of religious phenomena and traces them all back to nonreligious factors. Insofar as such an approach makes a claim to discern the true content and social significance of religion it may be called a reductionistic theory. In classic form this is true of "the orthodox variants of a Marxist theory of religion."

"Functionalism" mediates between these two positions, taking seriously the intentionality of religious phenomena but interpreting them with reference to their contribution to the solution of basic social problems. One of its chief advantages is that it can account for specificity in religious traditions and need not deal only with high levels of abstraction; at the same time it can also account for change and development. For Theissen's view of early Christianity this means that such an approach offers the best prospects for explaining how the earliest movement which arose in Palestine could survive and thrive—"be functional"—in utterly different surroundings.

The centerpiece at the functionalist's table is some kind of basic distinction between "conscious *motivations* for social behavior and its objective *consequences*,"[33] and the assumption that these are not necessarily the same. The former is subjective, conscious, intentional; the latter is actual and objective (if not always easily recognized), but not intentional. This distinction is widely known as the difference between manifest and latent functions,[34] but Theissen uses the terminology of "subjective intention" and "objective function." "The objective function of a religious phenomenon is seldom identical with its intention, even though it be mediated through human intentions. To a much greater extent it is to be sought in the unintended consequences of religious intentions."[35] The view has undeniable advantages for a historian seeking to deal with sociological issues. It offers a rough parallel to that basic distinction between the historian's concern for what is individual and unique and the sociologist's concern with typical and collective behavior. Functionalism, therefore, has the advantage of integrating what is important in other theories of religion, both the phenomenological and the causal-genetic, while it also offers the best prospects of integrating the proper but different interests of history and sociology.

In Theissen's view, functionalism concentrates on whatever "serves basic needs within a discrete social frame of reference." Among all social manifestations, only those which are socially effective are of interest or truly functional, an opinion which also registers his hesitancy to commit himself to a wider or more comprehensive scope of theory than is necessary to undertake the task at hand. It is important, however, to understand the "social frame of reference," the broader whole or context apart from which any reference to the function of specific actions, ideas, or symbols would make no sense. For early Christianity the broadest social frame of reference is the society of imperial Rome, but there are also narrower frames which can be used as the point of departure: Palestinian society, for example, or the Christian communities themselves. Within the frame of reference emphasis falls on serving "social needs," which Theissen typologizes as of two fundamental types, the production of order and the control of conflict. These polar opposites are not regarded as mutually exclusive virtues (or vices), as if viewed from an ideological presumption of what the social frame should be like. Instead, they are regarded as two ends of a continuum along which all actual social organisms seek an accommodation or balance of forces.

To the ideas of conflict and integration Theissen adds another axis marked at one end by the creative function of religion and at the other by its restrictive function. This yields a grid of theoretical perspectives on religion on which he is able to locate most of the classical theories, and by means of which he can underline the centrality of the functionalist approach,[36] thus underscoring his overarching concern for the development of a critical theory of religion.

Our concern, however, is with the role of sociological theory and social concepts in Theissen's work, to which we were brought originally by his use of the terms "conflict" and "integration" in describing the problems Paul faced at Corinth and the solutions he offered. It is clear that Theissen sees the conflicts at Corinth not in terms of the traditional exegesis of 1 and 2 Corinthians, by which they are regarded as evidence for the clash of theological ideas, but in terms of this broader sociological understanding of conflict and integration.

Despite the short shrift Theissen gives to causal-genetic theories of religion, there remains the question of whether this emphasis on conflict signals a deeper commitment to Marxist theory than might initially be apparent.[37]

There can be no doubt that the theme of conflict has proven a useful tool in Theissen's hands, and in ways which go beyond the bounds of the general polarity between Palestinian and Pauline Christianity to which we have already alluded. Specifically, he has described the relationship between "following" Jesus and the phenomenon of social uprooting in first-century Palestine which results primarily from economic factors. By attending to the socio-ecological conflict between urban and rural worlds, he has offered an interpretation of Jesus' temple prediction (Mk. 14:58). Political conflict plays a central role in his understanding of Mt. 5:38–48 par.[38]

Putting this accent on conflict in full perspective would require a broad assessment of conflict theory in contemporary sociological thought. Short of that, it must be remembered that such theory, first in the hands of Georg Simmel and more recently through the work of Lewis Coser,[39] has been elaborated and refined in ways which move far beyond the rather narrow view of conflict that characterized Marx. The corollary of this is that Marxism continues to emphasize a preeminent form of conflict, economic conflict. By contemporary standards this itself is something of a "reductionism" not unlike that attending Marx's interpretation of religion. It contrasts sharply with the diversity of conflicts to which modern sociologists attend and which Theissen identifies. There we find a range of disparities exploited, sometimes fruitfully and sometimes more tentatively, to point up the connections between the symbols, actions and ideas of religion and the wider world of social, economic, political, and ecological realities. When they are adduced by Theissen, such connections remain intact; ultimately the one set of categories is not to be substituted for the other.

Finally, not only the range and integrity of such connections are evident in Theissen, but also the quality or texture of the relationship itself. This is clearest when he points to economic stress and conflict as an ingredient in the formation of a religious movement. Such is the case with the depressed and stressful economic circumstances of Palestine which produce the Jesus movement and its itinerant charismatics, with their radical ethic renouncing goods and embracing poverty. While he points to the general role of economic circumstances that can contribute to the rise of this ethic, Theissen does not suggest that only these circumstances can motivate such a posture. In fact, those whom we can identify from the synoptic Gospels are relatively well off. This leads Theissen to conclude that in such instances the renunciation of property and the adoption of this wholly dependent style of life represent a voluntary acceptance of the ethic rather than one made inevitable by economic circumstances. Thus the relationship between the economic circumstances and the religious behavior is indirect rather than direct, a view which can be challenged[40] but which nevertheless conforms to the evidence of the Gospels themselves.[41]

This last illustration brings us back to the point where we began. Gerd Theissen's scholarship is, whatever else, the work of a New Testament scholar. His attention to the traditional concerns of exegesis—historical analysis and literary criticism—marks him as just that. His interest in the sociology of early Christianity also picks up a theme which has been embedded in New Testament scholarship for more than two generations. It is an interest which he pursues by leaning more on the side of social history than on abstract social theory, but such theory as he needs he is able to articulate and willing to defend without apology.

Expanding the range of concerns through which we interpret texts is not easily done. Nor can its results, and their reception, be foreseen. Hippolyte Taine's *Histoire de la littérature anglaise* pointed to what he called the "milieu" of literature and what today would be called the social basis of literature, which must be understood in explaining its production. Taine's reception among his nineteenth-century colleagues was marked by heated controversy and not a little resistance. Today he is considered a founding father of the sociology of literature. Flaubert said of Taine's book that whatever it left unsettled, it put to an end the uncritical notion that books fall from the sky like meteorites.[42] They don't, of course, and neither did the New Testament. Theissen himself has recently made the same point: "For those who can only understand the New Testament as an echo of the divine order it will necessarily come as disillusioning to have it shown to be the echo of social conflicts as well. On the other hand, those who can on principle accept the idea that even our innermost convictions are related to social conflicts as they are experienced and endured will find it easier to accept such connections in the New Testament. The essays which follow have as their purpose neither to disillusion in some maliciously pleasurable manner, nor to strengthen anxiety about theological causality. Their purpose is enlightenment about the social origins of our religion."[43]

NOTES

1. R. Scroggs, "The Sociological Interpretation of the New Testament: The Present State of Research," *NTS* 26 (1980): 164–79; A. J. Malherbe, *Social Aspects of Early Christianity* (Baton Rouge and London, 1977), 1–28; L. E. Keck, "On the Ethos of Early Christians," *JAAR* 42 (1974): 435–52; W. A. Meeks, "The Social World of Early Christianity," *CSRB* 6 (1975): 1–5; J. Z. Smith, "The Social Description of Early Christianity," *RelStR* 1 (1975): 19–25.

2. A bibliography of Theissen's major works will be found at the end of this Introduction. In what follows we will refer to these works only by the date indicated in that bibliography.

3. Theissen, 1978b.

4. The other is Theissen, 1974b.

5. The literature is extensive. S. M. Lipset has discussed the prospects for "historical sociologists" with attention to American history in "History and Sociology: Some Methodological Considerations," in S. M. Lipset and R. Hofstadter, *Sociology and History: Methods* (New York, 1968), 20–58. T. C. Cochran has written frequently on the connection, as in *The Inner Revolution: Essays on the Social Sciences in History* (New York, 1967). An earlier voice in Germany was O. Hintze, now available in his *Soziologie und Geschichte: Gesammelte Abhandlungen zur Soziologie, Politik und Theorie der Geschichte*, ed. G. Oestreich, *Gesammelte Abhandlungen*, Bd. II (Göttingen, 1964[2]). W. Schulze has provided an introduction to many facets of the problem in *Soziologie und Geschichtswissenschaft: Einführung in die Probleme der Kooperation beider Wissenschaften* (München, 1974), which includes an ample bibliography.

6. A. Deissmann, *Light from the Ancient East: The New Testament Illustrated by Recently Discovered Texts of the Graeco-Roman World*, trans. L. R. M. Strachan from the "fourth" German edition (London, 1927).

7. Ibid., 69.

8. Ibid., 9.

9. L. Rydbeck, *Fachprosa, vermeintliche Volkssprache und Neues Testament* (Uppsala, 1967). A brief analysis will be found in Malherbe, *Social Aspects*, 39–41.

10. E. A. Judge, *The Social Pattern of Christian Groups in the First Century: Some Prolegomena to the Study of New Testament Ideas of Social Obligation* (London, 1960).

11. Ibid., 60.

12. E. A. Judge, "The Early Christians as a Scholastic Community," *JRH* 1 (1960): 4–15, 125–37; idem, "St. Paul and Classical Society," *JAC* (1972): 19–36.

13. Malherbe, *Social Aspects*, 29–59.

14. S. J. Case, *The Social Origins of Christianity* (Chicago, 1923), vi.

15. Ibid., 24.

16. Keck, "Ethos," 437. In this same essay Keck goes on to remark that Case's colleague, Shailer Matthews, with his emphasis on "social mind" and "pattern" in theological thought, is more suggestive for contemporary work than is Case.

17. O. Cullmann, "Les récentes études sur la formation de la tradition évangélique," *RHPhR* 5 (1925), translated as "Die neuen Arbeiten zur Geschichte der Evangelientradition," and reprinted in his *Vorträge und Aufsätze 1925–1962*, ed. K. Froelich (Tübingen/Zürich, 1966), 41–89.

18. M. Dibelius, *From Tradition to Gospel* (New York, 1934), Eng. trans. B. L. Woolf from *Die Formgeschichte des Evangeliums* (Tübingen, 1933[2]).

19. R. Bultmann, *The History of the Synoptic Tradition* (New York, 1963), Eng. trans. J. Marsh from *Die Geschichte der synoptischen Tradition* (Göttingen, 1958[3]).

20. G. Iber, "Zur Formgeschichte der Evangelien," *ThR*, n.s. 24 (1957–58): 322.

21. A brief review of other early contributions will be found in Keck, "Ethos." Cf. also F. C. Grant, *The Economic Background of the Gospels* (London, 1926).

22. E. Güttgemanns, *Offene Fragen zur Formgeschichte des Evangeliums* (München, 1971[2]), 22–34. Eng. trans. William G. Doty, *Candid Questions Concerning Gospel Form Criticism* (Pittsburgh, 1979).

23. K. Kautsky, *The Foundations of Christianity*, Eng. trans. H. F. Mins (New York, 1953).

24. Ibid., 12.

25. M. Robbe, *Der Ursprung des Christentums* (Leipzig, 1967); P. Alfaric, *Origines sociales du Christianisme* (Paris, 1959); H. Kreissig, "Zur Zusammensetzung der frühchristlichen Gemeinden im ersten Jahrhundert u.Z.," *Eirene* 6 (1967): 91–100; A. Robertson, *The Origins of Christianity*, rev. ed. (New York, 1962).

26. Robertson, *Origins*, 132.

27. Cf. especially Theissen, 1977b and 1973.

28. Theissen, 1973, 78, and his recent statement in 1979c, 13.

29. E. Troeltsch, *The Social Teaching of the Christian Churches*, Eng. trans. O. Wyon (London and New York, 1931), I:78.

30. An exception is his essay "Theoretische Probleme religionssoziologischer Forschung . . ." (1974b).

31. Ibid., 37.

32. This has been expressed at some length in Theissen, 1978a, (= 1979b).

33. R. K. Merton, "Manifest and Latent Functions," chap. 1 of his *Social Theory and Social Structure*, 2d rev. ed. (Glencoe, Ill., 1957), quoted from the reprint in N. J. Demerath III and R. A. Peterson, eds., *System, Change and Conflict: A Reader on Contemporary Sociological Theory and the Debate Over Functionalism* (New York, 1967), 53.

34. Ibid., 9–75.

35. Theissen, 1974b, 39.

36. Ibid., 42

37. Theissen has recently addressed this issue more systematically in 1979c, 25–30.

38. Theissen, 1977b; 1976a; 1979d.

39. L. Coser, *The Function of Social Conflict* (Glencoe, Ill., 1956). Simmel's essay is found in a translation by K. H. Wolff in E. C. Hughes, ed., *Conflict and the Web of Group Affiliations* (Glencoe, Ill., 1955).

40. L. Schottroff and W. Stegemann, *Jesus von Nazareth—Hoffnung der Armen* (Stuttgart, 1978).

41. Cf. n. 37 above.

42. H. Levin, "Literature as an Institution," *Accent* 6 (1945–46), reprinted in E. and T. Burns, *Sociology of Literature and Drama* (Harmondsworth, England, 1973), 57.

43. Theissen, 1979c. 29–30.

A Bibliography of the Major Works of Gerd Theissen

1969 *Untersuchungen zum Hebräerbrief,* StNT 2, Gütersloh.

1971 *Ergänzungsheft* to R. Bultmann, *Die Geschichte der Synoptischen Tradition,* ed. G. Theissen and Ph. Vielhauer, Göttingen.

1973 "Wanderradikalismus: Literatursoziologische Aspekte der Überlieferung von Worten Jesu im Urchristentum," *ZThK* 70 (1973): 245–71; reprinted in 1979a, 79–105. For Eng. trans. cf. 1976c.

1974a *Urchristliche Wundergeschichten: Ein Beitrag zur formgeschichtlichen Erforschung der synoptischen Evangelien,* StNT 8, Gütersloh.

1974b "Theoretische Probleme religionssoziologischer Forschung und die Analyse des Urchristentums," *NZSTh* 16 (1974): 35–56; reprinted in 1979a, 55–76.

1974c "Soziale Schichtung in der korinthischen Gemeinde: Ein Beitrag zur Soziologie des hellenistischen Urchristentums," *ZNW* 65 (1974): 232–72; reprinted in 1979a, 231–71; Eng. trans. below, 69–119.

1974d "Soziale Integration und sakramentales Handeln: Eine Analyse von 1 Cor. 11:17–34," *NT* 16 (1974): 179–206; reprinted in 1979a, 290–317; Eng. trans. below, 145–174.

1974e "Soteriologische Symbolik in den paulinischen Schriften: Ein strukturalistischer Beitrag," *KuD* 20: 282–304.

1975a "Legitimation und Lebensunterhalt: Ein Beitrag zur Soziologie urchristlicher Missionare," *NTS* 21 (1975): 192–221; reprinted in 1979a, 201–30; Eng. trans. below, 27–67.

1975b "Die soziologische Auswertung religiöser Überlieferungen: Ihre methodologischen Probleme am Beispiel des Urchristentums,"

Kairos 17 (1975): 284–99; reprinted in 1979a, 35–54; Eng. trans. below, 175–200.

1975c "Die Starken und Schwachen in Korinth: Soziologische Analyse eines theologischen Streits," *EvTh* 35 (1975): 155–72; reprinted in 1979a, 272–89; Eng. trans. below, 121–43.

1976a "Die Tempelweissagung Jesu: Prophetie im Spannungsfeld von Stadt und Land," *ThZ* 32: 144–58; reprinted in 1979a, 142–59.

1976b "Synoptische Wundergeschichten im Lichte unseres Sprachverständnisses: Hermeneutische und didaktische Überlegungen," *WPKG* 65: 289–308.

1976c "Itinerant Radicalism: The Tradition of Jesus Sayings from the Perspective of the Sociology of Literature," Eng. Trans. by A. Wire of 1973, with abbreviated notes, in *The Bible and Liberation: Political and Social Hermeneutics* (= *Radical Religion* II, 2/3), Berkeley, 84–93.

1977a *Soziologie der Jesusbewegung: Ein Beitrag zur Entstehungsgeschichte des Urchristentums*, TEH 194, München. Eng. trans. 1978b.

1977b " 'Wir haben alles verlassen' (Mc X, 28): Nachfolge und soziale Entwurzelung in der jüdisch-palestinischen Gesellschaft des 1. Jahrhunderts n. Chr.," *NT* 27: 161–96; reprinted in 1979a, 106–41.

1978a *Argumente für einen kritischen Glauben—oder: Was hält der Religionskritik stand?* TEH 202, München Eng. trans. 1979b.

1978b *Sociology of Early Palestinian Christianity*, Eng. trans. by J. Bowden of 1977a, Philadelphia (= *The First Followers of Jesus*, London).

1979a *Studien zur Soziologie des Urchristentums*, WUNT 19, Tübingen.

1979b *A Critical Faith: A Case for Religion*, Eng. trans. by J. Bowden of 1978a, Philadelphia (= *On Having a Critical Faith*, London).

1979c "Zur forschungsgeschichtlichen Einordnung der soziologischen Fragestellung," in 1979a, 3–34.

1979d "Gewaltverzicht und Feindesliebe (Mt 5, 38–48/Lk 6,27–38) und deren sozialgeschichtlicher Hintergrund," in 1979a, 160–97.

1

Legitimation and Subsistence: An Essay on the Sociology of Early Christian Missionaries

[For Professor D. Ph. Vielhauer on his sixtieth birthday, 3 December 1974.]

As nobody could suspect that the primitive Christian movement would one day transform and shape our entire culture, its missionaries were not the esteemed founders of Christianity, but homeless, roving propagandists without roots or a means of livelihood. They embodied a form of socially divergent behavior which was estranged from society's fundamental norms and necessities. One need only recall the demands on the disciples to forsake home, possessions, security, and family. By doing so they preached and lived a freedom from basic social responsibilities of a sort which could be put into practice only by those who had removed themselves from the stabilizing and domesticating effects of a continuing life of work—not by virtue of the privilege of possessions, but by means of the ascetic poverty of an insecure marginal existence comparable to the life of the itinerant Cynic philosopher.[1] Even the most dedicated ascetic, however, requires subsistence. If he himself does not labor, then he is dependent on others who labor for him. In that way he remains firmly tied to this world, however much he may otherwise distance himself from it. The question of subsistence therefore goes to the root of his spiritual existence and touches at the credibility of the way of life he expounds.

Thus it is hardly accidental that this question assumes considerable proportions in the instructions to primitive Christian itinerant preachers (cf. the commissioning speeches, Lk. 10:3ff. and pars.), or that it dominates community rules covering relations with itinerant charismatics (Mt. 10:40–42; *Didache* 11) and can become a central theme in the quarrels among competing itinerant preachers (1 Cor. 9—11; 2 Cor. 10—13). The fact is that the social legitimacy of itinerant preachers depends to a great extent on how they provide for their own subsistence.

In this essay the thesis will be put forward that there were two types of primitive Christian itinerant preachers, to be distinguished as itinerant charismatics on the one hand and community organizers on the other. The most important difference between them is that each adopts a distinctive attitude to the question of subsistence. The first type arose in the social circumstances of the Palestinian region. The second, represented by Paul and Barnabas, arose in the movement of the mission into Hellenistic territory. Both types work side by side but come into conflict in Corinth.

ITINERANT CHARISMATICS

The Jesus movement was a renewal movement internal to Judaism. It was addressed to all Jewish congregations and originally had no interest in forming groups separate from Judaism. It is thus a misunderstanding to speak of primitive Christian communities in the earliest period. The bearers of what later came to be understood as "Christianity" were, rather, itinerant missionaries, apostles, and prophets who could depend on small groups of sympathizers. What they represented was not the only inner Jewish renewal movement marked by a pronounced socially divergent posture. At that time those who wished to renounce their social existence in order to adopt a different style of life were confronted with several possibilities. They could become beggars, thieves, guerrillas, Essenes—or, just as well, apostles, prophets, or missionaries. Sometimes they might try out a variety of these in succession, as did Simon the Zealot (Lk. 6:15).[2] There were robbers and beggars everywhere, of course, but what is extraordinary is that movements which seen from the outside might appear to be dedicated merely to such things could actually become bearers of the religious and social renewal of an entire society.[3] This unusual significance of socially divergent behavior in Palestinian society of the time is no doubt linked with the same deep-seated social crisis which found explosive expression in the Jewish War. We cannot stop here to analyze that crisis in detail but will only single out some factors which were significant for the emergence and shaping of the primitive Christian charismatic stance.

Socio-political Factors

It proved impossible in Palestine to bring different governing structures into a balanced relationship. On the one side stood those "Western" political structures on which the Roman Empire was based: The polis, which prevailed only in the Hellenistic cities of the Mediterranean and in the territory east of the Jordan;[4] and Roman provincial administration, repeatedly discharged through the rule of native "kings."[5] On the other side stood two "indigenous" forms of governance: theocracy, that is, the rule of a native priestly (or lay) aristocracy,[6] and the monarchy of the Hasmonaeans and Herodians, which stood in some tension to both the aristocracy and the people.[7] This is not the place to inquire into the reasons why it proved impossible to fashion such structures of government into the basis for a stable political order, or to ask why the integration of Jewish-Palestinian society into the Roman Empire failed. The fact remains that the effort failed, to which the Jewish War stands as testimony. Symptomatic of such failure are those radical theocratic movements which arise at the beginning of the century and which, seizing on old traditions, proclaim the replacement of all structures of governance by the governance of God. These radical theocratic movements could appear in an activist-legalist guise (such as Zealot guerrilla fighters);[8] they could also appear, however, in the form of enthusiastic messianic prophets awaiting God's miraculous intervention.[9] The Jesus movement can be characterized as representing their quietistic wing. At its center stood the universal Kingdom of God which was to come in a miraculous manner without the inducement of violent acts, and which already was announced in the present through exorcisms and healings (cf. Lk. 10:8–9; 11:20).

Socio-economic Factors

Socio-economic factors are also responsible for the failure to stabilize the land politically and for the resulting rise of radical theocratic movements. Numerous hints suggest that religiously inspired forms of socially divergent behavior spread most readily among those strata and groups which suffered under social and economic pressure.[10] Thus the elder Pliny reports of the Essenes that they above all would accept "refugees" weary of life who "through the adversity of fate were driven to adopt their way of life" (*Historia naturalis* V, 17, 4). With the Zealots we encounter an explicitly revolutionary social program. They took up a position of resistance to the regular levying of taxes by the Romans, promised the abolition of debts, and destroyed the archive in which debts were recorded (Josephus, *Bellum Judaicum* II, 427). Within the Jesus movement can be found a radical critique of wealth. The movement's followers understood that it was difficult for the rich to join, and the "rich young man" shrinks from the requirement that disciples lead a homeless existence (Mk. 10:17ff.).

But it would be wrong to look only among the lower strata for the emergence of socially divergent behavior. Social and economic pressure can be felt in all strata and will indeed be felt most intensely where the possibility of a "better" life is recognized but the prospect of social decline threatens. The sons of well-off families are to be found among the desperadoes of every age.[11] Even the primitive Christian itinerant charismatics are not drawn exclusively from the poorest classes; the father of James and John, for example, is able to take on hired laborers in addition to his two sons (Mk. 1:20). Nor is socio-economic pressure an exclusively class-specific problem, for it can unsettle an entire society even if it falls most severely on the lowest classes. In any event, its causes are largely matters which pervade the whole of society. We can here leave open the question of the role played by the ruinous land policies of Herod the Great,[12] the role of double taxation by the state and the priestly aristocracy,[13] the significance of a concentration of land ownership in the hands of a few (often foreign) landlords, and the importance of poor harvests and drought.[14] Within the framework of our theme, there is another phenomenon which commands our attention: The most important religiously inspired movements of socially divergent behavior in Palestine were able to solve the problems of subsistence in nonconformist ways.

The Qumran community, for example, lived apart from society in a cooperative association which eschewed private ownership.[15] The Zealots took by force their share of the land's productivity. Just as they elevated robbery, widespread at the time, to the rank of a religious and social program,[16] so the Jesus movement elevated the equally pervasive institution of begging. Its missionaries, in fact, expected to receive lodging and food as "compensation" for preaching and healing (Lk. 10:17ff.). They did not have much to offer that was very concrete. Not everybody could be healed, and preaching consisted of words. A synoptic saying promised heavenly reward to whoever received them (Mt. 10:40–42), which is to say that support was given without visible hope of return. This was certainly no ordinary mendicancy, but charismatic begging which trusted in God to sustain his missionaries (Mt. 6:25ff.).

Socio-ecological Factors

The struggle of a society with its natural environment and its social configuration must also be taken into account when assessing the origin and development of socially divergent behavior. Were it possible to confirm the supposition so frequently expressed, that Palestine at this time was overpopulated,[17] this would also be a factor in the origin of the Jesus movement. Those who were dissatisfied with the prospects for life in the area could emigrate—the astounding scope of the Diaspora is in part to be explained by such emigration—or they could join the Zealots or the Essenes, or they could become Christian charismatics. What should be noticed is the particular relationship to the environment which characterizes each of these different patterns of socially divergent behavior. We can no more imagine the Zealots without their mountain hideouts than the Qumran community without the desert oasis of Ain Feshka or the baptist movement without the river Jordan. One characteristic of the Jesus movement is its being rooted in the rural world (or better, hinterland) of settled Palestine.[18] The world reflected in the images of its parables is rural.[19] The ethos of homelessness is portrayed by comparison with foxes, birds, and lilies (Mt. 8:20; 6:25–34). The story about plucking ears of grain (Mk. 2:23–28) shows how itinerant charismatics in a rural setting can help themselves to food.

In general, it can be said that the norms of this early Christian itinerant-charismatic style presuppose a rural milieu. In Luke 10 we read of "cities" (RSV "towns"), to be sure, but quite apart from the fact that in the synoptic Gospels small places often are inappropriately called cities, in this instance the places could not have been very large since the entire town is made liable at the Day of Judgment for rejecting the traveling missionaries, to be punished like Sodom and Gomorrah. Unless we are to assume that an archaic notion of collective punishment is at work here, the entire town must have had at least some knowledge of the itinerant charismatics. A hint in this same passage about the pattern of subsistence is also revealing. Somebody marching off without money or food, and making not the slightest provision in advance, can nonetheless count on finding accommodations among sympathizers at the end of the day. Large cities are, for the most part, separated from one another by more than a day's journey. Yet the *Didache* still advises that an apostle be given bread only ἕως οὗ αὐλισθῇ—enough to last "until the next night's lodging" (11:6–7), indicating that it still thinks in terms of villages not far removed from each other.[20]

Socio-cultural Factors

The various forms of religiously inspired socially divergent behavior—and similarly the Pharisaic movement, which is better integrated into society—should be regarded as multiple efforts to preserve Jewish society's cultural identity in the face of political subjugation and the threatened loss of religious and cultural independence.[21]. The essence of this independence was to be found in that complex of traditions, norms, and institutions which we call the Law. The various groupings and movements within Jewish society in the first century C.E. can be understood as different attempts to secure validity for this Law, whether by means of an interpretive adjustment to the manifold and altered circumstances of life (Pharisees), or by means of a consistent implementation of the Law in an unusually disciplined community cut off from society (Qumran), or by means of the political implementation of a radicalized first commandment which authorizes acts of terrorism against those seen as violating it (Zealots).[22] In each case we have an intensification of the Law.[23] While reacting to the confrontation with a politically imposed alien culture by intensifying those norms which are characteristic for Jewish society, however, those who do so simultaneously and involuntarily call into question the religious and cultural unity of this society. This is so because the heightened norms can be realized by only a small portion of the society, while the rest must necessarily compromise and lose social esteem, whether as the "am-ha-arez," the people of the land who do not know the Law, or as the "children of darkness" who have gone astray. Thus the effort to preserve cultural and religious identity by emphasizing and heightening the Law leads to the very loss of this identity and results instead in many groups, each of which claims that it alone represents the true Israel.

With the appearance of the Baptist and the Jesus movement a counterforce, born of this inner contradiction, begins to take shape. As with other renewal movements, here too we find a heightening of the Law. This leads, however, not to the condemnation of others but to a sentence of destruction on all humanity which in turn creates a new solidarity, the solidarity of those dependent on grace. Above all it would be inimical to such a movement to mark itself off from other groups within society and organize itself separately. Here, instead, everyone is accepted. It is no accident that this movement found approval particularly among the socially despised, those very people whose means of earning a living dictated that they compromise themselves in regard to the Law. Such are obviously the tax collectors and prostitutes, but also all the other "sinners," that is, all who found it impossible to honor the norms of Jewish society.

This becomes very important for the question of subsistence. Unlike the Qumran community or the Zealots, representatives of the Jesus movement have confidence in being voluntarily supported by those to whom their message is addressed. Their trust in

God, who surely will not allow his charismatic to perish (Mt. 6:25ff.), is a concrete example of trust in a society where they will always find people motivated to support them (Mt. 10:40–42). They would be supported by the tax collectors, for example, who were compromised by virtue of their position in a system of taxation which exploited the land. Like Jesus himself, those itinerant charismatics who were his disciples would eat and drink with such people (Mt. 11:19; Mk. 2:15ff.); or, more precisely, they would accept hospitality from such. Nor is it accidental that the one patron of the young movement who is characterized in terms of her social status, Joanna the wife of Chuza, is married to an official in Herod's government (Lk. 8:3).[24] She certainly did not belong to those circles most beloved by the people. The fact that she is specifically singled out, however, suggests that patrons from such elevated strata were more the exception than the rule.

The confidence of these charismatics in obtaining support was justified in other and more fundamental ways as well. Lodging and sustenance would be guaranteed to them εἰς ὄνομα προφήτου, δικαίου or μαθητοῦ (Mt. 10:40–42), not because they themselves belonged to the poor and needy, but because they stood in a special relationship to God. We have termed this "charismatic begging." Such "begging," however, could appeal for its support to the same motivations as might begging of a more ordinary sort, to that devotion to poverty according to which God commends the poor in a special way to the care of others: "Has not God chosen those who are poor in the world . . . ?" (James 2:5). H. Bolkestein has shown how this piety of poverty is related to the particular political and social structures of the East and was widespread in Egypt as well as in Palestine.[25] Within the framework of the democratic and republican institutions of both Greece and Rome charity was addressed to the general public, which is to say to all citizens. By contrast, where the lower classes are wholly dependent on the "justness" of the upper classes, justness becomes mercy and grace. Particularly in Israel the poor person qualified as somebody entrusted in an unusual way to God's protection. In this setting the term *poor* could become an honorific name for a religious group.[26] In this setting Jesus could pronounce the poor to be blessed (Lk.

6:20). In this setting, therefore, it was possible for early Christian itinerant charismatics to authenticate themselves, by means of demonstrable poverty, as "sent" by God and thereby receive support. The motivation for supporting them was latent in the sociocultural circumstances.

There can be no doubt that the origin and configuration of the Jesus movement, spread as it was primarily by itinerant charismatics, was connected with the political, economic, ecological, and cultural circumstances and contradictions of Jewish-Palestinian society in the first century C.E. This connection by no means justifies reducing the movement to its social conditions. The examples of the Zealots and Essenes make it clear that in the face of such conditions other responses were possible. All of these are attempts to structure life in a meaningful way under existing conditions, even if that means radicalizing, transcending, or calling into question the dominant mode of life. The various religiously inspired currents of socially divergent behavior in Palestine cannot be understood apart from this demand for a meaningful human social life. Whoever forsakes house and home, wife and children to roam the land as an itinerant charismatic not only is driven by the pressure of social conflicts but is also pursuing the promise of a new life—following a call. These two motives are hardly separable.

THE COMMUNITY ORGANIZERS

Sooner or later relativizing the Law, which began within the Jesus movement, was bound to relativize the distinction between Gentile and Jew, since the boundaries of the Law were also the boundaries of Judaism. Unlike the Hellenistic effort at reform which took place at the beginning of the second century B.C.E.,[27] this was not an external but an internal conquest of cultural boundaries between Jews and Gentiles, emerging from within the center of Judaism itself and bringing to the fore its universalistic tendencies. Hellenistic Jewish Christians were the first to turn to Gentiles (Acts 11:20). The protagonists of the Hellenistic mission, however, were Barnabas and Paul, who began with a methodical mission to the Hellenistic cities of the Mediterranean world. Both agreed in renouncing their privilege of being supported (1 Cor.

9:6).[28] To what extent is this renunciation connected with the altered social circumstances of their mission? Can other peculiarities of the Pauline mission be correlated with this?

Socio-political Factors

The Hellenistic mission was operative almost exclusively in cities with a republican constitution, subordinate to Rome's imperial power but also benefiting from it.[29] Urbanization and Romanization, or Hellenization, went hand in hand. Those structural contradictions which characterize the political situation of Palestine are missing here. Thus it is not surprising that the radical theocratic element within the early Christian movement retreats almost completely. The proclamation of the kingdom of God, a staple in the preaching of Palestinian itinerant charismatics (Lk. 10:9), is almost wholly absent in Paul. The βασιλεία-idea is found only four times. Meanwhile, the political structure is accepted without reservation (Rom. 13:1ff.) and Paul, being a citizen of Tarsus and of Rome, is fully integrated into the political texture of the Roman Empire.[30]

Socio-economic Factors

While Palestine was caught in a tightening economic squeeze in the first century, the urban Mediterranean world was experiencing an economic boom.[31] It was not necessary to belong to the very uppermost classes in order to achieve a certain degree of prosperity. In this atmosphere early Christianity quickly penetrated the higher strata of society to encompass some, if only a few, of those who were "wise, powerful, and of noble birth" (1 Cor. 1:26). Paul and Barnabas themselves might serve as examples. Paul was only a cloth worker, to be sure, but he possessed citizenship of both Tarsus and Rome. Since we learn from one of Dio Chrysostom's addresses to the Tarsians that the right of citizenship was in general withheld from cloth workers, it seems that Paul enjoyed an unusual, privileged status.[32] A gift to the Jersualem community testifies to the position of Barnabas (Acts 4:36). It must have been especially large, or it would not have been worth remembering. In addition, there are the "God-fearers" who are economically well-off, such as the Centurion of Caesarea and Lydia the purple-merchant. And finally, the governor of Bithynia observes that Christianity encompassed all classes (Pliny, *Epistulae* X, 96, 6).

A familial love-patriarchalism, which places a high value on the obedience of women, children, and slaves and has little room for the nonfamilial ethical radicalism of the synoptic tradition, is characteristic of these communities with their marked social stratification.[33] In this setting charismatic begging was inappropriate. The heads of households will have been interested in something else: "If anyone will not work, let him not eat" (2 Thess. 3:10). Such is the counsel of a letter coming from one of these communities, a piece of advice which appeals explicitly to the example of Paul. The consequences of this definitional relationship can also be seen operating in other directions. Because household-oriented patriarchalism, which values solidity, had so little empathy for roving charismatic beggars, it may have seemed fitting that Paul and Barnabas appeared on the scene as respectable working men.[34]

Yet that is not the whole story. It is a known fact that other missionaries, who *did* accept support, were also well received in the Pauline congregation. More decisive than the socio-economic status of those to whom the mission addressed itself was the status of the missionaries themselves. Paul was a craftsman, the "other apostles and the brothers of the Lord and Cephas" (1 Cor. 9:4) more likely fishermen (like Cephas) or farmers. One recalls the members of the Lord's family who, according to Hegesippus (Eusebius, *Historia eccelesiastica* III, 18, 4–20,7), were brought before Domitian as alleged messianic pretenders and questioned about their possessions:

> They said that all they possessed was nine thousand *denarii* between them, the half belonging to each, and they stated that they did not possess this in money but that it was the valuation of only thirty-nine *plethra* of ground on which they paid taxes and lived by their own work. Then they showed him their hands, adducing as testimony of their labour the hardness of their bodies and the tough skin which had been embossed on their hands from incessant work. [20, 2–3]

It is immediately evident that fishermen and farmers turned itinerant preachers had to give up their work if they were to missionize in rural environs. They could not pack up and carry along their fields and lakes as one might one's tools. Peter the fisherman is forced by necessity to accept the "privilege of support"; Paul the craftsman can afford to renounce it.[35]

Socio-ecological Factors

The transition from a rural movement to a mission in the urban world brought with it increased distances. Paul, it seems, only went from city to city and scarcely worked at all as a missionary in the rural villages. In part that is because in such regions the older ethnic languages still prevailed while in the cities Greek would be understood,[36] although for Greece itself this distinction would naturally not be relevant. Another reason is that Paul was himself rooted in urban culture. For him, cities are representative of the entire world: Corinth of Achaia (1 Cor. 16:15), for example, or Ephesus of Asia (16:19). Anyone like Paul who wished to travel from city to city in order to missionize the world as it was then known could not put into practice that radical renunciation of planning and foresight required by the commissioning speeches: ship's passage must be paid for; stuck in a city without money, one could hardly proceed to "help oneself." There are no prospects for plucking ears of grain. Barnabas and Paul needed money to carry out their mission. The fact that they were provided with the necessary means not (or not only) by the congregations but through their own work is quite in keeping with charismatic asceticism, even if it conflicts with the literal norms governing itinerant charismatics.

There were other possibilities as well for adjusting the mission to its new circumstances. This is shown by the actions of missionaries in competition with Barnabas and Paul who allow themselves to be supported by the congregation. They too faced the problem of bridging great distances, which they accomplished with the help of "letters of recommendation" mentioned in 2 Cor. 3:1. Such letters, however, are useful only if there is an addressee. Therefore, they turned first of all to existing congregations. Wherever Paul had founded a community, other itinerant preachers turned up later with bewildering regularity. One must assume that they let the congregations pay for their travel between cities. The *Didache* still envisions a missionary's being given provision enough to reach the next destination (11:6), and rules of this sort would lend themselves to elaboration. To Paul and Barnabas, however, whose work was to found communities, such letters of recommendation were of little use.

Socio-cultural Factors

While the itinerant charismatics in Palestine turned to the entire population and could count on the presence of a latent motivation to support them, Barnabas and Paul understood themselves to be missionaries to the Gentiles, men who had stepped beyond the boundaries of their own people. On the one hand, this meant that they had turned to people with foreign traditions, customs, and self-understandings; they were breaking new ground and for that very reason financial independence seemed advisable. On the other hand, they had to take into account the resulting conflicts with their own people (cf. Acts 13:50), and this drastically reduced chances of receiving support from that quarter.

As it happens, in the Hellenistic world at this time a paradigm was available in the figure of the Cynic itinerant preacher. Paul and Barnabas were well enough educated to anticipate which social categories would be ascribed to them: they would be seen as "philosophers" roaming the land. Among such philosophers there were, naturally, serious men; there were also imposters and cheats.[37] One useful criterion for distinguishing the two types was their attitude toward money. Since the time of Socrates it had been a familiar *topos* that the truly wise man takes no money for his wisdom, and Paul makes use of this idea in 2 Cor. 10—13. By attributing avarice to his competitors (cf. also 2 Cor. 2:17) he automatically ranks them among the Sophists, in opposition to whom the true wise man had always spoken out.[38] Paul also uses here the *topoi* of Cynic itinerant philosophers in a positive way. Like them, he lays claim to ἐλευθερία (1 Cor. 9:1; cf. Epictetus, *Dissertationes* 22, 48). Like them he lays claim to being self-sufficient: "I have learned, in whatever state I am, to be content (αὐτάρκης εἶναι)" (Phil. 4:11). The connection here with the philosophical tradition of the αὐταρκία of the wise man is unmistakable: Socrates too was considered αὐτάρκης καὶ σεμνός (Diogenes Laertius II, 24).

Such departure by Paul and Barnabas from the norms of early

Christianity's itinerant-charismatic posture is in all likelihood related to the altered socio-economic, socio-ecological, and socio-cultural conditions which the mission encountered in the urban Hellenistic world. That the change is related to these conditions, however, does not mean that it is determined by them. Other missionaries operated differently under the same conditions. Furthermore, we must assume that the renunciation of financial support was not just "causally" determined but was rooted in principle and deliberately intended, amounting to a significant adaptation of traditional norms to fit altered circumstances. Behind it there is to be found a deliberate missionary design. The renunciation is not the fundamental principle but is itself subordinated to a more comprehensive goal. It is true that in 1 Cor. 9:15–18 Paul practically makes his own salvation dependent upon his not having accepted any reward for preaching the gospel, but that does not prevent him from accepting support from Macedonian congregations (Phil. 4:10–20; 2 Cor. 11:9). The renunciation arose from concrete conditions in order to make the pioneering mission as effective as possible in this new territory. Where these conditions are absent (as, for example, among congregations already founded) it can be revoked, but it is just then that Paul also emphasizes his fundamental freedom and independence, his *autarkeia* (Phil. 4:11). Thus Paul represents a type of missionary who can be described as the goal-oriented community organizer, breaking new ground and establishing independent groups apart from Judaism rather than "grazing" among existing groups of sympathizers. It is his intention to missionize the entire world in this fashion, all the way to Spain, and every other consideration is subordinated to this monumental task.

THE CONFLICT BETWEEN ITINERANT CHARISMATICS AND COMMUNITY ORGANIZERS

The conflict between Paul and other competing missionaries in Corinth does not arise from personal animosities. It is a conflict between different types of missionaries which displays traits independent of the individuals involved. Whether Paul is coming to terms with the followers of Peter and Apollos in 1 Corinthians or with newly arrived missionaries in 2 Corinthians, in either case he must defend himself against the charge that he did not act like a real apostle and allow himself to be supported by the community (1 Cor. 9:3ff.; 2 Cor. 11:7ff.; 12:13). Independently of the fact that his competitors probably represented among themselves various theological viewpoints, together they shared this claim to the right of apostolic support. Regardless of the fact that Paul justifies his renunciation of such support by appeal to a very personal "necessity" which has been placed upon him (1 Cor. 9:16), he shares this necessity with Barnabas with whom he has undertaken the mission to the Mediterranean world (Acts 13:1ff.) but from whom theological differences of opinion have separated him (Gal. 2:13). Despite variations in situation, personnel, and theology, two types of missionaries meet in 1 and 2 Corinthians, types which can be distinguished by reference to their position on this issue of the right of support.

To say this is not to deny the differences in the situation in the two letters. If we proceed not from theological notions but from the social roles of the groups and individuals interacting in the two letters, the question of whether in both 1 and 2 Corinthians Paul is struggling against the same front must be answered by noting a distinction. In 1 Corinthians his attention is primarily directed not against his missionary competitors but against their followers in Corinth (1 Cor. 1—4). In contrast, the opponents in 2 Corinthians are itinerant missionaries who are not resident in Corinth but allow the Corinthians to furnish them with letters of recommendation (2 Cor. 3:1). It is methodologically impermissible to use statements about the resident "gnostics" in Corinth (1 Cor. 8:1—11:1) to interpret passages in 2 Corinthians which refer to itinerant charismatics. What can be compared in each case are (1) statements in 1 and 2 Corinthians about groups within the local congregation, and (2) statements about itinerant missionaries in the two letters.[39] It must of course be kept in mind that groups resident within the community will reflect the opinions of the traveling missionaries and, vice-versa, that these itinerant missionaries will be seen through the eyes of the locally resident Christians.[40]

At issue in the controversy among missionaries and their

followers is the matter of apostolic legitimacy. In order to analyze the controversy we can distinguish three forms of legitimacy. In each case the missionary must relate his pattern of life (including the question of his support) to divine commandments, events, and figures. In doing so he can choose to emphasize his existence, or his origin, or his accomplishments. Thus we may distinguish between (1) a charismatic legitimation based on a style of life qualified in a special way, (2) a traditional legitimation based on origin (by means of commissions and traditions which have been received), and (3) a functional legitimation based on work which has been accomplished or is yet to be done. For the most part these various modes of legitimation appear in combination but nevertheless offer practical categories for examining in terms of their typical characteristics the self-understanding of the missionaries who are competing in Corinth. For such a reconstruction we are largely dependent on Paul's statements. His objectivity in repeating what others have said is to be doubted. Whoever can intemperately defame his competitors as false apostles and servants of Satan, and even feel obliged to anticipate their eternal fate (2 Cor. 11:14f.), will have a distorted perspective on many things. Since the question of support keeps coming up, however, we can call on a wider group of texts to reconstruct the ideas and attitudes which were originally part of the controversial right to support, in order to test how far these ideas and attitudes are still visible behind Paul's polemic.

Charismatic Legitimation

In the synoptic commissioning speeches Christian missionaries are put under obligation to a demonstrable asceticism. They may not make the slightest provision for life but must trust God's grace as simply and completely as do the birds of the air and the lilies of the field. Foresight is distrust in the face of God's grace. The missionary stands under the demand for charismatic poverty. If in this light we read Paul's remarks in 1 Cor. 9 about his "right to support," his remarkable argument makes sense. What is remarkable is that Paul feels he must justify in such detail his right to support, even though he came under attack in Corinth precisely because he renounced it.

Paul begins with the general observation that nobody works without a reward. He says this on human authority (1 Cor. 9:8), but the revealed law also supports the claim "The ox which is treading on the grain is not to be muzzled." "Ox" here is to be read allegorically as referring to the apostle (9:9–11). But this argument too is apparently not yet sufficient. In 9:13 Paul further supplements what he says by appealing to the general right of the priests to receive a share of the sacrifice, and concludes by quoting a word of Jesus from the synoptic tradition (9:14). Why does he go to such lengths to justify this privilege of receiving support? Why does he pile up the arguments on a matter about which he and the Corinthians agree? It is, after all, not his exercise of the privilege which is under debate, but his renunciation of it![41]

The saying of Jesus must be read carefully: "In the same way, the Lord *commanded* that those who proclaim the gospel should get their living by the gospel" (9:14, emphasis added). Even in the Pauline variation on the saying what is mentioned is not an apostolic privilege but an apostolic duty, not a commandment that communities support their apostles but the obligation of missionaries to practice charismatic poverty, a poverty which renounces regular begging but—in reliance on one's own religious and social status as an "apostle," a "prophet," and so forth—makes one dependent on others' generosity, which cannot be calculated in advance. Thus Paul's renunciation of the "privilege" of support might be seen in a quite different way: the charge could be leveled at him that he has deliberately evaded the requirement of charismatic poverty, and that his work as a craftsman displays a lack of trust in the grace of God, who will also supply the material needs of his missionaries. Seen this way Paul is dependent on his work; he is not free and is no real apostle (9:1), for he has offended against the norm of the primitive Christian ideal of itinerant charismatics set down by Jesus himself.

In opposition to all of this Paul is at pains to show that the requirement of charismatic poverty is in reality the missionary's *privilege*. To do that, however, he must reinterpret Jesus' word, which he does with the help of general experience and Old Testament exegesis.[42] Just as the priest enjoys the privilege of a portion of the sacrifice, so the Lord too ordered: οὕτως καὶ ὁ κύριος διέταξεν . . . (9:14). By means of this introduction Paul takes the original meaning of this saying and actually stands it on its head, even if he otherwise renders it faithfully. In *such* fashion (οὕτως)—that is, by analogy to Old Testament privileges—the logion was never meant to be understood. Our assumption, that Paul has been reproached not for renouncing a privilege but for an offense against the norms of the early Christian itinerant charismatic movement, can be checked in three ways: by testing (1) whether reproaches were raised against Paul which point in this direction; (2) whether the self-understanding of his competitors was shaped by the fact that they fulfilled the norms of the early Christian itinerant charismatic movement; (3) whether Paul's defense elsewhere can also be understood as a response to objections of this sort.

OBJECTIONS RAISED AGAINST PAUL

The cry "Am I not free? Am I not an apostle?" in 1 Cor. 9:1 implies objections of that very sort, behind which may stand ideas which have their analogy in popular philosophy. The Cynic itinerant preacher, who also has freed himself of concern for property, family, and his own means of support, qualifies as somebody both "free" and "sent." Epictetus discusses the question whether one can be happy with the Cynic way of life and answers:

> Behold, God has sent you one who shall show by practice that it is possible. "Look at me, I have no house or city, property or slave; I sleep on the ground, I have no wife or children, no miserable palace, but only earth and sky and one poor cloak. Yet what do I lack? Am I not without pain and fear, am I not free?" [*Diss*. III, 22, 46–48]

It is clear that the Cynic itinerant preacher also understands himself to be free and sent from God. He too takes no care for his subsistence and lives by means of "dignified" begging. And if Paul was reproached for not being free, it may have been his labor as a craftsman which his critics had in mind. Such people can be regarded as in some ways not free: βαναυσία ἦθος ἀποτρέπει ἐλεύθερον, "the practice of mechanical art repels the man whose soul is free" (Plato, *Leges* 741e).[43]

In 2 Cor. 10:2 we encounter the charge that Paul lives "according to the flesh" (κατὰ σάρκα, RSV "acting in worldly fashion") and wages a worldly war.[44] This too may simply mean that he is too concerned with his livelihood and with worldly things, trusting too little in Christ. It should be noted that the term "to wage war" (στρατεύεσθαι) occurs otherwise only in 1 Cor. 9:7, where Paul asks, "Who serves as a soldier (στρατεύει) at his own expense?" Paul emphasizes, of course, that he is speaking on human authority (κατὰ ἄνθρωπον, 9:8), but is not what is said on human authority likely to be done in a human way? The phrases κατὰ ἄνθρωπον and κατὰ σάρκα correspond to one another. Furthermore, Paul assures his readers that his weapons of warfare are not "worldly" (σαρκικά, 2 Cor. 10:4), which recalls 1 Cor. 9:11 where he describes his support as "material benefits" (τὰ σαρκικά). The similarities to 1 Cor. 9 go further. In 2 Cor. 10:8 Paul speaks about his "authority" (ἐξουσία), which the Lord had given him for building up and not destroying the community. He may have in mind his "right to . . . food and drink" (1 Cor. 9:4; cf. ἐξουσία in 9:5, 6, 12, 18), that is, his claim to community support. Finally, it should be noted that in both passages the idea of "authority" (ἐξουσία) is found in conjunction with the notion of boasting (καύχημα, 9:15, 16; cf. 2 Cor. 10:8).[45] Were some perhaps offended by Paul's boasting of his renunciation of what was his right, that is, by his transgression of the norms of the early Christian institution of the itinerant charismatic?

It seems quite certain that Paul was not just generally rebuffed but suffered a specific reproach which called into question his status as an apostle. Whenever he speaks of the superlative apostles (2 Cor. 11:15; 12:11) he goes on to speak about his renunciation of his right to support,[46] and does so in such a way as to defend himself against the charge of ἁμαρτία or ἀδικία: "Did I commit a sin (ἁμαρτίαν) in abasing myself so that you might be exalted, because I preached God's gospel without cost to you?" (2 Cor. 11:7). "For in what were you less favored than the rest of the churches, except that I myself did not burden you? Forgive me this wrong (ἀδικίαν)!" (2 Cor. 12:13). The catchword ἁμαρτία may in this instance come from the Corinthian community, since Paul usually uses it to refer to the comprehensive power of sin rather than a specific transgression. Here a concrete norm is being presupposed, and the superlative apostles probably distinguished themselves by their zealous obedience to this norm—the requirement of charismatic poverty.

Even in 1 Corinthians Paul presupposes specific objections when he writes: "But with me it is a very small thing that I should be judged by you or by any human court. I do not even judge (ἀνακρίνω) myself. I am not aware of anything against myself, but I am not thereby acquitted. It is the Lord who judges me" (1 Cor. 4:3–4). Here again Paul's apostolic attributes as a "servant of Christ" and "steward of the mysteries of God" (4:1) are under debate. Here too he is being compared with other apostles (3:22–23; 4:6ff.). What he has in mind is not a regular legal proceeding—ἡμέρα, the day of judgment, could be metaphorical—but the situation is comparable to a formal indictment, a concrete ἀνακρίνειν. All of these elements recur in 1 Cor. 9:1ff. When Paul writes, "This is my defense (ἀπολογία) to those who would examine (ἀνακρίνουσιν) me" (9:3), he has in mind the charge that he is not a proper apostle because he allows himself to be concerned for his own support (9:1ff.). The catchword "defend oneself" (ἀπολογεῖσθαι) comes up again in 2 Cor. 12:19 after Paul has justified his "injustice" in not accepting support from the Corinthians. In my view there can be no doubt that one concrete norm is always to be found behind the accusation and the defense: it is the requirement of charismatic asceticism, the "privilege of support."

THE SELF-UNDERSTANDING OF PAUL'S COMPETITORS

In 2 Cor. 10:7 Paul takes note of his competitors' self-understanding. They are confident of belonging to Christ (Χριστοῦ εἶναι). An informative parallel to the phrase Χριστοῦ εἶναι, so much puzzled over, is to be found in the requirement for offering hospitality to primitive Christian itinerant charismatics: "For truly, I say to you, whoever gives you a cup of water to drink because you belong to Christ (ὅτι Χριστοῦ ἐστε, RSV "bear the name of Christ"), will by no means lose his reward" (Mk. 9:41). Itinerant preachers qualify as those who belong to Christ and are for that reason to be shown hospitality. Belonging to Christ's family is something they can rely on, which means that as missionaries they can count on finding people who will provide their food and lodging. As a result they can devote themselves wholly to their commission without being distracted by other concerns. When Paul rejects the accusation that he behaves "in a worldly fashion" along with the claim that only his competitors trust in Christ (that is, behave "in a spiritual fashion"), each claim can be used to shed light on the other. The charge against Paul reads that he is too concerned with his material existence instead of making it something wholly dependent on his belonging to Christ.

The presumed self-understanding of these competitors is attested by other passages as well. According to 2 Cor. 11:23 they claim to be διάκονοι Χριστοῦ, which could signify essentially the same thing as Χριστοῦ εἶναι.[47] Epictetus describes the itinerant Cynic preacher as also "God's servant," and asks

> whether the Cynic should not be undistracted entirely, devoted to the service of God (διακονία τοῦ θεοῦ), able to move freely among men, not tied down to private obligations nor involved in personal relations which if he violates he will cease to keep his character as a good man, and if he maintains (them) he will destroy the messenger (ἄγγελος) and scout and herald (κῆρυξ) of the gods . . . [*Diss*. III, 22, 69]

The Cynic, relieved of everyday responsibilities, also lives by trusting to God's grace: "Does God so disregard His own creatures, His servants (διάκονοι), His witnesses . . .?" (*Diss*. III, 26, 28). The Cynic too lives entirely on the basis of God's will: "My will is always to prefer what comes to pass, for I consider what God wills better than what I will. I shall attach myself to Him as His minister (διάκονος) and follower (ἀκόλουθος). My impulses and my wishes are one with Him; in a word, my will is His will" (*Diss*. IV, 7, 20). Here too we find an elevated ethos of independence from earthly necessities based on an unqualified trust in God's will. The early Christian itinerant charismatic movement originating in Palestine could link up in the Greek world with the ethos of the Cynic itinerant preacher. This ethos was also valued in the Corinthian congregation, which explains the accumulation of popular philosophical *topoi* in 2 Cor. 10—13.[48]

Although the term "servant" is not used for the itinerant charismatics of the synoptic Gospels, we find there another self-designation used by Paul's Corinthian competitors: ἐργάται (2 Cor. 11:13).[49] The early Christian itinerant missionaries are "laborers" in a quite specific sense: "The laborer deserves his food" (Mt. 10:10; Lk. 10:7). To be sure, he must offer the gospel free of charge (Mt. 9:9), but it goes without saying that in return he will be guaranteed his food and lodging. The alleged "false apostles" and servants of Satan (2 Cor. 11:13, 15) in Corinth thought the same thing.[50]

PAUL'S DEFENSE

Of interest here are only those arguments by which Paul ascribes to himself a charismatic legitimation. We have already noticed that he reinterprets the requirement of charismatic itinerant asceticism so that it becomes a privilege (1 Cor. 9:7ff.). In a similar manner he can then regard his offense against apostolic norms as the renunciation of a privilege. It is important to notice, however, that Paul does not intend this renunciation to be understood in an ethical sense, however true it may be that it should serve as a pattern for the behavior of those in Corinth who are "strong." Rather, the ulterior purpose of his argument is to portray his renunciation as a divine destiny distinguishing him personally, as a religious qualification—indeed, as a charisma. God himself has required that Paul transgress the usual norms of the primitive Christian itinerant charismatic movement.[51] He has no choice. He is under a sacred obligation. He is a marked man (1 Cor. 9:15–18). For that very reason, however, he fulfills Christ's command and is ἔννομος Χριστοῦ (9:21); he is not someone who transgresses against Christ's "law." The command which Paul has renounced means, of course, that the itinerant charismatic can devote himself entirely to the mission which he serves by preaching the gospel, but even this Paul can claim for his own behavior. If as a free man he became a slave to slaves and weak to the weak, he did so only for the sake of preaching the gospel. He subordinates everything else to that (1 Cor. 9:19ff.). If he has perhaps offended against the letter of the law, still he is for all of that no less ἔννομος Χριστοῦ (9:21).

This line of argument was apparently not persuasive in Corinth. In 2 Corinthians the old objections crop up again. It is instructive to see how Paul now reacts to the charge that he is no "servant of

Christ," that is, that he does not surrender himself fully to the risk of apostolic existence. Heatedly he replies: "Are they servants of Christ? I am a better one—I am talking like a madman—with far greater labors, far more imprisonments, with countless beatings, and often near death" (2 Cor. 11:23). There then follows an impressive *peristasis* catalog in which Paul enumerates all the risks he has taken. Thereafter, no one can doubt that he has regularly put his life at stake (the σάρξ) in order to fulfill his obligation as a missionary. It is noteworthy that in a comparable catalog in 1 Cor. 4:9–13 he counted working with his hands among his tribulations (4:12). In 2 Cor. 11:23ff. this important point is missing, and not by accident. It was just this issue which gave rise to the objection that he lived "in a worldly fashion" rather than exclusively for, and by, the gospel; it would not have been smart to resurrect this sore point as an argument in his defense.

Seen in its totality, Paul's point of view is perfectly comprehensible. The obligation of charismatic asceticism was de facto often enough only a privilege, and became more and more so as more Christian communities sprang up. Renouncing this "privilege" might offend against the letter of Jesus' command but was in keeping with its spirit. The opposite point of view, however, is also comprehensible. Paul clearly violated the norm. His competitors were scarcely "false apostles, deceitful workmen," and servants of Satan (2 Cor. 11:13, 15), as Paul disparaged them. They were normal early Christian missionaries, who held more closely to the rules for itinerant charismatics than did Paul. That they too departed from these rules can be seen from the letters of recommendation, which leads to the next point.

Traditional Legitimation

Next to their charismatic legitimation Paul's competitors emphasized, apparently in a secondary manner, their traditional legitimation. They referred to themselves as "Hebrews . . . Israelites . . . descendants of Abraham" (2 Cor. 11:22). It was known in Corinth that Paul was a Jew; he too was a Hebrew, an Israelite, a descendant of Abraham. The question could only be whether he was a "genuine" Hebrew, Israelite, and son of Abraham.[52] The accumulation of these terms suggests that the reference is not to any and every Jew, but to Jews in some specific sense of that term. It must have been in this special sense that Paul was deficient. It would have been known that Paul was a Diaspora Jew from Tarsus who held Roman citizenship. Nor could his strained relationship with Judaism have remained hidden. Regarding proximity to Palestinian Judaism he was—quite apart from the matter of spatial distance—in a position comparable to that of the Jews living in Corinth. Moreover, Roman and Tarsian citizenship point to a high degree of integration into the non-Jewish society; in some way he will have been represented as a Jew estranged from Judaism. It is therefore also probable that his opponents were not themselves Diaspora Jews but came from Palestine and represent that land where Jesus himself lived.[53] It is possible that Paul's objection that they preached another Jesus (2 Cor. 11:4) refers to a christology close to that of the synoptic tradition, especially since in 2 Cor. 5:16 he makes it clear that he does not regard Christ "from a human point of view." At the very least, traditions which were in close proximity to the commissioning speech may have maintained their currency among Paul's competitors.[54]

On yet a second point Paul's competitors appeal to a traditional legitimation. They came bearing letters of recommendation and received such letters from the Corinthian community (2 Cor. 3:1). Thus they always represented some specific Christian community. Paul did not. Originally, of course, he was dispatched along with Barnabas by the community in Antioch (Acts 13:1ff.), but in his letters this relationship to Antioch no longer plays any role. There may have been some disagreement. Paul had at any rate separated himself from Barnabas and perhaps at that same time from his original home church (cf. Gal. 2:13).

Paul's objection that his competitors have entered foreign territory is related to these letters of recommendation. Letters presuppose someone to whom they are addressed, and even if these letters carry but a general address they are still useful only if some specific people feel that they are directed to them. By definition a missionary armed with letters of recommendation must be entering unfamiliar territory. On the one hand, that is not in keeping with the original norms of the itinerant charismatic movement. Whether one makes provision by means of money or recommendations, in practice it comes to the same thing. On the other hand, it must be remembered that the itinerant charismatics in Palestine did not wish to found new communities. They directed their attention to the "lost sheep of the house of Israel" (Mt. 10:6).

Functional Legitimation

Paul is well aware that in terms of functional legitimation he surpasses all competitors: "I worked harder than any of them" (1 Cor. 15:10). And when he adds, "though it was not I, but the grace of God which is with me" (15:10), he expresses a very self-conscious "humility." Wherever Paul is attacked, he refers to his "workmanship." This is what proves he is a legitimate apostle: "Are you not my workmanship in the Lord? If to others I am not an apostle, at least I am to you; for you are the seal of my apostleship in the Lord" (1 Cor. 9:1–2). In 2 Cor. 3:2 he argues in a similar way in the face of these letters of recommendation: "You yourselves are our letter of recommendation, written on your hearts, to be known and read by all men."

By justifying primarily in a functional way his renunciation of his right to support, Paul is being consistent. He says that he accepted no support "rather than put an obstacle in the way of . . . Christ" (1 Cor. 9:12). What obstacle he has in mind is evident in 1 Thess. 2:5: Paul wants to avoid the suspicion that he works under the cloak of greed (ἐν προφάσει πλεονεξίας) or "peddles" the gospel, as do others (2 Cor. 2:17). That is why he works day and night (1 Thess. 2:9). By means of his renunciation of the right of support he wants to save as many as possible (1 Cor. 9:23). That is his "share" in the gospel. He has renounced his material share, but not his share in its success. His reward is to be found in those who are saved rather than in material support. The συγκοινωνὸς γίγνεσθαι ("that I may share") of 1 Cor. 9:23 corresponds exactly to the τῷ θυσιαστηρίῳ συμμερίζεσθαι ("share in the sacrificial offerings") of 9:13.

It becomes especially clear from 2 Cor. 10:12–18 that this kind of functional legitimation is decisive for Paul. Here he speaks expressly of the "measure" (RSV "limits") which God has given him, of a μέτρον τοῦ κανόνος (10:13), a norm to which he orients his behavior and through the fulfillment of which he knows himself to be legitimated. It is this norm which he thinks justifies his boasting. Its content is, first of all, ἐφικέσθαι ἄχρι καὶ ὑμῶν, that is, to succeed in getting as far as the Corinthians with his mission. But his commission extends yet further. In accordance with his "measure" (κατὰ τὸν κανόνα ἡμῶν) he hopes his field will be enlarged, "so that we may preach the gospel in lands beyond you" (10:16). His "canon" is the missionizing of the entire gentile world (cf. Gal. 2:9; 1:16). In contrast, he accuses his competitors of measuring themselves by reference to themselves (2 Cor. 10:12). Here too he is thinking of a "measure," and it is reasonable to assume that his competitors take as the guide to their behavior the traditional words of Jesus about the *vita apostolica*. The phrase κατὰ τὸ μέτρον τοῦ κανόνος would then correspond to κατὰ τὸ δόγμα τοῦ εὐαγγελίου in *Didache* 11:3, the content of which is the apostle's obligation to charismatic asceticism: he may receive hospitality only in terms of the bare necessities (*Did*. 11:4–6). This δόγμα τοῦ εὐαγγελίου refers to the apostle's style of life, not to his accomplishments. Anyone who seeks to legitimate himself by appealing to the norms of a style of life is certainly vulnerable to the reproach that he measures himself by himself—namely, by the normative marks of his *vita apostolica*.

Naturally, Paul's competitors have also appealed to "workmanship." Paul must expressly point out that "the signs of a true apostle were performed among you in all patience, with signs and wonders and mighty works" (2 Cor. 12:12), apparently to defend himself against objections that he himself performed no such signs.[55] Perhaps his competitors were superior in this regard. Miracles belong to the basic equipment of the missionary according to the commissioning speech in the synoptic Gospels (Mt. 10:8), and elsewhere they are taken as signs of the apostles (Mk. 3:15; 16:15ff.). Paul himself performed miracles—unless one were to accuse him of lying in 2 Cor. 12:12—but he sees them in relationship to his missionary accomplishments, as is evident from Rom. 15:18–19: "For I will not venture to speak of anything except what Christ has wrought through me to win obedience from the Gentiles, by word and deed, by the power of signs and wonders, by the power of the

Holy Spirit, so that from Jerusalem as far round as Illyricum I have fully preached the gospel of Christ." His work is the mission to the Gentiles. He speaks of other miracles, unrelated to this task, only in foolishness (2 Cor. 12:1ff.). He is legitimated not by them but by his missionary accomplishments. It is worth pondering that the very apostle who, like no other, rejects the idea of legitimation by means of works seeks in a concrete situation to be legitimated just that way, by his accomplishments.[56]

In conclusion, Paul's competitors appeal to a charismatic legitimation which is supplemented by a traditional one, while Paul, in contrast, represents a different form of apostolic legitimacy, a functional form which he combines with elements of a charismatic form—in which he takes his charismatic deficit, his "weakness," and elevates it to the status of a sign of his apostolic existence. These two forms of legitimation go hand in hand with different ways of arguing the question of subsistence. For the community organizer even this question is subordinated to an effective mission, while for the itinerant charismatic an orientation to the norms of the *vita apostolica* is a value in its own right. The conflict between these two types of missionaries may have run something like this. Itinerant charismatics arriving in Corinth made a claim on support from the community. The members reacted at first by pointing to Paul: our apostle Paul never raised any such claims. In response, the itinerant charismatics could point to the words of Jesus as a justification for their position. As regards Paul, that left but two choices. Either they must convert him to their style of life or deny him his claim to apostolicity. Possibly they tried the first; at any rate Paul protests, "And what I do [namely, forgoing my right to subsistence] I will continue to do, in order to undermine the claim of those who would like to claim that in their boasted mission they work on the same terms as we do" (2 Cor. 11:12).[57] Above all, however, they contested Paul's apostolicity—not out of personal malice, but in self-defense. If Paul were ultimately to prevail with his understanding of the *vita apostolica*, it would be at the expense of the material foundation underlying the primitive Christian institution of the itinerant charismatic. Who, after being freed from the requirement of earning a living for twenty years or so, would then have been willing or able to work—even under extreme necessity?

The theological question of an apostle's legitimacy is indissolubly linked with the material question of the apostle's subsistence. Certainly there once was a religious motive behind the choice of the life of the itinerant charismatic. But the decision brought with it certain circumstances of life on which one then became dependent, even in one's theological line of argument. Paul's material independence doubtless afforded a greater scope for his theological argument as well.

EXCURSUS: ON THE SOCIOLOGICAL STRUCTURE OF THE CORINTHIAN PARTIES

This conflict among competing missionaries would remain something of a puzzle were we not also to look into its effects on the community. Paul clearly addresses himself directly to the congregation in both letters. The origin of the conflict lies in the fact that various missionaries have achieved influence within the community,[58] giving rise to group divisions and arguments. The missionaries themselves have moved on. Apollos is no longer in Corinth when 1 Corinthians is written (1 Cor. 16:12), and the missionaries of 2 Corinthians have been given letters of recommendation to help them on their further travels (2 Cor. 3:1). In their wake they leave problems which also must have had causes within the Corinthian community itself. What gave rise to the group divisions within the congregation?[59]

Paul himself seems to trace the groups back to a special relationship between those baptized and those who baptized them. In order to point out the absurdity of something like a "Paul party" he explicitly assures his readers that he baptized only a very few in Corinth (1 Cor. 1:12–17). It is usually assumed that the Corinthian groups thought of themselves as enjoying a relationship with their apostles like that of members of a mystery cult.[60] This interpretation may be correct, but it does not preclude a more comprehensive analysis. All that is certain is that the groups did regard themselves as enjoying a special relationship with their apostles.

This raises the question of who within a congregation would enter into a special relationship with itinerant apostles? The first to come to mind are those who offer the missionaries food and lodging. In that case, their relationships to the missionaries cannot be strictly like those within a mystery cult, for they have a manifestly material basis. And if some members of the community extol "their" missionary, what more are they doing than extolling their own magnanimity? Naturally, nobody wishes to spend money for a second-class missionary; for that reason all regard as the most important missionary the one they have supported (and by whom they have surely been influenced theologically). What is more, if the missionary were important, so would his followers within the community be. Thus the disagreement among different parties may be a matter of scrapping for position within the pecking order. Paul sees its origin in the fact that the Corinthians are "puffed up" in favor of one against another (1 Cor. 4:6).

Can something more be said about the sociological background of these tussles for prestige within the congregation? We may at least voice the suspicion that the protagonists of the various parties were Christians from the upper strata, the few "wise", "powerful", and "of noble birth" whom Paul mentions in 1 Cor. 1:26. The following considerations suggest that this was the case:

1. We know the names of those whom Paul baptized and, since Paul himself connects this baptismal association with partisan affiliation, the probable members of his party. They were certainly not poor people. Crispus was a synagogue ruler prior to becoming a Christian (Acts 18:8–9).[61] Since his conversion influenced many others, he must have been a man others looked up to. Gaius we find in Rom. 16:23 playing "host" to Paul "and to the whole church," which means that he had large accommodations at his disposal. Tertius writes the letter to the Romans in Gaius's house, suggesting that it was not unusual to find services of this sort being performed there. According to 1 Cor. 16:15–18, Stephanas had devoted himself to "the service of the saints," and he visits Paul in Ephesus with two members of his family (or slaves). It thus appears that Paul confined his baptizing to a few influential and important members of the community. At least in regard to the party strife it is these with whom he is concerned, and it is interesting to note that he does not mention by name the members of Stephanas's house even though he has baptized them. He is concerned only with the head of the family. The important people in the "Paul party" occupy a relatively high social position. It seems reasonable to draw an analogous inference about the other parties, especially if we take into account a second argument.

2. Gaius is also one of those specifically named by Paul as belonging to his circle. Later, Paul stayed at his house (Rom. 16:23). The missionaries in competition with Paul, however, needed more than lodging. They required support and so were all the more dependent on these Christians who were economically well-off. Their hosts had to be able to accommodate them and have some money to spare after meeting their own needs. That would be all the more true if these competing missionaries also ac-

cepted money for continuing their journey. And in what other way, except by their own labor, could they acquire the provisions and money they needed? But once respected "homeowners"[62] had become followers of Apollos or Peter, their houses could then become meeting points and centers for smaller groups within the community. The congregation would also come together in one place, of course (1 Cor. 11:20), but in Rom. 16:23 Paul emphasizes that Gaius is host to the *entire* congregation, from which it may be indirectly concluded that elsewhere there were houses in which only a portion of the congregation gathered.

3. If the conflict among followers of various apostles is a struggle for position within the congregation, carried on primarily by those of high social status, then the train of thought in 1 Cor. 1—4 becomes more comprehensible, especially the transition from the theme of *schismata* (1:10–17) to that of the preaching of the cross (1:18ff.). From the preaching of the cross Paul derives a revaluation of all norms of social rank. It is precisely the nobodies, those who are weak and have no standing, whom God has chosen. To a great extent the congregation is gathered from just such levels, from people who enjoy no status in their world, that is, in antiquity's society. Yet in the matter of partisan allegiance Paul addresses himself to the few who are wise, powerful, and of noble birth (1:26). And when he contrasts his own social situation in 1 Cor. 4:9–13 with that of the Corinthians—more precisely, with that of the "wise," the "strong," and the "reputable" (RSV "held in honor") Corinthians (4:10)—it is not accidental that he mentions working with his hands, suggesting that among those whom he addresses are Christians who do not need to support themselves with their own labor. Meanwhile, the context (1 Cor. 3:18—4:9) makes it clear that Paul is speaking to those who are responsible for the party divisions.

4. In 1 Cor. 9 Paul combines his appeal to the strong about renouncing rights with a defense of himself against attacks occasioned by his renunciation of the right to support. Here too he must defend himself against unfavorable comparisons with other apostles, and so he produces that apology (9:3) which comes to mind when he thinks of a "human court" (4:3). The objections to Paul have been raised by members of the other parties. If the complaint that laboring with his own hands keeps him from being free (9:1) originates with them, we can hardly imagine them to be a group of people who would thereby implicate themselves too. That in what Paul is saying here he addresses himself to the strong also counts in favor of our thesis, for these, in all probability, belong to the upper strata.

5. Paul's informants about the partisan controversy are "Chloe's

people." The letter, which comes from the community itself, contained scarcely a hint about that problem and was probably composed by people possessing some degree of culture, since it contains popular philosophical *topoi* (1 Cor. 8:1; 10:23). By contrast, the oral reports seem to have been brought by people who look at the problems of the Corinthian community from "below." In both 1 Cor. 1:12ff. and 11:17–34 Paul obviously takes the side of those members of the community who come from the lower strata, who are without influence or standing (1:26ff.), who "have nothing" (11:22). In all probability the problems have been described to him by members of the community who themselves belong to the lower strata or who at least can see the matter from that perspective. As far as party strife is concerned, we may even conclude from the names of the informants ("Chloe's people," 1:11) that they are likely to have been slaves, since members of a family would have used their father's name, even if he were deceased. The party strife is apparently viewed negatively by these people, which is not surprising if it is an affair involving some of the more prominent members of the community who are competing for the most influence within the congregation.

In 2 Corinthians we hear nothing more about this strife among parties. Instead, almost all the Corinthians now seem united in a position opposing Paul. In its structure, however, this new conflict is comparable to the old. The attitude opposing Paul results from the respect now being accorded to the newly arrived "superlative apostles." These apostles are scarcely likely to have found shelter with those Christians who showed up at the Lord's Supper with "nothing" (1 Cor. 11:17ff.). Nor are those attracted to them the least cultured of people. They can evaluate letters, and they raise certain objections to Paul's appearance and rhetoric. Paul responds with arguments employing a clutch of allusions drawn from popular philosophy, which not everybody would have understood.

All these observations taken together justify the assumption that the protagonists of the Corinthian parties were members of the upper classes. Naturally, these in turn had their followers from the lower classes. A person of high social station is often influential in shaping the views of others. What causes the conflict is their desire to puff themselves up against one another (1 Cor. 4:6). In all probability we can assign that desire to the few there who were "wise", "powerful", and "of noble birth" (1 Cor. 1:26; 4:10).

We can now summarize our conclusions. Two different types of primitive Christian itinerant preachers, to be distinguished as itinerant charismatics and community organizers, came into conflict in

Corinth. The occasion of the conflict was a difference in attitudes on the question of the itinerant preachers' charismatic poverty and their claim to support from the community. Paul's competitors represent a type or pattern rooted in Palestinian soil and shaped by the ethos of the commissioning speech. Barnabas and Paul, by contrast, represent a type which is firmly established in the urban, Hellenistic world and is appropriate to the requirements of the initial stage of missionary work in this region. Among such people, socio-ecological, socio-economic, and socio-cultural factors have led to a transformation of the *vita apostolica* and its norms—specifically, to a renunciation of support. Subsequently, representatives of the other type, itself now undergoing some change, moved into the urban, Hellenistic missionary territory now opened up. The conflict between these two types of primitive Christian itinerant preachers could encompass the entire Christian community because it was overlaid with class-specific differences and tendencies already present within the Corinthian congregation. In this conflict it should not be forgotten, however, that both are part of what is essentially the same kind of social posture. Both embody a specific form of religiously inspired, socially divergent behavior. In both instances we are dealing with outsiders. This fact becomes built into Paul's self-portrait. He places himself on the low end of the social hierarchy. Indeed, he finally locates himself outside all of society by describing himself as "the refuse of the world, the off-scouring of all things" (1 Cor. 4:13). In this he is probably on a par with his competitor Peter, whose nickname "Barjona" may have been practically synonymous with "outlaw."[63]

All these people had left behind that social world in which they once lived. A great religious unrest, doubtless connected to the social conflicts of that era, turned them out onto the highways and made of them roving itinerant preachers, outsiders and "outlaws." Here on the margins of society they pursued a new form of life with what were often eccentric views and visions, words and actions. They understood themselves to be the "salt of the earth." And, in fact, they were the *cor inquietum* ("the restless soul") of a society marked by conflict. They were the "soul of soulless conditions" (Karl Marx),[64] the spirit of yet other groups which the world's history has otherwise passed over in silence. By studying them one learns this at least: when a religion ceases to be the *cor inquietum* of a society, when the thirst for a new form of life is no longer vital in it, when it becomes the antispirit amid spiritual and dispirited conditions, then there is something to be said for the proposition that this religion has expired. When that happens, no kind of interpretive art can rekindle it, and the question becomes all the more important: "If salt has lost its taste, how shall its saltness be restored?" (Mt. 5:13).

NOTES

1. Cf. ["Theissen, 1973 = Theissen, 1976c. Wire's translation renders the full text but only a greatly abridged version of the notes—Trans.] The ideas expressed there are further developed in what follows.

2. To be sure, in Mt. 10:4 and Mk. 3:18 "Cananaean" occurs, but that may be a transliteration of "ha kannai" (the Zealot). This variation in surnames is much more likely to stem from an original "Zealot" than the reverse, "Zealot" from "Cananaean." Any connection between the Jesus movement and the Zealots would have been inopportune after the Jewish war. Cf. J. Klausner, *Jesus of Nazareth: His Life, Times, and Teaching* (New York, 1929), 206.

3. Socially divergent behavior occurs in every society and is a completely "normal" occurrence; nothing short of absolute force could prevent it. Only an unusual increase in socially divergent behavior can be taken as a symptom of social disintegration and "anomie." Cf. R. König, "Anomie," in *Fischer-Lexikon Soziologie* (Frankfurt, 1958), 17–25. On the central importance of anomie for the sociology of religion cf. P. Berger, *The Sacred Canopy: Elements of a Sociological Theory of Religion* (Garden City, N.Y., 1967).

4. On the polis in Palestine cf. A. H. M. Jones, "The Urbanization of Palestine," *JRS* 21 (1931): 78–85; idem, *The Cities of the Eastern Roman Provinces* (Oxford, 1937), 248ff.; A. Alt, "Hellenistische Städte und Domänen in Galiläa," Galiläische Probleme 3, in *Kleine Schriften zur Geschichte des Volkes Israel*, (München, 1953), II:384–95; V. A. Tcherikover, "Was Jerusalem a 'Polis'?" *IEJ* 14 (1964): 61–78. For further literature see M. Hengel, *Judaism and Hellenism* (Philadelphia, 1974), II:17 n. 149.

5. The instability of the social and political situation is proven by the frequent changes in the form of governance. From 63 to 40 B.C.E. Judea, Galilee, and Peraea were under Roman provincial administration. Twice during that period a change in relations was brought about, by Gabinius in 57 B.C.E. and by Caesar in 47 B.C.E. From 40 B.C.E. until 6 C.E. native

monarchs ruled; from 6 to 41 C.E. Roman governors, from 41 to 44 C.E. again a native monarch, then again a Roman governor. Only in Galilee did local princes last, from 40 B.C.E. to 44 C.E.

6. Jeremias, *Jerusalem in the Time of Jesus* (Philadelphia, 1969), 181ff., has analyzed the institutions and customs of this theocratic circle.

7. The problems of Jewish monarchy are analyzed by A. Schalit, *König Herodes*, SJ 4 (Berlin, 1969), esp. 146ff., 298ff.; idem, "Herodes und seine Nachfolger,"*Kont*. 3 (1966): 34–42.

8. M. Hengel, *Die Zeloten: Untersuchungen zur jüdischen Freiheitsbewegung in der Zeit von Herodes I bis 70 n. Chr.* (Leiden, 1961).

9. Ibid., 235ff. In my opinion, however, these messianic prophets should be more sharply differentiated from the Zealots. The latter had a religious and social program which could be pursued independently of particular messianic pretenders. In contrast, the movements around messianic prophets collapsed with the death of the leader. Cf. R. Meyer, *Der Prophet aus Galiläa* (Leipzig, 1940 = Darmstadt, 1970).

10. So also Klausner, *Jesus,* 189: The unemployed "waxed poorer and poorer, sinking into mendicancy, crushed and depressed, hoping for miracles, filling the streets of town and village with beggary and piety or (in the case of the more robust) with brigandage, highway-robbery and revolt; outcasts, haunting the caves and desert places and the rocks and crevices of the mountains."

11. The hypothesis that the Jesus movement arose from social conflict can scarcely be refuted by referring to a few Christians who were better off, contrary to R. Schumacher, *Die soziale Lage der Christen im apostolischen Zeitalter* (Paderborn, 1924).

12. So, especially, Klausner, *Jesus,* 135ff. Cf., however, A. Schalit, *König Herodes,* 322–28.

13. F. C. Grant, *The Economic Background of the Gospels* (Oxford, 1926), 87–110, in particular points to this.

14. A list of periods of want is found in Jeremias, *Jerusalem,* 140ff.

15. Cf. W. R. Farmer, "The Economic Basis of the Qumran Community," *ThZ* 11 (1955): 295–308; 12 (1956): 56–58; L. M. Pakozdy, "Der wirtschaftliche Hintergrund der Gemeinschaft von Qumran," in *Qumran-Probleme,* ed. H. Bardtke (Berlin, 1963), 167–91.

16. M. Hengel, *Zeloten,* 26–35, provides an overview of the widespread scope of robbery and in doing so places the Zealots in a more general setting, without neglecting their characteristic traits.

17. Cf. Grant, *Economic Background,* 81–87; Hengel, *Judaism and Hellenism,* I:16, 47. S. W. Baron, *A Social and Religious History of the Jews* (New York, 1952), 1:370–72, gives a survey of the debate about the density of the population of Palestine at that time.

18. Cf. A. Deissmann, *Light from the Ancient East* (London, 1927), 246–47; idem, *Das Urchristentum und die unteren Schichten* (Göttingen,

1908[2]), 23ff.; A. N. Sherwin-White, *Roman Society and Roman Law in the New Testament* (Oxford, 1963), 120–43; E. A. Judge, *The Social Pattern of the Christian Groups in the First Century* (London, 1960), 10–17.

19. M. D. Goulder, "Characteristics of the Parables in the Several Gospels," *JThS* 19 (1968): 51–69, finds the world of the village, and of nature, presupposed only in the Marcan parables, while particularly in Luke more pronounced urban traits begin to emerge. Many parables from Luke's special tradition, however, are also set in a rural milieu, e.g., Lk. 10:30–37; 13:6–9; 16:1–8; 17:7–10. The fact that the parables are rooted in the rural world is the more remarkable as Jesus himself was an artisan, a sphere of life from which images are altogether absent.

20. What W. Bauer, "Jesus der Galiläer," in *Aufsätze und kleine Schriften* (Tübingen, 1967), 91–108, has demonstrated about Jesus also holds for the early Jesus movement. He calls attention to the fact that "from the beginning, Jesus was able to gain no ground in the cities. Nazareth will have no part of him, and Chorazin, Bethsaida, and Capernaum reject him. The tradition is altogether silent, however, concerning Sepphoris, Tiberias, Gabae, and Taricheae" (106).

21. The Jesus movement belongs to a type of messianic movement which arises out of the confrontation between two cultures where it is a matter of preserving some sense of self-esteem in the face of a politically superior culture. Cf. W. E. Mühlmann, *Chiliasmus und Nativismus* (Berlin, 1961); R. Linton, "Nativistic Movements," *American Anthropologist* 45 (1943): 230–40.

22. The Sadducees may also be understood from this standpoint. They wished to preserve the institutions of Jewish theocracy from which they profited as members of the upper classes. On the sociological background of the different currents in Jewish-Palestinian society, cf. P. Alfaric, *Die sozialen Ursprünge des Christentums*, ed. G. Pätsch and M. Robbe (Darmstadt/Berlin, 1963), 43–75, on which M. Robbe, *Der Ursprung des Christentums* (Leipzig/Jena, 1967), 57–71, bases his Marxist interpretation. It is a serious failure of both authors that they do not recognize the independence of the Essenes from the Christian movement.

23. So, correctly, Hengel, *Zeloten*, 233–34: the Jesus movement, the Pharisees, and the Zealots may be interpreted in a comparable way through "the motif of the eschatological sharpening of the Torah." Cf. the detailed investigation of this phenomenon by H. Braun, *Spätjüdisch-häretischer und frühchristlicher Radikalismus*, BHTh 24 (Tübingen, 1957).

24. Her prominence in Luke corresponds to the author's tendency to connect early Christianity with women from the upper strata; cf. M. Hengel, "Maria Magdelana und die Frauen als Zeugen," in *Abraham unser Vater: Festschrift für O. Michel* (Leiden, 1963), 243–56, esp. 245–46.

25. H. Bolkestein, *Wohltätigkeit und Armenpflege im vorchristlichen Altertum* (Groningen, 1967 = Utrecht, 1939).

26. The thesis of K. Holl, "Der Kirchenbegriff des Paulus in seinem Verhältnis zu dem der Urgemeinde," *Gesammelte Aufsätze* (Tübingen, 1928), II:44–67, that "the poor" was an ecclesiological title of the early community, has been critically examined by L. Keck—with negative results: "The Poor among the Saints in the New Testament," *ZNW* 56 (1965): 100–137; idem, "The Poor among the Saints in Jewish Christianity and Qumran," *ZNW* 57 (1966): 54–68. Yet it is beyond dispute that the term *poverty* is here not a purely sociological term but resonates with a religious interpretation of the social condition.

27. Cf. the detailed analysis of the social and religious aspects of this attempted reform in Hengel, *Judaism and Hellenism*. He correctly concludes about early Christianity, "At this point, though in a very different way from the reform attempt after 175 B.C.E., the door really was thrown open to the 'nations'" (I:313).

28. H. Conzelmann, *History of Primitive Christianity* (Nashville, 1973), 159, assumes, with some justice, that Barnabas was Paul's teacher on this matter. G. Dautzenberg, "Der Verzicht auf das apostolische Unterhaltsrecht: Eine exegetische Untersuchung zu 1 Kor. 9," *Bib*. 50 (1969): 212–32, has also inquired into the sociological grounds for this decision. The information that Paul turned to those of the lower strata, whom he then did not wish to burden, is not a very satisfying explanation since Paul doubtlessly also turned toward the higher strata (see below). Ch. Maurer, "Grund und Grenze apostolischer Freiheit: Exegetisch-theologische Studie zu 1. Korinther 9," *Antwort. K. Barth zum 70 Geburtstag* (Zurich, 1956), 630–41, completely disregards the sociological aspects.

29. Cf. Jones, *The Cities*, passim; Judge, *Social Pattern*, 10ff.

30. Acts 17:7 suggests some of the difficulties which could result from preaching about a "kingdom of God."

31. N. Brockmeyer, *Sozialgeschichte der Antike* (Stuttgart, 1972), 110: "The far-reaching urbanization of the empire during the early and peak phases of the imperial era occasioned a cultural and civilizing development which was singular for antiquity and which would again be achieved only in the modern period."

32. Cf. W. Bienert, *Die Arbeit nach der Lehre der Bibel* (Stuttgart, 1954), 302ff.

33. The absence of the synoptic tradition from the Epistles is, in my opinion, also determined by a sociological threshold which hindered the dissemination in the urban Mediterranean world of those traditions which arose in Palestine. If one gathers up all the sayings which *(a)* point to a radical-theocratic stock of ideas, thus all the sayings about the "kingdom of God," *(b)* are stamped by the nonfamilial ethical radicalism of Palestinian

itinerant charismatics, or *(c)* are bound to the cultural (including linguistic) conditions of this region, then little remains. The absence of the tradition is in no way to be attributed to Paul's personal decision. That is correctly emphasized by W. Schmithals, "Paulus und der historische Jesus," *ZNW* 53 (1962): 145–60, and H. W. Kuhn, "Der irdische Jesus bei Paulus als traditionsgeschichtliches und theologisches Problem," *ZThK* 67 (1970): 295–320.

34. Naturally there was also in Palestine a patriarchalism of the household, but it left no mark on the Jesus movement, which bore instead the imprint of itinerant charismatics. In the cities, on the other hand, resident Christians quickly became the strategic agents of early Christianity. Here the communities were much larger and developed their own structures of authority while the small groups of sympathizers in Palestine (cf. Mt. 18:20) depended much more on itinerant authorities.

35. A fisherman could also be hired on as a hand (cf. Mk. 1:20), of course, but the Palestinian itinerant charismatics worked primarily in rural regions (cf. Mt. 10:5–6). Furthermore, life on the sea could be combined with missionary ambitions only with difficulty, while the work of the artisan provided greater opportunities for contact with others. M. Weber, *The Sociology of Religion* (Boston, 1963), 95, described "wandering apprentices" as the characteristic agents of the spread of early Christianity.

36. Cf. K. Holl, "Das Fortleben der Volkssprachen in Kleinasien in nachchristlicher Zeit," in *Gesammelte Aufsätze* (Tübingen, 1928), II:238–48.

37. In 1 Thess. 2:1–12 Paul is probably distinguishing himself from such types; he does not fail to mention his work as an artisan (2:9). On the ethos of itinerant Cynic philosphers and beggars, cf. H. Bolkestein, *Wohltätigkeit*, 212–13.

38. Cf. H. D. Betz, *Der Apostel Paulus und die sokratische Tradition*, BHTh 45 (Tübingen, 1972), 100–117.

39. W. Schmithals, *Gnosticism in Corinth* (Nashville, 1971), regards Paul as fighting on the same front in both 1 and 2 Corinthians. This is not entirely wrong. The "gnostics" in 1 Corinthians and the supporters of the recently arrived itinerant preachers could have belonged to precisely the same circles. Similarly the itinerant preachers in 1 and 2 Corinthians belong to a comparable sociological type.

40. Cf. the methodological reflections of C. K. Barrett, "Christianity at Corinth," *BJRL* 46 (1963/64): 269–97, esp. 287; idem, "Paul's Opponents in 2 Corinthians," *NTS* 17 (1971): 233–54, esp. 251.

41. Schmithals, *Gnosticism*, 228 n. 152, perceives the problem: "But one never defends himself thus against charges which arise directly out of the fact that the apostle *has* the right." He goes on to draw the wrong conclusion, that Paul's apostolic rights were not disputed.

42. To be sure, this is frequently seen as an artificial intensification of arguments. Cf. the dicussion of W. Schrage, *Die konkreten Einzelgebote in der paulinischen Paränese* (Gütersloh, 1961), 234–35.

43. On the discrediting of the artisan's life in antiquity cf. Bolkestein, *Wohltätigkeit*, 191ff., 332ff., who explains that the negative judgment comes from the higher circles of those freed from manual labor. The manual laborers from the lower strata, however, would not have judged themselves so negatively. Socrates' opinion on manual labor is much more positive than that of his aristocratic student Plato. Cf. further F. v. d. Ven, *Sozialgeschichte der Arbeit*. Bd. I, *Antike und Frühmittelalter* (München, 1971).

44. This reproach is much controverted in the literature. (1) R. Reitzenstein, *The Hellenistic Mystery-Religions* (Pittsburgh, 1978), 459, is of the opinion that the parties attacked by Paul returned his reproach (that their strife betrays a fleshly character [1 Cor. 3:1–3]): Paul himself instigated strife and for that reason behaves in a fleshly manner. (2) Betz, *Paulus*, 96: An angel of Satan dwelt in Paul, causing his illness; thus he behaves in a fleshly manner. (3) Most think very generally of ignoble, un-Christian motives. So H. Lietzman, *An die Korinther I/II*, HNT 9 (Tübingen, 1949[4]), 140. H. Windisch, *Der zweite Korintherbrief* (Göttingen, 1924), 295, is more concrete: Paul was regarded as a sorcerer. D. Georgi, *Die Gegner des Paulus im 2. Korintherbrief: Studien zur religiösen Propaganda in der Spätantike*, WMANT 11 (Neukirchen, 1964), 232 n. 13, agrees. (4) Schmithals, *Gnosticism*, 165, wants to understand "according to the flesh" in a purely mythical sense: Paul was no pneumatic but a sarcic in terms of the Gnostic myth of origins.

45. Cf. Barrett, "Opponents," 246.

46. Barrett, ibid.: the theme of renunciation of support always follows "almost immediately upon Paul's emphatic assertion that he does not fall short of οἱ ὑπερλίαν ἀπόστολοι."

47. For the following cf. Georgi, *Gegner*, 31–38.

48. Cf. the fundamental investigation of these *topoi* in Betz, *Paulus*.

49. Cf. Georgi, *Gegner*, 49–51.

50. That one must distinguish between the false apostles and the superlative apostles, and that the latter reside in Jerusalem—the position of E. Käsemann, "Die Legitimität des Apostels," *ZNW* 41 (1942): 33–71, and Barrett, "Opponents," 252ff.—is improbable in my view. Cf. R. Bultmann, *Exegetische Probleme des zweiten Korintherbriefes* (Darmstadt, 1963), 20–32.

51. Cf. E. Käsemann, "A Pauline Version of the 'Amor Fati,'" in *New Testament Questions of Today* (Philadelphia, 1969), 217–35. Of course one cannot completely reject the ethical interpretation. Paul, however, wants first of all to show that his renunciation of support is a fate imposed by God.

52. Cf. on the question Georgi, *Gegner*, 51–82.

53. For the sociological analysis of Paul's opponents, whether they are Jewish Christians or Hellenistic Jewish Christians is not a critical matter. It is not even critical whether they personally come from Palestine. What matters is only that they represent that type of early Christian itinerant charismatic which originated in Palestine. Independent of that fact, their Palestinian origin is probable; so Käsemann, *Legitimität*, 33–71, and Barrett, "Opponents," 251. Even those exegetes who regard them as Hellenistic Jewish Christians reckon with a Palestinian origin: Georgi, *Gegner*, 58; G. Friedrich, "Die Gegner des Paulus im 2. Korintherbrief," in *Abraham unser Vater* (Leiden/Köln, 1963), 181–215. Schmithals, *Gnosticism*, 289–93, disputes the Palestinian origin.

54. The supposition that this has to do with a θεῖος-ἀνήρ christology, which corresponds to the christology of the synoptic miracle stories, is unconvincing. This thesis has frequently been put forward since Georgi, *Gegner*, 213ff.; see, among others, G. Bornkamm, "Die Vorgeschichte des sogenannten zweiten Korintherbriefes," in SHAW.PH (1961), 15–16 [abridged Eng. trans. in *NTS* 8 (1962): 258–64]; Friedrich, "Gegner," 181ff; Kuhn, "Jesus bei Paulus," 295–320.

(1) A θεῖος-ἀνήρ christology cannot be inferred from the performance of miracles by missionaries (2 Cor. 12:12). In the logia source the missionaries are commissioned to perform miracles (Lk. 10:9), although there is no θεῖος-ἀνήρ christology in that source. The temptation narrative even witnesses to a certain distance from such a christology (Lk. 4:1ff.).

(2) Neither can one infer a θεῖος-ἀνήρ christology from the mention of "another Jesus" (2 Cor. 11:4). Paul connects that phrase with his reproach that the Corinthians "submit" to such a proclamation. We also encounter this reproach in 2 Cor. 11:20: the Corinthians "submit" to claims of privileges by the opponents. Paul, in contrast, did not burden them. Barrett, "Opponents," 242, rightly concludes, "In the foreground stands the ethical test of behavior that is or is not consistent with the Gospel—a test which the Corinthians had omitted to apply."

(3) The quest after a δοκιμὴ τοῦ ἐν ἐμοὶ λαλοῦντος Χριστοῦ (13:3) more likely points to a mode of speech in the I-style, as we find it in the Logia source and the Gospel of John. The opponents are primarily bearers of the word, the sermon (11:4).

(4) The problem of the christology of the competing itinerant preachers should be separated from the question of their self-understanding. Here too, in my opinion, there is no hint that the opponents understood themselves as θεῖοι ἄνδρες. One might more appropriately call to mind the ethos of the Cynic itinerant philosophers. It is, in my opinion, inappropriate to extend the θεῖος-ἀνήρ concept so far that it also covers these propagandists, since on the whole this concept is not very precise. Cf. the

overview of M. Smith, who surveys the different types from Augustus to Anthony the Hermit: "Prolegomena to a Discussion of Aretalogies, Divine Men, the Gospels and Jesus," *JBL* 90 (1971): 174–99.

55. We must of course reckon with the possibility that this derives not from a *topos* of the competing itinerant preachers but from the congregation resident in Cornith, which is seeking criteria for evaluating missionaries—so Barrett, "Opponents," 245.

56. E. Käsemann, *Legitimität*, 59–60, polemicizes against the view that Paul is legitimated by his works. It is true that Paul ascribes everything to God's grace and that he boasts of his own contribution only "in foolishness." Nevertheless, he is justified by his accomplishments—God's accomplishments done through him. The reference to the grace of God is no restriction on Paul's almost unsurpassable self-consciousness as preacher of a unique, absolute truth to the whole world. Rather, it is a hypertrophy of this self-consciousness; he boasts, in fact, εἰς τὰ ἄμετρα (2 Cor. 10:13). Should a reproach of the opponents stand behind that, one ought not a priori to exclude the possibility that for once Paul's opponents made a pertinent observation.

57. Cf. Betz, *Paulus*, 102.

58. It is uncertain whether Peter was ever in Corinth; cf. C. K. Barrett, "Cephas and Corinth," in *Abraham unser Vater* (Leiden/Köln, 1963) 1–12. But at least there were missionaries in Corinth who appealed to Peter.

59. The existence of a Christ party is contested; cf. the review of opinion in Schmithals, *Gnosticism*, 117ff.:

(1) Such a party is not mentioned in 1 Clem. 47:3. But from that it follows at most that the author of 1 Clement could himself make nothing of a "Christ party," whether in his interpretation of 1 Corinthians or in his argument with the Corinthian congregation.

(2) It is passed over in 1 Cor. 3:22, where Paul, Apollos, and Cephas are subordinated to the community. The community, however, is in turn subordinated to Christ. Thus the passage makes perfectly good sense if it is assumed that there was a Christ party: not just some, but all, belong to Christ.

(3) The argument implicit in the question, "Is Christ divided?" cannot be aimed at a Christ party. If, however, the phrase ἐγὼ δὲ Χριστοῦ appears inappropriately in the Pauline argument, then it is all the more likely that Paul did not introduce it himself. If not the party then certainly the slogan must have been present in Corinth.

(4) To the extent that the bond of baptism characterizes the parties, these must be understood as very heterogeneous groups. Paul, Apollos, and Peter could have baptized in Corinth or actually did so. The Christ party could point to nothing analogous. Either this is not a party or it is a

group which is deliberately opposed to the party divisions. In that case, we have here the slogan of some individual Christians.

However that may be, Paul takes for granted a "Christ" slogan in Corinth and would leave himself open to ridicule were he here knowingly to insinuate something which does not correspond to the circumstances. In my opinion the decisive question is, Who uttered this slogan? and for that 2 Cor. 10:7 is relevant. The slogan does not arise from local Christians but (at least originally) from itinerant missionaries (cf. Mark 9:41). The apostles are representatives of Christ and "belong to" him. The Corinthian parties, in turn, understood themselves to be bound to an apostle and through him to Christ as well. In 1 Cor. 3:22–23 we see Paul reversing this relation: all the apostles belong to the community, but the community belongs (directly) to Christ.

60. Cf. U. Wilckens, *Weisheit und Torheit* (Tübingen, 1959), 12. Schmithals, *Gnosticism*, 289–92, presents some very weighty counterarguments.

61. I have analyzed the social status of the prominent Corinthians in "Social Stratification in the Corinthian Community: A Contribution to the Sociology of Early Hellenistic Christianity," pp. 000–00 below.

62. First Cor. 11:22 may be evidence for the existence of house owners. Their importance for the makeup of the community has been investigated by F. V. Filson, "The Significance of the Early House Churches," *JBL* 58 (1939): 103–12.

63. Cf. Hengel, *Zeloten*, 57.

64. "Introduction. Contribution to the Critique of Hegel's Philosophy of Right," *Karl Marx: Early Writings*, trans. and ed. T. B. Bottomore, Foreword by E. Fromm (New York/London, 1964), 44.

2

Social Stratification in the Corinthian Community: A Contribution to the Sociology of Early Hellenistic Christianity

To which social strata did the Christians of the Hellenistic congregations outside Palestine belong? Various opinions have been expressed on this problem. According to A. Deissmann, primitive Christianity was a movement within the lower strata. "The New Testament was not a product of the colourless refinement of an upper class. . . . On the contrary, it was, humanly speaking, a product of the force that came, unimpaired and strengthened by the Divine Presence, from the lower class (Matt. 11:25ff.; 1 Cor. 1:26–31). This reason alone enabled it to become the Book of all mankind."[1] E. A. Judge has expressed the opposite view: "Far from being a socially depressed group, then, if the Corinthians are at all typical, the Christians were dominated by a socially pretentious section of the population of the big cities."[2] Both judgments appeal to the makeup of the Corinthian congregation and both can be confirmed by means of a sociological analysis of all the information about this congregation. Both opinions are probably correct, because—and this is the thesis to be argued here—the Corinthian congregation is marked by internal stratification. The majority of the members, who come from the lower classes, stand in contrast to a few influential members who come from the upper classes. This internal stratification is not accidental but the result of structural causes. The social makeup of the Corinthian congregation may, therefore, be characteristic of the Hellenistic congregations as such.

To prove this thesis requires a systematic analysis of everything said about the Corinthian community, specifically, (1) statements about the whole congregation, (2) statements about individual members, and (3) statements about groups within the congregation. These results must then be interpreted, in the second part of this essay, by inquiring into the structural elements which render plausible the internal stratification of the Corinthian congregation, whether these are to be found in the social structure of the city of Corinth itself or arise from the structure of the Pauline mission. Finally, we will briefly discuss the significance of social stratification for the history and self-understanding of primitive Christianity and sketch some working hypotheses for further investigations in the sociology of religion.

THE SOCIOLOGICAL EVALUATION OF EVIDENCE FOR THE CORINTHIAN CONGREGATION

Statements About the Community as a Whole

Paul himself describes the social makeup of the Corinthian congregation: "For consider your call, brethren; not many of you were wise according to worldly standards, not many were powerful, not many were of noble birth; but God chose what is foolish in the world to shame the wise, God chose what is weak in the world to shame the strong, God chose what is low and despised in the world, even things that are not, to bring to nothing things that are, so that no human being might boast in the presence of God" (1 Cor. 1:26–29).

At first glance such a passage would seem to confirm the romantic idea of a proletarian Christian community, a religious movement of the lower classes. On closer analysis, however, we find that Paul mentions three categories of people: those who are wise, those who are powerful, and those of noble birth. The terms "wise" and "powerful" are linked to previously stated ideas about wisdom and foolishness, power and weakness. But noble birth (εὐγενεῖς) brings into play something entirely new, a specific sociological category which Paul especially emphasizes. When repeating the idea in vv.

27–28 he not only contrasts "noble birth" with "lower born," but sharpens the contrast between εὐγενεῖς and ἀγενῆ by two further designations: τὰ ἐξουθενημένα ("despised") and τὰ μὴ ὄντα ("things that are not"). Although it is true that by means of these designations social relationships are seen in a theological light,[3] the sociological implications of the concepts cannot be denied.[4] Among other things, "nothingness," οὐδενία, is a *topos* derived from the realm of philosophical ridicule.[5] The truly wise Socrates qualifies as "nothing" (Plato, *Phaedrus* 234e; *Theatetus* 176c). Epictetus follows in these footsteps when he anticipates others' opinions that he amounts to nothing: οὐδὲν ἦν ὁ Ἐπίκτητος (Epictetus, *Dissertationes* III, 9, 14; cf. IV, 8, 25; *Enchiridion* 24, 1). Thus when Paul writes that those whom society and the world (κόσμος, 1 Cor. 1:28) regard as nothing are in reality representatives of that true wisdom which is contained in Christ, his Greek diction reveals how others perceive the social status of those whom he is addressing. This becomes even clearer with the supplementary, appositive phrase τὰ μὴ ὄντα. In Euripides, Hecuba complains about the divine actions which humble the exalted and exalt the humble: ὁρῶ τὰ τῶν θεῶν, ὡς τὰ μὲν πυργοῦς ἄνω τὰ μηδὲν ὄντα, τὰ δε δοκοῦντ' ἀπώλεσαν ("I see the Gods' work/who exalt on high/that which was naught/ and bring the proud names low"). Andromache confirms this in her answer: . . . τὸ δ' εὐγενὲς εἰς δοῦλον ἥκει, μεταβολὰς τοιάσδε ἔχον ("high birth hath come to bondage—ah, the change, the change"; *Trojan Women* 612ff.). This contrast between μηδὲν ὢν and εὐγενές is also found in Sophocles (*Ajax* 1094–7): οὐκ ἄν . . . θαυμάσαιμ' ἔτι, ὃς μηδὲν ὢν γοναῖσιν εἶθ' ἁμαρτάνει, ὅθ' οἱ δοκοῦντες εὐγενεῖς πεφυκέναι ("I shall never marvel after this if any base-born fellow gives offense when those who pride themselves on their lineage [offend thus by their perverted utterances]"). Since this same idiomatic use of μηδέν to express an opinion about social rank is attested in Hellenistic Judaism (Philo, *De virtutibus* 173–74), we can assume that for Paul, too, the phrase τὰ μὴ ὄντα has a sociological significance, especially since it stands in contrast to εὐγενεῖς; thus the last of the three categories mentioned (wise, powerful, of noble birth) is of unmistakable sociological significance. Because this particular term in the series goes beyond the catchwords of the preceding context, it can be assumed that in the new paragraph (1 Cor. 1:26ff.) Paul has a social fact in mind and probably intends the first two categories to be understood sociologically as well. The "powerful" would be influential people; the "wise," those who belong to the educated classes (that is, "wise according to worldly standards") for whom wisdom is also a sign of social status. Unless Paul had also been thinking in these instances of sociological criteria he could scarcely have combined the three terms and, taking them collectively, contrasted to them the election of those who are not, the μὴ ὤν. Philo also combines references to the strong, powerful, and understanding in a similar way when he writes (*De somniis* 155), "Are not private citizens continually becoming officials, and officials private citizens, rich men becoming poor men and poor men men of ample means, nobodies becoming celebrated, obscure people becoming distinguished, weak men (ἀσθενεῖς) strong (ἰσχυροί), insignificant men powerful (δυνατοί), foolish men wise men of understanding (συνετοί), witless men sound reasoners?" In my opinion there can be no doubt about the sociological implications of the language of 1 Cor. 1:26–29.

If Paul says that there were not many in the Corinthian congregation who were wise, powerful, and wellborn, then this much is certain: there were some. As early as Origen this passage was cited as an objection to Celsus's opinion that in Christian gatherings one would find only the lower classes.[6] If the actual number of such people was small, their influence must be accorded all the more import. Were that not the case, Paul would scarcely think it necessary to devote a substantial portion of his letter to an exchange with their "wisdom." Nor could he identify these people with the whole congregation when writing: "We are fools for Christ's sake, but you are wise in Christ. We are weak, but you are strong. You are held in honor, but we in disrepute" (1 Cor. 4:10). Here again we find the same three categories—the wise, the powerful, the esteemed—even if the terminology has been modified. Moreover, here again these terms have a sociological significance, for Paul contrasts his circumstances with those of the Corinthians in terms bearing indisputable sociological implications. For example, Paul works with his hands, experiences hunger, has no permanent home, and is persecuted. He is "the refuse of the world, the offscouring of all things" (1 Cor. 4:11–13).[7] Paul puts himself at the bottom of the scale of social prestige but sees the Corinthians as occupying the top: *You* are clever, strong, honored. In doing so he addresses the entire congregation, although earlier he had said that there were "not many" who were wise, powerful, and of noble birth. It can only be concluded that the phrase "not many" doesn't mean very much. In 1 Cor. 1:26ff. Paul does not wish to contest the significance of those congregational members from the upper classes but simply objects to their all-too-well-developed consciousness of their own status. Naturally, he is right. These representatives of the upper classes were a minority within the congregation, but apparently a dominant minority. At the very least, several members of the Corinthian congregation who appear to be very active may be counted in their group.

Statements About Individual Members of the Congregation

We should be cautious in evaluating statements about individuals. Apocryphal legends may always want to know more about New Testament figures than the New Testament tells, but modern exegesis ought not to further this tendency. Instead, it should subordinate its (perfectly proper) curiosity to methodical criteria. In what follows, statements about holding office, about "houses," about assistance rendered to the congregation, and about travel can all serve as criteria for elevated social status. The first two of these have to do with position, the last two with activities. Each of the criteria raises specific problems.

REFERENCES TO OFFICES

From Acts 18:8 we learn that Crispus, one of the first Christians, was a synagogue ruler. His conversion to Christianity was probably of great significance for the founding of the community, setting off a small wave of conversions ("and many of the Corinthians, when they heard of it [RSV "hearing Paul"] believed and had themselves baptized [RSV "were baptized"] (Acts 18:8). Paul mentions Crispus in 1 Cor. 1:14 at the head of that short list of congregational members whom he has baptized but says nothing about his former position in the synagogue.

A synagogue ruler[8] was leader of the Jewish worship service, not head of the community as such. He controlled the reading of Scripture and the homilies (cf. Acts 13:15 where, however, several synagogue rulers are found). For our purposes it is particularly important to note that he had to assume responsibility for the synagogue building.[9] Since upkeep of the synagogue required money, there was reason to entrust this office to a wealthy man who would be in a position, should the occasion arise, to supplement the community's funds with his own contribution. This is confirmed by a number of inscriptions in which synagogue rulers have memorialized their expenditures for these Jewish houses of worship. In Aegina (that is, not far from Corinth) a certain Theodoros completely rebuilt a synagogue over a period of four years, admittedly with money provided by collections and synagogue possessions, as he expressly states (Frey no. 722 = *CIG* 9894; *IG* [Berlin, 1873ff.], IV, 190). But in Porto (Frey no. 548) and Acmonia (Frey no. 766) synagogue rulers also undertook repairs ἐκ τῶν ἰδίων, that is, using their own resources. An inscription at Side (Frey no. 781) is probably to be interpreted this way: A φροντιστὴς τῆς ἁγιωτάτης πρώτης συναγωγῆς ("superintendent of the most sacred premiere synagogue") has provided repairs. Certainly the best known is an inscription of Theodotus in Jerusalem (Frey no. 1404; cf. Deissmann, *Light*, pp. 439–41):

> Theodotus, the son of Vettenus, priest and ruler of the synagogue, son of a ruler of the synagogue, son's son of a ruler of the synagogue, built the synagogue for reading of the law and for teaching of the commandments, also the strangers' lodging and the chambers and the conveniences of waters for an inn for them that need it from abroad, of which (synagogue) his father and the elders and Simonides did lay the foundation.

That these synagogue rulers were esteemed men—even beyond the boundaries of the Jewish community itself—can be deduced from a funerary inscription of one Staphylus of Rome (Frey no. 265 = E. Diehl, *Inscriptiones latinae christianae veteres* [Berlin,

1925–31], no. 4886): *Staff(y)lo arc(h)onti et archisynagogo honoribus omnibus fu(n)ctus restituta coniux benmerenti fecit*. Ἐν εἰρήνῃ ἡ κοίμησις σου. The phrase *omnibus honoribus functus* is often found in funerary inscriptions and indicates that the deceased held high offices in the *municipium*, the colony, the polis, or an association.[10] A majority of those inscriptions preserved from synagogue rulers emphasize that those who held these offices rendered a service to the Jewish congregation through their initiative and generosity. They were certainly not the poorest members of the community. So we may assume in the case of the synagogue ruler Crispus that he possessed high social status, which would explain why his conversion had great influence on others.[11]

The status of Erastus, described at the conclusion of Romans as "the city treasurer" (οἰκονόμος τῆς πόλεως, 16:23), is more controversial. Did he hold a high municipal office to which he had been elected, or was he a less significant person employed in financial administration, possibly even a slave to be regarded as the city's property, an *arcarius rei publicae* ("public treasurer"; the *Vulgate* reads *arcarius civitatis*)?[12] The problem must be discussed at three levels. First, all New Testament statements must be evaluated, then the parallels outside the New Testament. Finally, and most important, is the analysis of inscriptional evidence pertaining to Corinthian offices.

Statements in the New Testament. The term οἰκονόμος is found in Gal. 4:2 in conjunction with ἐπίτροπος and in 1 Cor. 4:1 in conjunction with ὑπηρέτης. From this we learn little about the social status of an οἰκονόμος: he is in another's service (a father's, or Christ's) but given great authority. Another observation is more important. Only in Rom. 16:23 does Paul mention the worldly status of a member of the congregation. That the person he mentions, Crispus, was a synagogue ruler is something we learn not from Paul but from Acts. The same is true of the information that Aquila and Priscilla supported themselves as artisans (Acts 18:3). In the case of slaves, to be sure, Paul does allude summarily to social status, as in Rom. 16:10 (τοὺς ἐκ τῶν Ἀριστοβούλου), 16:11, and Phil. 4:22. Apart from that, he sometimes calls attention to the fact that a person is of Jewish descent. Otherwise, however, he is interested only in services rendered to the congregation. Only in the case of Erastus (Rom. 16:23) does he depart from this "rule." If in doing so Paul wished to stress Erastus's *dependent* status that would not be very tactful, especially since he had previously mentioned Gaius, who was sufficiently well-off to put his house at the disposal of Paul and the entire congregation. Therefore, an exceptional instance in which the worldly status of one member of the community is mentioned probably indicates status *worth* mentioning, that is, relatively high status.

In two other instances in the New Testament an Erastus is mentioned. In 2 Tim. 4:20 a deutero-Pauline author writes, "Erastus remained at Corinth." This Erastus would be Paul's traveling companion of Acts 19:22, where Paul sends Erastus together with Timothy to Macedonia and then goes himself via Macedonia to Achaia (that is, to Corinth) and Jerusalem. It is uncertain that these "Erastoi" are one and the same, and one could argue that several persons in the Pauline mission field bore this name, so that it was necessary for Paul to distinguish among them by means of a qualifying phrase such as that in Rom. 16:23. Paul himself, however, never mentions any other Erastus. What speaks *for* the common identity of all these "Erastoi" is their common connection with Corinth. If Erastus had once been in Ephesus (as Acts 19:22 presumes), his being greeted in the last chapter of Romans is appropriate, since this chapter quite possibly was addressed originally to the Ephesian congregation. With reference to our problem, we may conclude that an Erastus off on frequent trips is not likely to be a slave, and that even if these travels should be considered legendary it is unlikely that such legends grew up around a slave.[13]

Within the New Testament materials, the strongest argument in favor of Erastus's low social status remains the Vulgate translation. *Arcarius civitatis* means a low-level financial bureaucrat, usually a slave. This translation, however, could have been influenced by 1 Cor. 1:26ff., according to which one would certainly not expect to find among the congregational members a high public official. Moreover, the particular Latin idiom should be noted. The Romans now and then appropriated the term οἰκονόμος but reserved it for lower ranks.[14] This leads to the next point.

General linguistic usage. The meaning of the word οἰκονόμος varies according to time and place. In his epigraphic investigation of the term P. Landvogt concludes that in the Hellenistic period (and later) this term could signify an office of high standing,[15] whether by appointment as a royal official or by election in the Hellenistic cities. Only evidence for the latter, which comes primarily from western Asia Minor, is of interest for our purposes. Here the phrase οἰκονόμος τῆς πόλεως is amply testified to.

Philadelphia (Landvogt, 26–27): A τῆς πόλεως οἰκονόμος erected a stele. The inscription dates from the period of the empire.

Smyrna *BrM* [London. 1874–1916], III/2, 448 and 469; Landvogt, 28–29); At the end of the fourth century B.C.E. the οἰκονόμος, together with priests, presented an offering for which he provided the funds. He held a high office. For Roman times a ταμίας is attested in Ephesus (*BrM* III, 636).

Magnesia (O. Kern, *Inschriften von Magnesia* [1900], nos. 98, 99, 100, 101, 103, 97, 94, 89, 12; Landvogt, 31–36): There existed here in the second century B.C.E. a college of οἰκονόμοι with cultural and political duties. It administered municipal finances.

Priene (F. J. W. Hiller v. Gaertringen, *Inschriften von Priene* [Berlin, 1906], nos. 6, 18, 83, 99, 107, 108, 115, 117, 119; Landvogt, 36–44): An οἰκονόμος τῆς πόλεως is testified to from the fourth century B.C.E. to the first century C.E. by nos. 83, 99, 107, 108, 115, and 117. Together with the νεωποίης he controls the city finances and in the first century B.C.E. also assumes the latter's functions. The οἰκονόμος was elected annually.

Aphrodisia (*CIG* 2811; Landvogt, 44): an οἰκονόμος of the city council administered its treasury. The inscription comes from Roman times.

Stratonicea (*CIG* 2717; Landvogt, 44): At the time of the emperor Valerian (third century C.E.) an οἰκονόμος appointed by the city asked the gods if advancing barbarians would destroy the city. This too must have been a high municipal official.

Hierapolis (W. Judeich, *Altertümer von Hierapolis* [1898], no. 34; *IGRR* IV, 813; Landvogt, 47): Two οἰκονόμοι τῆς πόλεως provided for the erection of a column in honor of the provincial governor—thus in Roman times.

From an unknown location in Phrygia is preserved the oath of an οἰκονόμος τῆς πόλεως to the mother of the gods (*CIG* 6837; Landvogt, 48).

Apollonia (*SIG*² 545; Landvogt, 49): οἰκονόμοι, probably a college of officials, cover the expenses for an inscribed stele (second century B.C.E.).

In these instances the term οἰκονόμος (τῆς πόλεως) refers to a high position. It is held by officials who deal with financial matters, erect columns, but have different responsibilities in different cities. These are not simply treasurers, but alongside them will frequently be found the ταμίας. P. Landvogt describes the relationship between these two: "To judge from the fixed functions of the ταμίας and the name οἰκονόμος, the essential difference consists in this: (*a*) the ταμίας was exclusively a treasury official dealing with deposits and withdrawal of cash; (*b*) the οἰκονόμος was an official of managerial status who dealt with the actual material resources of the state, with property, valuable goods, and so forth. He combined functions which in Athens, for example, and other cities were divided among various officials. Since the οἰκονόμος, in his characteristic position as administrative official, is deeply involved in financial matters, his office easily becomes involved with that of the ταμίας who, in part, merely paid out what came in by authority of the οἰκονόμος. Thus the οἰκονόμος can replace the ταμίας but does not consistently do so."[16] The office of οἰκονόμος is well attested for the Roman period (in Philadelphia, Smyrna, Aphrodisia, Stratonicea, Hierapolis; the inscriptions from Priene are not far removed from the imperial period). The possibility of a similar office in Corinth cannot be ruled out.

Nevertheless, we cannot on this basis simply infer an elevated social status for Erastus, for alongside the οἰκονόμοι (τῆς πόλεως) already described there were others who certainly (or very probably) were slaves or freedmen. From Nicomedia has come a funerary inscription for a man who clearly was well-off but who was once *not* free, one Gajus Tryphon (*CIG* 3777; Landvogt, 26). From Cos come two inscriptions (W. R. Patton and E. L. Hicks, *Inscriptions*, no. 310; Landvogt, 24, cf. *CIG* 2512) which mention an οἰκονόμος τῶν Κώων πόλεως where there is no mention of the father's name and where the office is not held as a result of annual elections. The incumbents are probably slaves or freedmen. The inscriptions themselves come from the period of the later empire. The father's name is also missing in an inscription from Chalcedon (*CIG* 3793; Landvogt, 26: Διονύσιος, οἰκονόμος Καλχηδονίων, and in Philadelphia (*IGRR* 1630). In a list of officials from Sparta (*CIG* 1276; Landvogt, 23) a Φιλοδέσποτος οἰκονόμος is named, who is described in *CIG* 1239 as a slave (cf. the name, "one who loves his master").

It seems that on the basis of linguistic usage alone we cannot reach any unequivocal conclusions about Rom. 16:23. The inscription of closest geographical proximity, from Sparta, knows of a slave as οἰκονόμος in the service of the city.[17] Before drawing inferences from that for the circumstances in Corinth, however, something else must be considered. Corinth was a Roman colony, and its political circumstances were not comparable to those of an ordinary Greek city. On the other hand, Paul comes from Tarsus in Asia Minor and has spent a lot of time in just that part of Asia Minor where the evidence testifies that the οἰκονόμος held a prestigious office. If Romans 16 is addressed to the Ephesian congregation, then it is very likely that Paul takes over the linguistic conventions of that place;[18]

and it is entirely possible that he uses a Greek equivalent for an office which is described by a Latin name in Corinth. To be sure, evidence for the οἰκονόμος in Ephesus comes only from the fourth century B.C.E., but for a later period in this general neighborhood it can be found in Magnesia (second century B.C.E.), Priene (first century B.C.E), and Smyrna (second/third century B.C.E.). The question remains, Was there an office in Corinth to which Paul referred by the term οἰκονόμος, the incumbent of which was likely to be a person of elevated social status?

Offices in Corinth. Corinth was a bilingual colony in which Caesar had settled freedmen.[19] From the beginning of that period there must have been Greeks there, for excavations show that the older city had not been totally destroyed. The city's constitution is Roman and its official language Latin.[20] Not until Hadrian's time are the majority of inscriptions in Greek. This bilingual equality is particularly important with reference to our problem. While the Latin designations for office are officially mandated, we might under the circumstances expect a more flexible linguistic use of the Greek equivalents.

At the head of the colony (the constitution of which does not differ significantly from that of the *municipium*)[21] stand the *duumviri*[22] who are elected annually and the *duumviri quinquennalis*, particularly important persons who are chosen every five years and whose responsibility is to take a census. Since στρατηγὸς πενταετηρικός corresponds to this *duumviri quinquennalis* (Meritt, nos. 80, 81), we can interpret στρατηγός, found four times (Kent, nos. 371, 468; Meritt, nos. 95, 110), as *duumvir*. In point of fact, the Greek office of στρατηγός corresponds to that of the *duumvir*. His duties consist of convening the council and the assembly, presiding over meetings and elections, and generally representing the city's interest. On the basis of information from both inscriptions and coins we know the names of a series of Corinthian *duumviri*. For 50/51 C.E. (that is, at the time that the Corinthian congregation was founded) Cn. Publicius Regulus and L. Paconius Flam(inius) were *duumviri* (Edwards, nos. 51–53); in 52/53 C.E. Ti. Claudius Dinippus and Ti. Claudius Anaxilas (West, no. 54) were *duumviri*, although here there is some uncertainty.[23]

Next to the *duumviri* the most esteemed officials are the two aediles,[24] who together with the *duumviri* are sometimes referred to as the *quattuorviri*. Their duties included maintenance and oversight of public places and buildings, the provisioning of grain, and staging the games. The Corinthian Isthmian games, however, called for their own *agonothetai* (according to even the Latin inscriptions), a position of great prestige. At times of difficulty in procuring provisions, a *curator annonae* (Gr. ἐπιμελητὴς εὐθυνίας; cf. Meritt, nos. 76, 94) was also chosen. But under normal circumstances that task also belonged to the aedile. In the context of our concerns this office is of great significance, for as it happens there is evidence that a certain Erastus served as a Corinthian aedile. The inscription was found in 1929 and has been supplemented by finds from 1928 and 1947.[25] Kent's reconstruction (no. 232) reads, [*praenomen nomen*] *Erastus pro aedelit[at]e s(ua) p(ecunia) stravit* ("Erastus laid [the pavement] at his own expense in return for his aedileship"). The inscription was originally part of the pavement itself, written on two tablets which were reused in the mid-second century. It is unlikely that the Erastus mentioned had recently died, for as long as his identity was known it would have been rather too disrespectful to destroy this memorial to his service. It seems more likely that his pavement, for whatever reason, had to be destroyed or resurfaced, which would be plausible only after the passage of considerable time and would bring us back to the mid-first century C.E., the time when the Corinthian congregation was founded.[26]

There are justifiable grounds for hesitating to identify the Christian Erastus with the aedile Erastus. The decisive question is whether οἰκονόμος τῆς πόλεως (Rom. 16:23) corresponds, in terminology and in fact, to the Corinthian aedile. *Aedilis* is usually translated in Greek as ἀγορανόμος,[27] something which can be attested for Corinth itself. About 170 C.E. a certain Priscus, mentioned in several surviving inscriptions (Kent, nos. 199–201, 306; *IG* IV, 203), in return for his selection as aedile (ὑπὲρ ἀγορανομίας) had the buildings of the Isthmian cult restored, just as Erastus a century earlier, *pro aedilitate*, had streets or plazas paved. That raises the question, Why does Paul not write ἀγορανόμος if he wants to send greetings from the aedile Erastus? It may be objected that the Greek title ἀγορανόμος is first testified to in Corinth in the second half of the second century C.E., after Greek seems to have been the official language for quite some time. Since in the first century C.E. Latin was clearly the official language, it is not certain that at that time *aedilis* corresponded to ἀγορανόμος. However that may be, the argument stands that ἀγορανόμος is usually the translation of *aedilis*.

It could further be argued that for Paul the linguistic conventions of Corinth were less decisive than his own vocabulary,[28] which had been influenced by his experience in Asia Minor. The argument, however, is not sound, for ἀγορανόμος is an office known in the cities of Asia Minor as well, even where there is evidence of an οἰκονόμος (τῆς πόλεως) as in Philadelphia (*IGRR* nos. 1631, 1637, 1640), Smyrna (*IGRR* no. 1438), and

Hierapolis (*IGRR* nos. 810, 818, 820). A longer list would include as examples Akmonia (*IGRR* nos. 654, 657, 658), Thyatira (*IGRR* nos. 1210, 1244, 1248, 1250, 1255, 1257), Pergamum (*IGRR* nos. 352, 461, 477, and others).[29] In short, Paul the native of Asia Minor could have known the office of ἀγορανόμος at least as well as that of οἰκονόμος τῆς πόλεως.

These linguistic arguments touch on only one facet of the problem, however. We also must ask if the Corinthian office of aedile can be defined so far as its tasks are concerned in such a way that it could in fact be translated by the term οἰκονόμος. Kent thinks so: "Corinth was a unique colony in that she controlled the management of games which were internationally famous. She therefore administered the Isthmian festivals by means of a completely separate set of offices, and the Corinthian aediles, thus relieved of all responsibility for public entertainment, were in effect confined in their activities to local economic matters. It is possible for this reason that St. Paul does not use the customary word ἀγορανόμος to describe a Corinthian aedile but calls him οἰκονόμος (Romans xvi, 23)."[30]

But neither is this argument sound, for there are *agonothetai* not only in Corinth but, for example, in Akmonia (*CIG* 3858), Aphrodisias (*CIG* 2766, 2812, 2785, 2789), Ephesus (*CIG* 2961b, 2987b), and many other cities.[31] Corinth was distinguished by the fact that its games were internationally famous, not by the fact that it created an office to supervise them. Furthermore, aediles' responsibilities were not confined to "local economic matters." Their chief duty was oversight and maintenance of public places, and by carrying out this responsibility they made their impression on the public's awareness.

If we weigh the countervailing arguments, the possibility cannot be entirely ruled out that the οἰκονόμος τῆς πόλεως is equivalent to the Corinthian office of aedile; but neither can that be satisfactorily proven.

Thus far in the debate about identifying the inscriptional Erastus with the Christian Erastus an important aspect of the matter has been overlooked. The aedile is chosen for one year. It would have been mere chance were Erastus aedile in precisely that year when Paul wrote to the Romans while in Corinth. Significantly, most of those chosen for municipal offices have held other offices earlier. It is scarcely imaginable that the city's leadership (the aedile belongs to the *quattuorviri*, the municipal summit) would be entrusted to men who had not already proven themselves capable in more modest positions. Therefore, I think it most likely either that οἰκονόμος τῆς πόλεως is the Greek equivalent of a "Latin" office or that it is an office which bore a Greek title in Corinth at that time, one held prior to the office of aedile.

The first of these possibilities raises the matter of the quaestor.[32] The two quaestors were, juridically speaking, on a par with the aediles, but the office of aedile was more distinguished.[33] This is understandable, since as far as public esteem is concerned, a treasurer would find it hard to compete with somebody who could put up public buildings. It can be presumed that this was true in Corinth since the names of eleven aediles have been preserved there, along with the names of five honorary aediles, not counting those inscriptions where the name is lost.[34] By comparison, the office of municipal quaestor is mentioned only three (or four) times (West, no. 104a; Kent, nos. 168, 170; Kent, no. 119, may refer to a provincial quaestor).

It is characteristic of these inscriptions that in them we encounter the office as a part of the *cursus honorum*. In West, no. 104a, the sequence of offices runs *quattuorvir, quaestor, argyrotam(ias)*. In Kent, no. 168, *quaestor, aedile, duumvir, duumvir quinquennalis, agonothet*. In Kent, no. 170, it is possible that we have presented the career of Antonius Sospes, known to us from Plutarch (*Quaestiones convivales* VIII, 4, 1–4; IX, 5, 1–2). He was quaestor, military tribune, *agonothet* repeatedly, and finally, *duumvir*. As a rule, in the *cursus honorum* the lower offices were held first.[35] But there are many examples which depart from the rule. Twice the "quaestor" stands at the beginning of the *cursus honorum* (where, however, the fragmentary character of the inscriptions should be noted). On another occasion this office is found next to that of aedile (for in West, no. 104a, an aedile apparently refers to himself proudly as *quattuorvir;* had he been *duumvir* he would not have remained silent about that fact, and the positions subsequently occupied make this interpretation most likely, for quaestor and ἀργυροταμίας are both positions which entrust the incumbents with administrative and financial responsibilities). We can conclude from this that many *duumviri* were previously aediles, many aediles had been quaestors, and many quaestors had already held some other office. Only in the case of an exceptional career, however, or because of inordinate pride, is an entire *cursus honorum* recounted. The aedile Erastus almost surely had also already occupied some lesser office, possibly that of quaestor.

Thus the question arises, Could the office of quaestor be the equivalent of οἰκονόμος τῆς πόλεως? Here too there is a language problem. The usual counterpart to quaestor is ταμίας; but for our period this term is not attested. In Meritt, no. 5, ταμίας is inferred by analogy from other inscriptions, but this inscription itself comes from the Greek period. In Meritt, no. 106, the Greek inscription has been superimposed on an obliterated Latin inscription, and thus comes from a later period. Only the office of ἀργυροταμίας is testified to, but it stands alongside the quaestor's office.[36] We know that the οἰκονόμος in the cities of Asia Minor was close to the ταμίας and from time to time took over his function. In light of the (unofficial) Greek language customs of Corinth which do not exclude variations in Greek terminology, and in light of Paul's origins in Asia Minor, it is conceivable that the office of οἰκονόμος τῆς πόλεως in Rom. 16:23 corresponded to that of quaestor.

We cannot, however, finally settle on this possibility. Corinth, as a financial and commercial center of Greece, had a plethora of officials responsible for administering and balancing accounts. Possibly the lower offices carried Greek titles at an early date. In West, no. 104a, we find an *argyrotamias* in a Latin inscription. Perhaps there was an *oekonomos* as well.

Thus Erastus, later to be chosen aedile, could have occupied the office of οἰκονόμος τῆς πόλεως (perhaps that of quaestor) in the year in which Romans was written, an office which did not yet signify the pinnacle of a public career. I can see no compelling argument against this identification of the Christian Erastus. The name is not otherwise attested for Corinth, by inscriptions or literature, making a confusion of two persons less likely in this instance than with some other names. We can assume that Erastus belonged to the οὐ πολλοὶ δυνατοί. To have been chosen aedile he must have been a full citizen—and in a Roman colony that would mean Roman citizenship. His spending for the public indicates that he could claim a certain amount of private wealth. It is quite possible that he was a freedman as the inscription does not mention his father. Add to this the fact that he has a Greek name, and we may perhaps imagine him a successful man who has risen into the ranks of the local notables, most of whom are of Latin origin.

REFERENCES TO HOUSES

"Houses" provide information about private circumstances rather than public status. It is specifically said about two individual Christians that their "houses" were baptized, or became Christians, with them: Crispus (Acts 18:8) and Stephanas (1 Cor. 1:16; cf. 16:15ff.). Does it follow that these two may perhaps have owned slaves? A. Strobel contests the idea on the basis of Roman legal terminology.[37] According to Strobel, οἶκος corresponds to the Latin *domus*, that is, the members of a family who are actually related and have legal capacity. In contrast, *familia* includes slaves and chattel. Such is the case in Roman law. For the New Testament, however, the language of Roman law would be informative only on the basis of three kinds of inference: from juridical to non-juridical language, from the Latin meaning of a word to the Greek meaning, and from the general usage of the ancient world to Jewish and Christian usage.

It is doubtful that Roman legal terminology was the norm for Paul, especially since this terminology itself was not uniform. Ulpian (*Digest*, XXXIX, 4, 12, 2) explicitly says: "*familiae autem appellatione hic servilem familiam contineri sciendum est,*" ("the family slave is here understood to be included in the term *familiae*"), that is, he presupposes that the term *familia* does not *eo ipso* include slaves.[38] Apparently even in the juridical realm we cannot presume a fixed terminology. If not there, how much less in the everyday world?

In addition, drawing inferences from Latin words to Greek meanings is problematic. The meaning of a word is constituted by an entire field of sense-related concepts. On the Greek side there is nothing corresponding to the contrast in Latin between *domus* and *familia*. On the contrary, the Greeks had to adopt φαμίλια as a loanword (*BCH* 14, 370; *Inscr. Cos*. 141, 1; *IGRR* IV, 1454) thus indicating that οἶκος/οἰκία is not determined by the contrast with a Greek word which corresponds to the Latin *familia*. This can also be seen in Aristotle's definition: οἰκία δὲ τέλειος ἐκ δούλων καὶ ἐλευθέρων ("and the household in its perfect form consists of slaves and freedmen"; *Politica*, I, 2, 1). It is interesting to note that Aristotle specifically speaks of a "complete" house, as if aware of a narrower sense of the word. Indeed, it may be asked whether the occasional emphasis on the "entire" house is not designed deliberately to include the slaves (so Acts 18:8).

Finally, the possibility of a specific Jewish or Christian use of terms should not be excluded *a priori*. In Christian inscriptions *familia* now and then means "family" in our sense.[39] On one gravestone we read of a woman who was good to her slaves, and was an affectionate mother and diligent wife: "*haec bona familiis, mater pia, sedula coniux, hic corpus posuit . . .*" (Diehl, no. 190; cf. no. 168). *Familia* here serves as an overlapping concept covering children and spouse. Might not a new attitude toward slaves come to be reflected linguistically, so that it is more natural to consider them as part of the "house" while at the same time *familia* loses some of its close association with slaves? Finally, all Christians were called "brethren," and that could have had—at least linguistically—some consequences.

In view of all this, the way language is actually used in early Christianity must be the deciding factor. Who belongs to a "house?" First of all, it is striking that children are often specifically named alongside the "house" (Ignatius, *Ad Polycarpum* 8:2; Hermas, *Mandata* 12, 3, 6; Hermas, *Similitudines* 5, 3, 9; 1 Tim. 3:12). Does that mean that they don't belong to the house? That can hardly be maintained consistently.[40] To manage a "house" well means to have obedient children (1 Tim. 3:4). And when we read in a Jewish inscription, τὸν οἶκον καὶ τέκνα τέκνων (Frey, no. 765), it seems clear that the children actually belonged to the household and their being specifically mentioned means little. Otherwise, with the same argument wives would have to be excluded from the house: ἀσπάζομαι τοὺς οἴκους τῶν ἀδελφῶν μου σὺν γυναιξὶ καὶ τέκνοις (Ignatius, *Ad Smyrnaeos* 13:1). Deacons ought to be the husband of but one wife and manage their children καὶ τῶν ἰδίων οἴκων well (1 Tim. 3:12). Naturally, wives belonged to the house. A widow is greeted "with her entire house and her children" (Ign. *Ad Pol*. 8:2).

This emphasis on women and children does not mean that they are not already included within the concept of the house. To the contrary, such an emphasis presupposes the significance of mentioning the actual family members, that is, differentiating them from a broader background which is taken for granted. To this background could belong more distant relatives—or servants and slaves. Since the latter are never mentioned in their own right alongside the "house," it may be assumed that they make up part of that general background which is taken for granted and from which women and children are sometimes singled out for special notice. It is not accidental that slaves and servants are called οἰκέται (Rom. 14:4; 1 Peter 2:18; Luke 16:13). Nor is it accidental that they are mentioned alongside wives and children in the so-called *Haustafeln*, while other relatives play no role in such lists. In fact, the conjunction of wives, children, and slaves is so well attested (Col. 3:18ff.; Eph. 5:22ff.) that it can also probably be presumed in 1 Tim. 3:12. "Let deacons be the husband of one wife and let them manage well their children and households" (that is, the servants).[41]

For our purposes the Lucan and Pauline terminology are particularly important. Five times in Acts Luke mentions "houses" which have corporately converted to Christianity: the house of the centurion from Caesarea (10:2; 11:14); that of Lydia the purple-merchant in Philippi (16:15); that of the warden in Philippi (16:31); and that of Crispus the synagogue ruler in Corinth (18:8). Can it be accidental that houses are mentioned only with reference to such relatively well established Christians? This elevated social status is evident in the case of the centurion and the purple-merchant. Beyond that, the inclusion of slaves within the category of "houses" seems probable for Acts 10:2 and 11:14. The centurion is εὐσεβὴς . . . σὺν παντὶ τῷ οἴκῳ αὐτοῦ (10:2). He relates his vision to "two of his slaves and a devout soldier from among those that waited on him" (10:7). Luke surely doesn't want to say that the slaves were not themselves devout, although the soldier belongs to the God-fearers—as if the centurion would entrust his vision to slaves who were unbelievers. Rather, the predicate εὐσεβής is needed only for the soldier, since the slaves were already characterized in 10:2 as God-fearing. They belong to a God-fearing house, the inclusiveness of which was particularly emphasized: ". . . with his *entire* house." It is also possible that slaves belonged to the household of the purple-merchant in Philippi. We are told that the Christian missionaries met "women" by the riverside, among whom was Lydia the purple-merchant who heard the apostle there (more than once?) and was baptized "with her house." A. Strobel thinks it unlikely that slaves were present.[42] In my view, however, it is most likely that they were. When women left their houses they were accompanied if at all possible by male and female slaves. When he singles out specific houses Luke probably always has in mind its slaves and servants too. This is probably also true with regard to Crispus (Acts 18:8).[43]

Paul speaks of Stephanas's οἶκος (1 Cor. 1:16) and οἰκία (16:15). Thus it seems evident that the terms οἶκος and οἰκία are here synonymous. In at least one instance he includes slaves within these categories, for the οἱ ἐκ τῆς Καίσαρος οἰκίας (Phil. 4:22) are certainly not of the emperor's family. That Onesimus, the slave returned to Philemon, henceforth belongs once more to κατ' οἶκόν σου ἐκκλησίᾳ (Phlm. 2) is likewise taken to be self-evident. So it is quite possible that the house of Stephanas included slaves. It is not necessarily the case that Fortunatus and Achaicus are such.

Reference to someone's house is hardly a sure criterion for that person's high social status; but it is a probable one, particularly if other criteria point in the same direction. Crispus, for example, is already known as a man of some standing by virtue of his position as synagogue ruler. In Stephanas's case we hear that he has dedicated himself to the community's service (1 Cor. 16:15). That brings us to the next criterion.

REFERENCES TO SERVICES RENDERED

Terms like διακονεῖν, διάκονος εἶναι, or διακονία are used to describe Phoebe from Cenchreae, Stephanas and his house and—in connection with the Jerusalem collection—the entire congregation (cf. 2 Cor. 8:4; 9:1,12; Rom. 15:31). In the case of the collection we are dealing with material expenditure, and that is probably true for the other instances as well. Stephanas and his house dedicated themselves to serving the saints: εἰς διακονίαν τοις ἁγίοις (1 Cor. 16:15). Similarly, the congregation is obliged to take up the collection τῆς διακονίας τῆς εἰς τοὺς ἁγίους (2 Cor. 8:4). From the parallel in language we may probably infer a parallel in fact. Stephanas and those who accompany him had made up for Paul the ὑστέρημα of the Corinthians (ἀνεπλήρωσαν, 1 Cor. 16:17). The same phrase is found in Philippians: Epaphroditus, λειτουργὸς τῆς χρείας (Phil. 2:25; cf. 4:10–20), has brought material support to Paul. Having fallen ill while visiting Paul he has risked his life ἵνα ἀναπληρώσῃ τὸ ὑμῶν ὑστέρημα τῆς πρός με λειτουργίας (Phil. 2:30). As in 1 Cor. 16:17, Paul speaks here of "your deficiency" although on the most plausible reading of matters, the deficiency is his. But such paradoxes are usual in Paul. Since ὑστέρημα also is used in connection with the collection (2 Cor. 8:14; 9:12) it is reasonable to assume that in Ephesus Paul received some material support from Stephanas. It is true that in 2 Cor. 11:9 Paul writes that he did not allow himself to be supported by anyone in Corinth, but he adds explicitly, "when I was with you," from which it could almost be concluded that when away from Corinth he did allow the Corinthians to support him. Nevertheless, we must also reckon with the possibility that this was not the case. According to 1 Cor. 16:18 Stephanas and his circle refreshed Paul's "spirit" along with that of the congregation's—which doesn't sound much like material gifts.

In Rom. 16:1 Phoebe is described as διάκονος τῆς ἐκκλησίας of the Corinthian port city of Cenchreae, a person who has helped Paul and many others (16:2). For that reason the community which Paul is addressing ought to help her ἐν ᾧ ἂν ὑμῶν χρῄζῃ πράγματι, "in whatever she may require from you." The term πρᾶγμα frequently means "business" in the economic sense of that word, and the generalizing relative clause all the more hints that something more than just congregational matters are involved. At the least, the statement could be understood as a recommendation to support Phoebe in her "worldly" business. This support would reciprocate Phoebe's service to Paul and others. Thus her services too consisted of "earthly" things, σαρκικά.

Yet we must also be careful with these arguments. We can scarcely infer high social status from catchwords like διακονεῖν or διάκονος. Even slaves may have been called "servers" in Christian congregations. Pliny tortured two of them to gain more precise information about the eccentric "superstition" of the Christians: "*ex duabus ancillis, quae ministrae dicebantur*" ("from two maid-servants who were called deaconesses"; *Epistulae* X, 96). His mode of interrogation suggests that these are not free persons, although that is not entirely certain.[44] Nor is it certain that a Greek διάκονος corresponded to the Latin *minister*. These considerations, however, are not decisive for our problem. In the case of the Corinthians Phoebe and Stephanas a further criterion can be mentioned. Both of them make journeys.

Among the Corinthians not only these two are recognized for having rendered service to Paul and the congregation, even if the term διακονία is used only with reference to them. Providing hospitality for Paul is itself a service, and we know of at least four Corinthian Christians with whom Paul stayed: Gaius, Aquila, Priscilla, and Titius Justus. Paul writes the letter to the Romans from the house of Gaius, ξένος μου καὶ ὅλης τῆς ἐκκλησίας (Rom. 16:23). This Gaius is one of those few whom Paul himself has baptized. His "services" parallel those of Philemon. In Philemon's case, too, a congregation, the ἐκκλησία κατ' οἶκον (Phlm. 2), meets in his house and there, too, Paul stays, or at least reserves a room (Phlm. 22). The fact that Philemon owns a slave who has run away may not prove his wealth, but it does nothing to disprove it. Paul, however, in offering to make good any damages suffered because of Onesimus's actions, hints that this is hardly to be considered seriously. We have the impression that Philemon has not been too badly disadvantaged by this runaway slave.

Returning to Gaius, it is interesting to observe that in his case Paul speaks not of a "house-congregation" (as in Phlm. 2) but of the "whole congregation." From this it could be concluded that the congregation also met at other places, but in smaller groups. The Christians at Cenchreae, for example, would have met at Phoebe's house. In any event, the whole congregation met at Gaius's, and that presupposes that he had sufficient space at his disposal,[45] since the congregation at Corinth was large, a λαὸς πολύς (Acts 18:10). Thus we may infer high social status for Gaius. In addition, there is the matter of other people found frequenting the house. From here Tertius writes the letter to the Romans. That makes it appear as if other tasks were customarily performed in this house. There also seem to have been contacts with the "city-treasurer" Erastus, whose greetings are conveyed at the very end of Romans as if he had just stopped by, since these greetings give the impression of being appended.

At the beginning of his mission Paul stayed with Aquila and

Priscilla,[46] a Jewish couple who shortly before this had found it necessary to leave Rome because of Claudius's edict. The evidence suggests that they were scarcely insolvent. Later on, in Ephesus, they gathered a "house-congregation" around themselves (1 Cor. 16:19; Rom. 16:3), and according to Acts 18:26 Apollos enjoyed their hospitality and was later recommended by them to the Corinthian community. One can only speculate about why they so quickly left Corinth. Business considerations possibly played some role, for it is noteworthy that Paul quits their house in Corinth once he is in the position, by means of a gift from Macedonia (Acts 18:5; cf. 2 Cor. 11:8), to devote himself completely to the mission. That he stopped working is understandable, but why did he not stay on with Priscilla and Aquila? A controversy seems out of the question, for later the relationship appears to be still very good. Perhaps the answer lies in the location of the house. It is expressly said of the house of Titius Justus, to which Paul moves, that it was adjacent to the synagogue. Excavations to date have not uncovered the synagogue, but an inscription, "synagogue of the Hebrews," has been found[47] in the neighborhood of the agora suggesting that the synagogue probably occupied a central location by virtue of which it would have been propitious for the Pauline mission. Moreover, whatever helped or hindered the mission would have a similar effect on the more worldly pursuit of commerce. For example, excavations have revealed that around the agora were the boutiques of individual craftspeople, the whole constituting a commercial center. It is entirely possible that Aquila and Priscilla, as newcomers in Corinth, could not find a suitable spot to locate their business establishment. That is, of course, mere conjecture, but one worth juxtaposing to the idea that Paul possibly worked as an "employee" of Aquila and Priscilla in one of the shops which have been excavated by the agora.

Paul's third host is Titius Justus. E. Haenchen assumes that quite apart from its location this house offered certain advantages. Unlike Aquila's and Priscilla's place of business, this location would allow Paul to discourse all day without interruption and to have his own private room. To be sure, nothing is said about this and we simply don't know.[48] We have no information about the social status of Titius Justus. It can only be assumed that it was not inferior to that of Aquila and Priscilla, as Paul would hardly have made claims on anyone who would have found it a greater burden than they had. The opposite is more probable.

Like houses, these services rendered to the mission and to the congregation constitute no absolutely certain criterion. The willingness of the new congregations to make sacrifices should not be underestimated. Nevertheless, such services are a good criterion if, independently of the willingness to make sacrifices, they entail certain presuppositions (as in the case of Gaius) or if they can be supplemented by further criteria. For example, Phoebe, Aquila, and Priscilla, along with Stephanas, make journeys, and Stephanas managed a "house."

REFERENCES TO TRAVEL

We come across several Corinthians on "journeys": Aquila and Priscilla (Rom. 16:3; 1 Cor. 16:19; Acts 18:18–19); Phoebe (Rom. 16:1–2); Erastus (Acts 19:22); Stephanas with Achaicus and Fortunatus (1 Cor. 16:15–18); Chloe's people (1 Cor. 1:11). Perhaps Sosthenes (1 Cor. 1:1) should be added, if he is identical with the Corinthian synagogue ruler of the same name (Acts 18:17). In Phoebe's case a journey to Rome is not out of the question. Otherwise, it is a matter of traffic between Ephesus and Corinth. We must necessarily be cautious in drawing conclusions about the social status of people who travel. Business trips can be made by dependent workers; others who travel are simply sailors, companions of the wealthy, and so forth. Chloe's people could have been slaves or freedmen. Here too we must rely on supplemental information and the coalescence of several criteria. Such supplemental criteria are always given, however, except in the case of Chloe's people.

We may assume that at least some Corinthian Christians were merchants. Others, such as Aquila and Priscilla, may have changed their place of residence for business reasons. Some, possibly, were sufficiently free from the need to earn a living that they could invest their time and money in travel. Paul, for example, simply assumes that the Corinthian community could manage to bring its own collection to Jerusalem (1 Cor. 16:3). Even if journeys as such are no certain criterion, their frequency is worth noting. Of seventeen persons (or circles of people) named, we find nine engaged in travel.[49] That cannot be an accident.

Once we have discovered a group of Corinthian Christians of upper social status it becomes all the more important to ask whether any names have been preserved of the many who were *not* "powerful and of noble birth"? The evidence is meager. It is not impossible that Stephanas's companions were slaves.[50] One difficulty of this assumption is that Paul enjoins the community to be subject to them.[51] To be sure, he makes this request in a general reference to "every fellow worker and laborer" (1 Cor. 16:16) and only subsequently mentions Achaicus and Fortunatus. Nevertheless, the possibility that they are family members must also be taken seriously.

In the case of Tertius we might assume that he is a slave-scribe but that is only an assumption. From the late third century we have a funerary inscription of an ὀρθόγραφος Nikias (Kent, no. 305): "I proved myself the best writer in the army (or: in the competition?); but I exchanged my bridal chamber for a grave."[52] He certainly was no slave. He mentions his father and was soon to be married when he died. Even though this is a much later inscription, the suspicion still arises that Tertius may have been a comparable ὀρθόγραφος, who wrote the letter to the Romans ἐν κυρίῳ (suggesting that he also wrote letters ἐν σαρκί). Perhaps the phrase ἐν κυρίῳ indicates that he did it free for Paul. In any event, nothing is said that would put Tertius among the proletarian or such. Perhaps he was a scribe employed in the imperial provincial administration.

There remain Chloe's people as representatives of the lower strata. It has been debated, of course, whether or not they came from Corinth at all since Paul overlooks them at the end of his letter. But from this it follows only that they were no longer with Paul when the letter was written. They scarcely belong in Ephesus—if it is assumed that Romans 16 contains a list of greetings to people in Ephesus—for they are not mentioned there although two groups of slaves are. In any event, they are known in Corinth. Paul does not have to "introduce" them, and on the basis of their information he is willing to raise serious objections against the congregation. But who were "Chloe's people"? There are three possible answers.

They could be family members. The phrase οἱ Χλόης would then correspond to the phrase οἱ τοῦ Ζεβεδαίου (John 21:2). This same phrase can be used to indicate that a woman is someone's wife (John 19:25; Mk. 15:40; Mt. 1:6). There is, however, a difficulty with this explanation: families bear the father's name and Chloe is a woman. If she were a widow, her sons would continue to bear the father's name. In fact, a mother could even come to be known by her son's name (cf. "Mary of Joses," Mk. 15:47, with Mary the "mother of Joses," Mk. 15:40). Rom. 16:13, where Paul greets Rufus and "his mother and mine," shows that Paul inclines toward language oriented to the male line. In my opinion we can reasonably exclude the possibility that we are dealing with Chloe's sons or other family members.

Paul is probably referring to members of Chloe's house in some wider sense, as is true in the closest New Testament parallel. In Acts 16:33 the phrase οἱ αὐτοῦ ἅπαντες means the same thing as οἶκος (16:31). Members of the family are, of course, included in the reference. It is emphasized, however, that the *entire* household is involved (16:33, 34); the wider concept of house, including servants and slaves, is probably intended. Within the Pauline letters themselves the closest parallel would be groups of slaves addressed summarily (Rom. 16:10, 11; Phil. 4:22). It is understandable that Paul uses ἐκ with the genitive each time. Not all the slaves or freedmen of Aristobulus, of Narcissus, or of Caesar, were Christians. Paul specifically sends greetings to τοὺς ἐκ τῶν Ναρκίσσου τοὺς ὄντας ἐν κυρίῳ (that is, insofar as they are Christians). Οἱ Χλόης are probably slaves or dependent workers.[53] Their visit to Ephesus has a much different quality from the visit of Stephanas who comes to Paul, brings news, perhaps even the congregational letter, and possibly returns to Corinth to complete the errand. That Paul neither mentions Chloe's people again, nor thanks them for their visit, could indicate that they stopped by Ephesus only incidentally while engaged in other business. But of course that is supposition. If

Chloe's people, however, *were* representatives of the lower classes, it would be understandable that Paul, in responding to their report, should stress that in Corinth there are not many who are wise, powerful, or of noble birth (1 Cor. 1:26).

A third interpretation, however, is improbable.[54] Since οἱ Χλόης parallels the groupings around various missionaries and those described in the phrase ἐγω δε Χριστοῦ, F. R. Hitchcock has supposed that they were fellow members of a mystery religion. Χλόη, in fact, can be shown to be another name for Demeter and there was a cult of Demeter in Corinth. But it is not at all likely that Paul would take a report originating with such people and play it off against the Christian congregation. In doing so he would, in a sense, be setting Gentiles as judges of the affairs of the community, a position he flatly rejects in 1 Cor. 6:4. Besides, complaints coming from such a source would scarcely matter much to the Corinthians.

We can now give a summary of what we know about those Corinthian Christians known to us by name. Apart from Chloe's people we have (at a maximum) sixteen names. However, it is not always certain that those named come from Corinth. Lucius (Rom. 16:21) is frequently identified with Luke, Luke being a familiar form of Lucius. Similarly, it has been assumed that Sosipater (Rom. 16:21) is the Sopater of Beroea mentioned in Acts 20:4. Sosthenes, who is mentioned alongside Paul in the prescript of the first letter to Corinth, could only be regarded as a Corinthian if identified with Sosthenes the synagogue ruler in Acts 18:17, which is by no means certain.

Achaicus:	1 Cor. 16:17; companion of Stephanas.
Aquila:	Rom. 16:3; Acts 18:2, 18, 26; 1 Cor. 16:19; house-congregation; small business establishment; travel; support of apostles.
Erastus:	Rom. 16:23; financial official of the city; probably later chosen aedile and, in consequence, made a public gift; travel.
Fortunatus:	1 Cor. 16:17; companion of Stephanas.
Gaius:	Rom. 16:23; 1 Cor. 1:14; his house served the entire church and Paul. Connections with Erastus?
Jason:	Rom. 16:21.

Crispus:	1 Cor. 1:14; Acts 18:8; synagogue ruler; manager of a "house"; his conversion to Christianity influenced others.
Lucius:	Rom. 16:21.
Priscilla:	See Aquila.
Phoebe:	Rom. 16:1–2; services rendered to Paul and the church; travel.
Quartus:	Rom. 16:23.
Sosipater:	Rom. 16:21.
Sosthenes:	1 Cor. 1:1; Acts 18:17 (?); synagogue ruler; travel.
Stephanas:	1 Cor. 1:16; 16:15; manager of a house; services rendered to the church; travel.
Titius Justus:	Acts 18:7; lodging for Paul.
Tertius:	Rom. 16:22; scribe.
Chloe's people:	1 Cor. 1:11.

Of the seventeen persons (including one group) listed, nine belong to the upper classes according to the criteria discussed above. In three instances, three of the criteria apply: houses, services rendered and travel for Aquila, Priscilla, and Stephanas. In four cases, two criteria apply: offices and travel for Erastus and Sosthenes; office and "house" for Crispus; services rendered and travel for Phoebe. In two cases, one criterion fits: services rendered for Gaius and Titius Justus, on the basis of whose character, however, a certain position in life seems a perfectly reasonable conclusion. Of these nine, Sosthenes possibly was not a Corinthian. In contrast to these there is only a small group of people of probably inferior social status, Chloe's people. This also may be true of Achaicus, Fortunatus, and Tertius, but is by no means certain. The social standing of Jason, Lucius, and Sosipater remains an open question, and we are not even certain if the last two belonged to the Corinthian community.

The result is clear. The great majority of the Corinthians known to us by name probably enjoyed high social status. We need not for that reason cast doubt on Paul's statement that "not many" Corinthians belonged to the upper strata (1 Cor. 1:26). In the letters it is understandably the important people who are most likely to be mentioned by name, who keep in touch with Paul (that is, were free to travel) and who exercise influence within the congregation. Thus we may conclude that in all probability the most active and important members of the congregation belonged to the οὐ πολλοὶ σοφοί, δυνατοί, and εὐγενεῖς. Those of the lower strata scarcely appear as individuals in the Corinthian correspondence. This makes all the more important an analysis of statements about divisions within the congregation.

Statements About Divisions Within Corinth

1. The most revealing statements doubtless are those about the groupings which emerge at the Lord's Supper.[55] Some Christians apparently bring their "own" meal while others (described as μὴ ἔχοντες, 1 Cor. 11:22) have nothing and go hungry. Paul asks the first group, "Do you not have houses to eat and drink in?" thus raising the question of who in Corinth would have had houses. Had Paul simply wanted to recommend that each should eat alone he could have used an expression such as ἐν οἴκῳ (11:34, 14:35) or παρ' ἑαυτῷ (16:2). Further, one wonders if Paul would have expressed himself so awkwardly that he could be misunderstood as if recommending to the "hungry" that they eat their fill at home—a cynical suggestion, to say the least. On the contrary, Paul's question is directed only to those who have enough to eat and drink. Thus it is not out of the question that the phrase οἰκίας ἔχειν conveys the notion of home ownership. That is not certain, to be sure. All that is certain is that at the Lord's Supper there emerged social differences, a split between the "haves" and the "have nots."

2. There are direct statements about the material and financial achievements of the Corinthians. In urging the collection[56] Paul is clear about taking into account individuals' differing financial circumstances. Each should put aside on the Sabbath what he or she can (1 Cor. 16:2). In my opinion it follows from the controversy about apostolic support that some Corinthian Christians have considerable means at their disposal, for we learn that the Corinthians have evidently provided hospitality for several missionaries: Apollos, Peter (or missionaries who make their appeal in his name),

the opponents of Paul who show up in 2 Corinthians, and the superlative apostles (2 Cor. 11:5). Now such generosity is imaginable even under modest circumstances if one presumes an uncommon willingness to make sacrifices. Yet those who can indulge in the luxury of reproaching other missionaries for *not* accepting hospitality, and can do so not once but repeatedly (1 Cor. 9:1ff.; 2 Cor. 10—13), must have a tidy sum to call their own. It is apparently not the entire congregation which raises such objections. In 1 Cor. 9:3 Paul only defends himself before some, τοῖς ἐμέ ἀνακρίνουσιν. Hence it can be assumed, in my opinion, that the spokesmen of the Corinthian parties, that is, protagonists among the followers of other missionaries, belonged to the upper classes—but that will not be pursued here.

3. In 1 Cor. 6:1–11 we hear about litigation among Corinthian Christians. The object of such suits are βιωτικά, probably affairs of property or income.[57] Such litigation would hardly be undertaken by those who have no property. Further, it must be kept in mind that members of the upper classes generally have greater confidence in receiving justice from a court or prevailing in their interpretation of the law, especially since they can pay for good attorneys[58] and have a better grasp of complicated legal matters. Perhaps Paul hints at the status of the litigating Christian[59] when he asks, in irony, "Can it be that there is no man among you wise enough to decide between members of the brotherhood?" (1 Cor. 6:5). Whoever considers himself "wise" ought at least to be wise enough to settle such disputes.

4. "Wisdom" and "knowledge" are certainly understood theologically, both by Paul and the Corinthians, as revealed knowledge for salvation. That, however, does not preclude the prospect that the "wise" are also educated in the ordinary sense. Often enough in the history of religions it can be observed that just such educated classes are most open to the idea of a form of knowledge which saves.[60] In Corinth there may have been something like an intellectual enthusiasm for the Eastern saving wisdom, of the sort which can often be observed in educated or ostensibly educated people. Perhaps that is why Paul stresses that this wisdom is a foolish offense to all people, East and West, Jew and Greek (1 Cor. 1:23). There

are, in fact, concrete hints that the Corinthians did not lack at least an average cultural background. This is indicated by sayings in 1 Corinthians which echo sentiments common in popular philosophy of the time: "The wise man is king." "Everything belongs to the wise man." "Knowledge makes one free."[61] It is also indicated by Paul's apology in 2 Cor. 10—13 which is full of *topoi* taken from popular philosophy and which it is assumed the readers will recognize.[62] When scruples about taking part in a pagan celebration can be brushed aside by means of such a "philosophical" saying as "we all possess knowledge" (1 Cor. 8:1), that points to a particular setting in life (*Sitz im Leben*) for such sayings. The city treasurer Erastus (and all the more, the aedile Erastus) could have kissed his public office goodbye had he on principle rejected invitations to feasts at which pagan rites and meat sacrificed to idols were unavoidable.[63] The "liberal" position on eating such meat may be looked for among the higher strata, the more rigid position among the lower strata—an assumption which cannot be fully discussed here. For our purposes it is sufficient to recognize that in Corinth "the wise" and others who do not belong to that group are in opposition to one another, and that the "wise" and the "gnostics" are more likely to be found in the upper strata.

5. The advice to slaves in 1 Cor. 7:21ff. indicates that these too belonged to the congregation (cf. 1 Cor. 12:13), whether as part of the retinue of a Christian master or independently. This latter possibility is consistent with Paul's advice about mixed marriages in 1 Cor. 7:8ff., which presupposes that Christians live in the houses of pagans and that the Christian congregation is not simply the union of several households.

Analysis of the statements about divisions within the congregation confirms our assumption of internal social stratification. Here, as earlier in the case of those Corinthian Christians known by name, those belonging to the upper levels stand out more clearly. The "wise" have a sharper profile than the weak, who lack knowledge and insight. The wealthy, who have their ἴδιον δεῖπνον are addressed more directly than are the μὴ ἔχοντες. And although we can still hear the criticism aimed at Paul's style of life, those who agreed with his strategy of rejecting support remain silent. Once again those groups whose members we can assume belonged to the upper classes prove themselves the most active. But clearly they are to be distinguished from other groups which remain more in the background but which are nevertheless in the majority according to 1 Cor. 1:26. There are structural causes of this social stratification which can be observed in the Corinthian congregation, causes which have their roots both in the social structure of the city of Corinth itself and in Paul's mission.

THE SOCIOLOGICAL INTERPRETATION OF THE EVIDENCE

The Social Structure of the City of Corinth

After its destruction in 146 Caesar refounded Corinth as a Roman colony in 44 B.C.E.[64] There he settled mostly freedmen but not exclusively: ἐποίκους πέμψαντος τοῦ ἀπελευθερικοῦ γένους πλείστους, "sending people for the most part who belonged to the freedmen class" (Strabo, VIII, 6, 23). Veterans were probably also among the colonists. In any event the settlers were Roman citizens, a Roman colony by definition possessing such citizenship.

Under these circumstances the Roman element was dominant, even if there may have been Greek slaves, for example, among the freedmen. Thus it is certainly no accident that eight of the seventeen surviving names of Corinthian Christians are Latin: Aquila, Fortunatus, Gaius, Lucius, Priscilla, Quartus, Titius Justus, and Tertius. To be sure this tells little about ethnic origin, as Aquila and Priscilla were obviously Jews. Jews constituted a third group of people alongside Romans and Greeks (cf. West, no. 111; Philo, *De legatione ad Gaium* 281f.; Acts 18:1ff.). According to Apuleius (*Metamorphoses* XI) the Isis cult could be found in Corinth in the second century C.E., so perhaps Apollos the Alexandrian ran across fellow Egyptians there as early as the first century.

It is especially important for the founding of the congregation that this city had no continuity in its tradition. Nothing in Corinth was more than a century old, whether the constitution, buildings, families, or cults. In this period many families were socially ascendant, their grandfathers and great-grandfathers quite possibly having been slaves. Such a city is rather receptive to new endeavors.[65] It is also easy to imagine that relatively "established" circles could also be won over to new ideas, for the "new" Corinthians lived in a center of a country the culture of which had by that time become a "myth." They did not really *live* within this culture. If in many aspects of life they stood in continuity with Greek traditions, the use of Latin in their inscriptions and the construction of an amphitheater show how very un-Greek, in other ways, was their style of life. Such circumstances are particularly unsettling to those strata of society for which culture (real or imagined) is a part of social status. Possibly some of their members were particularly receptive for that reason to new wisdom from the East, seeing in it the fulfillment of all claims to wisdom and knowledge.[66] Surely it is no accident that Paul had no success in the tradition-conscious city of Athens, according to Acts 17, but won "many people" for the Christian faith in Corinth. In a newly founded, culturally heterogeneous city the desire for a new cultural and social identity is much more likely to arise than in the established cultural center of Athens.

Corinthian citizens were not only on the rise socially; the city had also experienced a rapid economic upturn,[67] as excavations confirm. The oldest houses are still quite simply built, while later structures are laid out more handsomely. It is at just this time, in the first century, that the Corinthians are busily engaged in construction, donating buildings and amenities. Of twenty-seven instances testified to by inscriptions, seventeen fall in the short period between Augustus and Nero.[68] Since in most instances the donor cannot be shown to come from outside Corinth, it may be assumed that local citizens took responsibility for such municipal benefactions. The Christian Erastus probably distinguished himself in just such manner.

An unmistakable indicator of this economic upturn is the resumption by Corinth of the Isthmian games, sometime between 7 B.C.E. and 3 C.E. After the destruction of old Corinth these games were continued in Sicyon. The *agonothetai*, elected as organizers and leaders of the games (from whom was expected financial assistance for that purpose), all seem to have been Corinthians. The games involved many people. Dio Chrysostom (*Orationes* 37, 8) mentions the θεωρόν, the festival pilgrim, second to the merchant—and in so doing signifies the close association between the games and commercial activity.

Corinth's wealth was based primarily on trade: ὁ δὲ Κόρινθος ἀφνειὸς μὲν λέγεται διὰ τὸ ἐμπόριον ("Corinth is said to be 'wealthy' on account of its commerce"), Strabo writes (VIII, 6, 20). It had the reputation of being a "great and wealthy city" (Strabo, VIII, 6, 23). This testimony from about the time of Christ's birth is supplemented for the second century C.E. by a speech of Aelius Aristides which praises Corinth as Greece's commercial center (Aelius Aristides, *Orationes* XLVI, 22–23). Dio Chrysostom (*Or.* 37, 8) was right in putting the merchant at the head of the list of Corinthian visitors. Thus it fits with the general picture of Corinth to link the frequent travels of members of the Christian community with business matters.[69]

A second factor in Corinthian wealth, inseparable from commerce, was banking. Plutarch (*Moralia* 831a) names three banking centers in Greece: Patrae, Corinth, and Athens.[70]

A third factor to be taken into account is production from artisans. Strabo calls particular attention to Corinthian τέχνας τὰς δημιουργικάς ("arts of the craftsman"; VIII, 6, 23). Metalworking had declined (Strabo, VIII, 6, 23), but Corinthian bronze, a distinctive bronze alloy, was still coveted. As an example of the rapacity of the Romans who rule the world Petronius (*Satyricon* 119) mentions, among others, the soldier who prizes Corinthian bronze, so it must still have been famous at that time. The older, Greek Corinth which had now disappeared was famous above all for its pottery; the new Corinth also saw growth in such craftsmanship, for at the end of the first century lamps were again being exported in increasing quantities.[71]

Finally, governmental administration must be mentioned as a fourth factor in Corinth's prosperity. Since 27 B.C.E Corinth had been the seat of the governor of Achaia, a fact which in itself brought many people to the city. Dio Chrysostom mentions the πρεσβυτής (envoy) third (*Or.* 37, 8), and since he distinguishes him from the διερχόμενος (passing traveller) we may assume that the provincial government sometimes was the destination of such "envoys." Scribes such as the Christian Tertius (Rom. 16:23) were certainly in demand by the state government.

It is conceivable that in such an aspiring city as this the social strata are more clearly differentiated from one another than in places where from time immemorial there have been well defined groups of wealthy families and groups of the poor. The rhetor Alciphron (*Epistulae* III, 24) gives evidence of a sharp distinction between rich and poor in the second century B.C.E.: οὐκ ἔτι εἰσῆλθον εἰς τὴν Κόρινθον. ἔγνων γὰρ ἐν βραχεῖ τὴν βδελυρίαν τῶν ἐκεῖσε πλουσίων καὶ τὴν πενήτων ἀθλιότητα ("I did not go further into Corinth, having learned in short order the sordidness of the rich there and the misery of the poor"). A community like the Christian congregation in Corinth, encompassing various groups and classes, was in all probability confronted with special problems of integration because of its internal stratification.

Social Conditions of the Pauline Mission

If Paul makes it quite clear that the majority of Corinthian Christians come from the lower strata, it is all the more noteworthy that all of those baptized by him belonged to the upper strata: Crispus, Gaius, and Stephanas. They must have been especially important for the Pauline mission; or, conversely, in them the mission fell on fertile soil. There is a sociological reason for this inherent in the Pauline mission itself. According to the Acts of the Apostles, which is credible on this point, Paul first turned to the Jews, then the Gentiles.[72] More precisely, he turned to the "God-fearers," Gentiles sympathetic with the beliefs and moral principles of Judaism who did not fully convert to Judaism or become circumcized, the σεβόμενοι or φοβούμενοι τὸν θεόν. The Acts of the Apostles tells how during the Corinthian mission Paul, when rejected by the local synagogue, declared, "From now on I will go to the Gentiles." Acts continues, "And he left there and went to the house of a man named Titius Justus, a worshiper of God" (σεβομένου τὸν θεόν, 18:7). This was probably a man of means, for with some justification it has usually been assumed that there were people of property in the circles of these "God-fearers." It is those very people whose work and social status implies social relationships with the Gentile world, relationships which as Jews they could maintain only with considerable effort,[73] who would have reason not to enter fully the Jewish community despite their inner concurrence with Jewish beliefs. One has only to think of the resulting problem of food taboos, or the drastic shrinkage of the "marriage market." On the other hand, it could be a real advantage for someone of lower social standing to convert completely to Judaism, that is, to become a proselyte. This assumption can be supported by inscriptions from Diaspora Judaism found in Italy, even if the chance character of what survives makes evaluation difficult.[74] Of a total of 731 inscriptions, 8 refer to proselytes and 7 (perhaps 8) to "God-fearers." Among the proselytes we find two slaves and an adoptive child; among the "God-fearers," no slaves, but a Roman of equestrian rank, a status we know was dependent on the level of one's wealth.[75] From this evidence K. G. Kuhn and H. Stegemann conclude: "Among the 'God-fearers' in the Jewish-Hellenistic diaspora the proportion of those of higher social status was greater than among the proselytes who, for the most part, come from the lowest strata of the people (for example, slaves)."[76] The reader of the New Testament can confirm this. God-fearers emerge now and again as leaders of Jewish and Christian congregations. One thinks of the purple-merchant in Philippi (Acts 16:14ff.) or the centurion of Capernaum—at the very least Luke's rendering here depicts what is a typical trait; cf. Lk. 7:5, where the pious centurion even had a synagogue built—and the centurion of Caesarea, Acts 10:1ff. It is these very people who show themselves receptive to Christianity.

The reasons are not hard to find. God-fearers had already demonstrated an independence with reference to their native traditions and religion.[77] They stood between differing cultural realms and were thus particularly receptive to the Christian faith, which crossed ethnic and cultural boundaries and offered an identity independent of inherited traditions. Judaism could not do this; within it these people would not be fully entitled.[78] Christianity, however, especially in its Pauline form, offered them the possibility of acknowledging monotheism and high moral principles and at the same time attaining full religious equality without circumcision, without ritual demands, without restraints which could negatively affect their social status.

Seen in this light, the conflict between Christianity and Judaism is easier to understand: the Christian mission was luring away the very Gentiles who were Judaism's patrons. According to the report in Acts, Paul was brought before the governor Gallio by the Corinthian Jews.[79] They charged him with persuading people to fear God in a fashion contrary to the Law. The phrase σέβεσθαι τὸν θεόν ("to fear God") in 18:13 is identical in language and content with the technical term σεβόμενοι τὸν θεόν, here simply expressed in a different verbal form. This can be understood to mean that Paul taught a way of being σεβόμενος τὸν θεόν which ignored the legal rules and restrictions, and involved no commitment to the Law. To the disciplined Jews this meant that Paul was selling a Judaism at reduced rates. In other ways too it must have been a bitter thing for the Jewish congregations of the Diaspora that Paul was successful with the God-fearers.[80] Not only did their contributions now benefit the Christian community, but the Jews, as a minority, had come to depend on the recognition and advocacy of such people in a foreign, gentile world full of anti-Jewish prejudices.

Such structural reasons for the participation of the upper classes in the Pauline communities are not wholly confined to those who were the object of the mission. They also have something to do with the missionary. Paul himself came from the upper strata.[81] By profession, it is true, he was only a simple craftsman, probably a tent-cloth maker from Tarsus. Nevertheless, he was a citizen of that city and of Rome as well (Acts 21:39; 22:28).[82] That is all the more noteworthy since normally cloth workers enjoyed neither privilege, as appears from a speech of Dio Chrysostom's (*Or.* 34, 21–23).[83]

> For instance, to leave now the discord of Council and Assembly, of the Youth and the Elders, there is a group of no small size which is, as it were, outside the constitution. And some are accustomed to call them "linen-workers" (λινουργούς), and at times the citizens are irritated by them and assert that they are a useless rabble and responsible for the tumult and disorder in Tarsus, while at other times they regard

> them as a part of the city and hold the opposite opinion of them. Well, if you believe them to be detrimental to you and instigators of insurrection and confusion, you should expel them altogether and not admit them to your popular assemblies; but if on the other hand you regard them as being in some measure citizens, not only because they are resident in Tarsus, but also because in most instances they were born here and know no other city, then surely it is not fitting to disfranchise them or to cut them off from association with you. But as it is, they necessarily stand aloof in sentiment from the common interest, reviled as they are and viewed as outsiders. . . . "Well then, what do *you* bid us do?" I bid you to enroll them all as citizens—yes, I do—and just as deserving as yourselves; and not to reproach them or cast them off, but rather to regard them as members of your body politic, as in fact they are.

Thus it appears that Paul's family had achieved what was contested for most cloth workers in Tarsus, the right to full citizenship in the city. In addition, however, Paul's family also possessed Roman citizenship and so doubtless enjoyed a privileged status. It is understandable that Paul would appeal to people whose social status was equivalent to his. Perhaps the fact that he was a Roman citizen enhanced his visibility and respectability, since from a legal point of view he was the equal of the citizens of Corinth.

Finally, practical requirements of the mission should be mentioned. It is true that because of his work as a craftsman Paul was relatively independent. But for his missionary task he was dependent on a place to live and rooms for congregational gatherings.[84] Larger rooms of that sort could only be provided by those who were reasonably well-off.

These are some of the structural reasons why Paul was able, in Corinth and elsewhere, to win for Christianity those who belonged to the upper strata. That does not alter the fact, however, that in the Corinthian congregation most Christians came from the lower classes. Some probably came in the retinue of an individual of high social standing, whether as family member, servant, or slave. Nevertheless, the inner social stratification of the Corinthian congregation cannot be attributed to that exclusively.[85] The advice to those in "mixed marriages" (1 Cor. 7:8ff.), for example, presupposes that the boundaries between Christianity and paganism or

Judaism could cut right through houses and families and separate spouses, parents, and children. Similarly, the advice to slaves (1 Cor. 7:21ff.) does not appear to be confined to slaves of Christian masters, since, unlike the situation in the deutero-Pauline letters (cf. Col. 3:18ff.; Eph. 6:5ff.) or in Philemon, here masters receive no advice about relations with slaves. Finally, 1 Cor. 11:20–34 contradicts the thesis that the internal stratification in the congregation can largely be traced back to differences of social status within Christian houses, for it is specifically assumed here that different houses have different social status. The wealthy are supposed to eat their "own meal" at home (11:22, 34). We can hardly assume that the μὴ ἔχοντες (11:22) are their fellow household members, or the problem of the relationship between the "haves" and the "have nots" would simply be repeated within the houses.

In conclusion it can be said that Hellenistic primitive Christianity was neither a proletarian movement among the lower classes nor an affair of the upper classes. On the contrary, what is characteristic for its social structure is the fact that it encompassed various strata—and thus various interests, customs, and assumptions. E. A. Judge has correctly emphasized this: "The interests brought together in this way probably marked the Christians off from the other unofficial associations, which were generally socially and economically as homogeneous as possible. Certainly this phenomenon led to constant differences among the Christians themselves . . ."[86] These differences, which in my view are particularly instructive in Corinth, cannot be investigated here. Finally, however, the results of our sociological analysis of information about the Corinthian congregation must be incorporated within the historical framework of the development of Christianity and ancient society, even if we can do no more than sketch some working hypotheses for further research.

The Hellenistic communities represent an advanced stage in the development of primitive Christianity. The oldest communities are to be found in the area of Palestine. Christianity's transition from the rurally structured world of Palestine to the urban, Hellenistic culture of the Mediterranean world was probably accompanied by its penetration of the higher strata of society. The primitive congregation's self-designation as πτωχοί (Gal. 2:10; Rom. 15:26) may not only express a "purely religious" self-understanding but may also deserve a literal interpretation. At any rate Paul gathers his collection for the "poor" in Jerusalem aware that he is providing real support (cf. Rom. 15:27; 2 Cor. 9:12). For example, the Galilean fishers and farmers who moved to Jerusalem were literally poor. Indeed, in leaving their Galilean home they gave up their means of earning a living. And I think it entirely conceivable that there was conflict in the community between the Jews of the Diaspora living in Jerusalem, presumably better off, and the "native" Jews, a conflict heightened by material concerns (Acts 6:1–6). The history of primitive Christianity was thus shaped even in the first generation by a radical social shift which altered important socio-cultural, socio-ecological, and socio-economic factors through the processes of Hellenization, urbanization, and the penetration of society's higher strata. If this is taken into account it can hardly be deemed an accident that the Hellenistic congregations only hesitantly accepted Palestinian traditions, which came from an entirely different social world. As is generally acknowledged, Paul knows only a few of the sayings of the Lord. And even if he had known more, the ethical radicalism of the Jesus tradition, with its ethos of surrendering family, property, and home, would have found little room to survive in the congregations founded by him.

In these congregations there developed an ethos obviously different from that of the synoptic tradition, the ethos of primitive Christian love-patriarchalism.[87] We encounter it particularly in the deutero-Pauline and pastoral Letters, but it is already evident in Paul (namely, in 1 Cor. 7:21ff.; 11:3–16). This love-patriarchalism takes social differences for granted but ameliorates them through an obligation of respect and love, an obligation imposed upon those who are socially stronger. From the weaker are required subordination, fidelity, and esteem. Whatever the intellectual sources feeding into this ethos, with it the great part of Hellenistic primitive Christianity mastered the task of shaping social relations within a community which, on the one hand, demanded of its members a high degree of solidarity and brotherliness and, on the other, encompassed various social strata. This primitive Christian love-patriarchalism, with its moderate social conservatism, made a lasting impact on Christianity. It prevailed against Montanism and Gnosis in the second century. It produced the church's fundamental norms and fashioned lasting institutions. It solved problems of organization and prepared Christianity to receive the great masses. Its historical effectiveness is rooted not least of all in its ability to integrate members of different strata. Members of the upper classes could find a fertile field of activity, so that ancient Christianity never lacked for distinguished leadership figures—beginning with Paul. But the lower strata were also at home here. They found a fundamental equality of status before God, solidarity and help in the concrete problems of life, not least of all from those Christians who enjoyed a higher station in life. Christian brotherhood probably would have been more radically carried out within socially homogeneous groups. That is much easier, however, than realizing a measure of brotherhood within communities which are sharply stratified socially. It was here that primitive Christianity's love-patriarchalism offered a realistic solution.

In the context of late antiquity this love-patriarchalism became significant for society as a whole. It offered a new pattern for directing and shaping social relationships in contrast to that of Greco-Roman antiquity.[88] The latter sought to solve the problems of social integration by means of a noble vision of a citizenry enjoying equality of status. This equality was at the center of politico-social conflicts. Again and again efforts were made to reduce social tensions to a tolerable level by extending citizenship to a greater number of people. We have already seen an example in Dio Chrysostom's suggestion (*Or.* 34, 21ff.) to the Tarsians that they extend the right of citizenship to all linen workers in order to avoid social conflict. Another example is the gradual extension of Roman citizenship until the edict of Caracalla in 217, which bestowed it on the entire population of the empire.[89] Political equality, however, was always circumscribed. Not only were slaves excluded, but resident aliens and foreigners as well. Furthermore, along with the tendency to extend citizenship to everyone in the empire went, simultaneously, a trend toward establishing new legal distinctions, as for example in the introduction of gradations in criminal penalties beginning with Hadrian. Above all, however, political and social developments led, especially in the great crisis of the third century,[90] to an impoverishment of the masses and an incipient "feudalization" of the higher strata, denying to this socially integrating pattern of political equality its social basis, namely, a broad swath of the urban bourgeoisie conscious of its rights as well as its responsibilities. The weakening of this group probably contributed not a little to the transition from enlightened monarchy in the second century to the absolute Dominate in the fourth century. It probably also contributed to that vicious circle of growing military threat on the empire's borders which increased internal social pressure, which in turn increased the difficulty of energetically resisting the threat.

Faced with such radically altered social relationships, the society of late antiquity could adopt a new pattern of integration[91] which had been developed in small religious communities within the Roman Empire—Christian love-patriarchalism. In it equality of status was extended to all—to women, foreigners, and slaves. For in Christ there was "neither Jew nor Greek, . . . neither slave nor free, . . . neither male nor female; for you are all one in Christ Jesus" (Gal. 3:28). At the same time, however, all of this was internalized; it was true "in Christ." In the political and social realm class-specific differences were essentially accepted, affirmed, even religiously legitimated. No longer was there a struggle for equal rights but instead a struggle to achieve a pattern of relationships among members of various strata which would be characterized by respect, concern, and a sense of responsibility. Thus even in the face of increasingly difficult social circumstances as the world of antiquity was coming to a close, in a period of growing social pressure, a new form of social integration was available. It held out the chance of a certain humanity to those who were becoming ever more dependent while at the same time it held fast to the idea of fundamental equality of status. Constantine was able to succeed with his religious policy only because Christian love-patriarchalism, as the creative answer to radical social changes, was able to have an effect even beyond the small Christian minority.

If the basic pattern of primitive Christian love-patriarchalism today appears insufficient for shaping our social relationships, it should nonetheless be given its historic due: it was a human attempt to shape social relationships. It never completely stifled other social forms and ethical traditions from Christianity, such as the ethical radicalism of the synoptic tradition or the vision of a spiritual community of brothers and friends bound together only by the love commandment, as in John's Gospel. The idea of political equality, coming from the ancient polis, could again and again be combined with such ethical traditions. Indeed, it could even strengthen them to the point that the fundamental demand for freedom and equality was raised on behalf of all people and combined with the specific Christian claim of brotherhood. Christianity cannot remain indifferent to this radicalization of ancient democratic traditions which has so irrevocably shaped our ethical and political consciousness.

NOTES

1. A. Deissmann, *Light from the Ancient Near East* (London, 1927), 144.

2. E. A. Judge, *The Social Pattern of Early Christian Groups in the First Century* (London, 1960), 60. Judge stresses, to be sure, that members of the lower strata also joined the Christian community as part of the retinue of those from the higher classes. Cf. further R. Knopf, "Über die soziale Zusammensetzung der ältesten heidenchristlichen Gemeinden," *ZThK* 10 (1900): 325–47; E. von Dobschütz, *Christian Life in the Primitive Church* (New York, 1904), 14; J. Weiss, *Der erste Korintherbrief* (Göttingen, 1910), xvi.

3. Without question, Paul is here applying the idea of creation from nothing to a social situation. On creation *ex nihilo* cf. 2 Macc. 7:28; Philo, *De opificio mundi* 81; *De specialibus legibus* IV, 187; 2 Baruch 21:4f.; Hermas, *Mandata* I, 1; Hermas, *Visiones* I, 1, 6; 2 Clem. 1:8: ἐκάλεσεν γὰρ ἡμᾶς, οὐκ ὄντας καὶ ἠθέλησεν ἐκ μὴ ὄντος εἶναι ἡμᾶς. The distinction between μή and μηδέν is not very relevant; cf. 1 Cor. 11:22 with 2 Cor. 6:10.

4. Cf. J. Bohatec, "Inhalt und Reihenfolge der 'Schlagworte der Erlösungsreligion' in I Kor 1 26–31," *ThZ* 4 (1948): 252–71.

5. For detailed discussion of this *topos* see H. D. Betz, *Der Apostel Paulus und die sokratische Tradition*, BHTh 45 (Tübingen, 1972), 123–30.

6. Origen, *Contra Celsum* III, 48.

7. περικαθάρματα should be understood in a sociological sense, as is κάθαρμα in Philo, *De virtutibus* 174. The meaning "propitiatory sacrifice" is attested only in later sources. Cf. H. Conzelmann, *1 Corinthians* (Philadelphia, 1975), 90 n. 49.

8. On the office of the ruler of the synagogue cf. E. Schürer, *Geschichte des jüdischen Volkes* (Leipzig, 1907[4]), II: 509–512, Eng. trans. *The History of the Jewish People in the Age of Jesus Christ (175 B.C.–A.D. 135)*, (Edinburgh, 1886–90), II: 433–36, rev. and ed. G. Vermes and F. Millar (Edinburgh, 1973–1979), and J. B. Frey, *Corpus Inscriptionum Iudaicarum* I (Rome, 1936), xcvii–xcix. It is noteworthy that Sosthenes, as the ruler of the synagogue, represents the case of the Jewish community before the procurator Gallio (Acts 18:17), since that was usually the task of the ἄρχοντες. Perhaps he held both offices.

9. That there was a synagogue in Corinth is shown by an inscription (cf. B. D. Merritt, *Greek Inscriptions, 1896–1927: Corinth, Results of Excavations conducted by the American School of Classical Studies at Athens VIII, 1* [Cambridge, 1931], no. 111). The style of the inscription, however, points to a later time (cf. 79).

10. Cf. Frey, *Inscriptionum,* 188.

11. Cf. E. Haenchen, *The Acts of the Apostles* (Philadelphia, 1971), 535.

12. H. J. Cadbury, "Erastus of Corinth," *JBL* 50 (1931): 42–58, argues for the latter possibility. The genitive τῆς πόλεως would in this case probably be taken as a possessive genitive.

13. Cadbury, ibid., 42ff., on the one hand regards the three Erastoi of the New Testament as identical but on the other hand maintains that Erastus was probably a slave. One cannot, in my opinion, hold both views at once.

14. So U. Wilcken, *Griechische Ostraka aus Aegypten und Nubien: Ein Beitrag zur antiken Wirtschaftsgeschichte,* Bd. I (München, 1899 = Amsterdam, 1970), 499: "The old, purely Greek titles were retained only in the lower posts, which stood under the κράτιστοι, like the οἰκονόμοι . . ." That is true chiefly, however, for Egypt. Cf. Strabo xvii, 1, 12 (concerning Egypt): παρέπονται δὲ τούτοις ἀπελεύθεροι Καίσαρος καὶ οἰκονόμοι, μείζω καὶ ἐλάττω πεπιστευμένοι πράγματα. This passage shows that on occasion higher responsibilities were also entrusted to the οἰκονόμος.

15. P. Landvogt, "Epigraphische Untersuchungen über den οἰκονόμος: Ein Beitrag zum hellenistischen Beamtenwesen" (diss., Strasbourg, 1908). The relevant inscriptions almost all come from Asia Minor. I have been able to find no inscription which really alters the picture and only add here a few inscriptions from Asia Minor. It is never clear, however, whether or not these have to do with civil servants and public functions: MAMA VII: 1; VIII: 136, 386, 399.

16. Ibid., 21.

17. For this reason Cadbury, "Erastus," 49, excludes the parallels from Asia Minor.

18. Cf. also W. A. McDonald, "Archaeology and St. Paul's Journey in Greek Lands. Part III: Corinth," *BA* 4 (1942): 36–48; he probably has in view the office of οἰκονόμος in Asia Minor: "The argument that *oikonomos* is translated *arcarius* in the Vulgata and that the *arcarius* in Roman cities was usually of servile origin, while the *aedile* was of higher social standing, loses its point when we take into account the fact that *oikonomos* to an easterner like Paul might denote one of very similar social position to a Roman *aedile*" (42 n. 2).

19. On the political goals of the colonization policy of the Caesars cf. F. Vittinghoff, *Römische Kolonisation und Bürgerrechtspolitik unter Caesar und Augustus*, AAWLM.G 14 (Mainz, 1951). On Corinth see 85–87. Cf. further A. H. M. Jones, *The Greek City from Alexander to Justinian* (Oxford, 1940), 61–64.

20. Cf. on that the careful reflections of J. H. Kent, *The Inscriptions 1926–1950: Corinth, Results of Excavations Conducted by the American School of Classical Studies at Athens VIII*, 3 (Princeton, 1966), 18–19. Four Greek inscriptions are published by Kent from the time from Augustus to Trajan (2 of which cannot be dated with certainty), as compared with 101 Latin inscriptions (of which 43 cannot be dated with certainty). By contrast, in the period from Hadrian to Gallienus only 17 Latin inscriptions (5 of which cannot be dated with certainty) can be identified, as compared with 35 Greek inscriptions (13 of which cannot be dated with certainty). Latin was able to catch on and hold its own because, among other reasons, Corinth had been the provincial capital of Achaia since 27 B.C.E.

21. Cf. W. Liebenam, *Städteverwaltung im römischen Kaiserreich* (Leipzig, 1900), 460–61; Vittinghoff, *Kolonisation*, 41–43: the difference between a colony and a *municipium* lay primarily in the fact of Roman establishment. Beyond that it was less a matter of different legal structures than of a difference in levels of respect. A colony belonged to the Roman people who made up the state. Above all, colonies received privileges. For that reason, *municipia* sought to become colonies but colonies did not seek to become *municipia*. On colonies, cf. further E. Kornemann, s.v. "coloniae," PRE 7, 511–88. The political structure of Corinth is comprehensively discussed by Kent, *Inscriptions*, 23ff.

22. On the *duumviri* cf. Liebenam, *Städteverwaltung*, 255ff.; for the corresponding στρατηγοί, 289–90.

23. Cf. A. B. West, *Latin Inscriptions, 1896–1927: Corinth, Results of Excavations Conducted by the American School of Classical Studies of Athens VIII*, 2 (Cambridge, 1931), 31–35. But Kent, *Inscriptions*, 25, proposes C. Julius Laconis f. Spartiaticus.

24. Cf. W. Liebenam, *Städteverwaltung*, 263–65; Kubitschek, s.v. "Aedilis," PRE 1, 448–64; Kent, *Inscriptions*, 27.

25. For discussion of the Erastus inscription cf. F. J. M. de Waele, *Mededeelingen v.h. Nederland. histor. Institut de Rom* 9 (1929): 40–48; idem, "Die Korinthischen Ausgrabungen 1928–1929," *Gn*. 6 (1930): 52–57. On p. 54 of the latter he identifies the Erastus of the inscription of Corinth with the Christian Erastus. In his review of R. Carpenter's *Ancient Corinth*, 1933, in *Gn*. 10 (1934): 223–30, however, de Waele retracts his opinion (226). Cf. further A. G. Roos, "De titulo quodam latino corintho nuper reperto," *Mn*. 58 (1930): 160–65. Cadbury, "Erastus," discusses in detail the identity of both Erastoi, with negative results. For the opposite view cf. McDonald, "Archaeology," 42 n. 2; O. Broneer, "Corinth: Center of St. Paul's Missionary Work in Greece," *BA* 14 (1951): 78–96; Kent, *Inscriptions*, 99–100, 27.

26. Kent, *Inscriptions*, 100, also accepts this date ("near the middle of the first century after Christ"), but without offering any justification for it.

27. Cf. Cadbury, "Erastus," 54.

28. So McDonald, "Archaeology," 42 n. 2.

29. Cf. further (also on other offices) the compilation of evidence in Liebenam, *Städteverwaltung*, 539ff.

30. Kent, *Inscriptions*, 27.

31. Cf. also Liebenam, *Städteverwaltung*, 542–45.

32. Cf. ibid., 265–66, 269, 298, 328ff.

33. Cf. ibid, 269.

34. Cf. the compilation in Kent, *Inscriptions*, 27–28.

35. Liebenam, *Städteverwaltung*, 269, cites *Digesta*, 4, 11: "ut gradatim honores deferantur, edicto, et, ut a minoribus ad maiores preveniatur, epistola divi Pii ad Titianum exprimitur." On the variations in the succession of offices cf. 269 n. 5. Numerous further examples of Corinthian "careers" can be found in Kent, *Inscriptions*. Cf. no. 150, *agonothet*, twice *duovir*, twice *pro duumviri* (= "prefect"); no. 152, *praefectus fabrorum*, priest of Jupiter, honorary aedile, *duovir*, *duovir quinquennalis*, *agonothet*; no. 153, aedile, *praefectus iure dicundo*, *duovir*, *duovir quinquennialis*, *agonothet*; no. 154, aedile, *praefectus iure dicundo*, *duovir*, pontifex, *agonothet*; no. 156, *augur*, *praefectus fabrorum*, aedile, *duovir*, priest, *isagogeus*, *agonothet*; no. 158, *duovir*, *duovir quinquennalis*, *augur*, priest, military tribune, *praefectus fabrorum*, *curator annonae* three times, *agonothet*; no. 166, honorary aedile, *duovir*, *agonothet*, *duovir quinquennalis*. Cf. further nos. 160–63.

36. On ἀργυροταμίας cf. J. Oehler, PRE 2, 802. For a collection of texts see Liebenam, *Städteverwaltung*, 565. West describes the office: "The *argyrotamias* was probably the official called curator Kalendarii in municipalities located in Latin speaking provinces. His functions were differentiated from those of the quaestor (ταμίας) by the fact that in his

charge were the productive funds of the community. He collected rents and other charges, loaned money, kept appropriate records, examined and listed the securities offered, and in other ways managed the endowments of the city" *Inscriptions,* (85).

37. A. Strobel, "Der Begriff des 'Hauses' im griechischen und römischen Privatrecht," *ZNW* 56 (1965): 91–100. Cf. the conclusion (99–100): "The house is exclusively represented in these texts as a union (= family) of adult, related persons having legal capacity, in which the legal and business capacities are united in the person of the father of the house."

38. On the "families" of slaves cf. F. Bömer, *Untersuchungen über die Religion der Sklaven in Griechenland und Rom I,* AAWLM.G 7 (Mainz, 1957), 57ff. In his study of the words *familia* and *domus* he presents (on 65 n.1) several arguments against Strobel. Less persuasive, to be sure, is his evidence that *domus* now and then could also include slaves. That does not follow, in my opinion, from the evidence in *CIL* III 7380 (= *Inscriptiones Latinae selectae,* ed. H. Dassau [Berlin, 1892–1916], 5682). ". . . populo et familiai Caesaris . . ." means here subject people who, by way of exception, are called a family of Caesar because in this case they were truly the "private property" of the emperor (cf. Dessau, *Inscriptiones*). Nor do *CIL* 9023 and Dessau 1091 change anything, in my opinion.

39. So Bömer, *Sklaven,* 65 n. 1.

40. The question of whether children belonged to "houses" has been heatedly discussed in the controversy over infant baptism. J. Jeremias, *The Origins of Infant Baptism,* SHT 1 (London, 1963), argues for the inclusion of children. Against that is K. Aland, *Die Säuglingstaufe im NT und in der Alten Kirche,* TEH 85 (München, 1963[2]); cf. further P. Weigand, "Zur sogenannten 'Oikosformel,'" *NT* 6 (1963): 49–74. The evidence collected by G. Delling in his careful and balanced study, "Zur Taufe von 'Häusern' im Urchristentum," *NT* 7 (1965): 285–311, need not be repeated here.

41. Also, according to Delling, "Taufe," 294, we have here a broader idea which "includes, besides the children named, either kinsmen or more particularly also servants, or both."

42. Strobel, "'Hauses,'" 99.

43. So also Delling, "Taufe," 299: "One may suppose that there were slaves in the house of Cornelius, of Lydia, of the jail keeper in Philippi (Acts 10:2; 16:15, 31); they are also specified for the house of the βασιλικός of Capernaum (John 4:53; cf. also v. 51)."

44. Cf. Bomer, *Sklaven,* 13.

45. Cf. F. V. Filson, "The Significance of the Early House Churches," *JBL* 58 (1939): 105–12. The Christian church constructed in Dura-Europos arose on the site of a private house, the size of which shows that it was the house of a well-to-do Christian. The Christians probably first gathered at his house, which was then later rebuilt into the church. Cf. E. Dinkler, s.v. "Dura-Europas," *RGG*[3] II, 290–92.

46. On that situation cf. W. Bienert, *Die Arbeit nach der Lehre der Bibel: Eine Grundlegung evangelischer Sozialethik* (Stuttgart, 1954), 310–11.

47. Merritt, *Inscriptions*, no. 111.

48. Haenchen, *Acts*, 539. F. J. de Waele, *Corinthe et Saint Paul*, Les antiquités de la Grèce (Paris, 1961), 94, sees Titius Justus as a rich Roman. Unfortunately he does not tell us how he comes to that conclusion. Moreover, Paul's taking up residence in his house could have been motivated by the fact that Titius Justus was a native, which allowed Paul to strike up better relations with other Corinthians, while Aquila and Priscilla, as immigrants, could offer no suitable "center of communication."

49. Travel also costs money. For that reason imperial permits were very much in demand, as can be inferred from Pliny, *Epistulae*, x, 45, 46. Himself a well-to-do governor in Bithynia, Pliny the Younger illegally procured for his wife an imperial permit when she, at the death of her grandfather, wished to return from Asia Minor to Rome. Trajan, the emperor, pardoned his friend (Pliny, *Epist*., X, 120–21).

50. According to Weiss, *Korintherbrief*, 386, Fortunatus and Achaicus are the names of freedmen. That, however, signifies little in a colony which was founded by freedmen.

51. So also Strobel, "'Hauses,'" 99.

52. De Waele, *Corinthe*, 101, supposes a school of *orthographoi*. This interpretation is based on the translation of στρατῆσι by "competition." Kent, *Inscriptions*, 119, translates differently.

53. These could also be freedmen. But even so one would rather expect the name of the *patronus*. "A woman's *liberti* took the *nomen* and *praenomen* of the father of their *patrona*" (so J. Marquardt, "Das Privatleben der Römer," *Handbuch der römischen Altertümer*, ed. J. Marquardt and T. Momsen [Leipzig, 1886[2]], VII, 1:22).

54. F. R. Hitchcock, "Who are 'the people of Chloe' in I Cor. 1:11?" *JThS* 25 (1923): 163–67.

55. That the tensions so prominent in 1 Corinthians were tensions between rich and poor Christians is usually not disputed; cf., for example, Weiss, *Korintherbrief*, 293; G. Bornkamm, "Lord's Supper and Church in Paul," *Early Christian Experience* (New York, 1969), 123–60, esp. 126 and 128; von Dobschütz, *Christian Life*, 19.

56. Von Dobschütz, *Christian Life*, also cites the collection as an argument that no inconsiderable number of well-to-do Christians belonged to the Corinthian community.

57. Cf. F. Preisigke, *Wörterbuch der griechischen Papyrusurkunden* (Berlin, 1925), I: 270; further, Epictetus, *Diss*., I, 26, 1–7.

58. Lawyers originally received no negotiated fee. Cladius, however, established that lawyers could also lay claim to fees within limits. (Tacitus, *Annales* XI, 7, 8). Cf. U. E. Paoli, *Das Leben im alten Rom*

(Bern/München, 1961²), 219–35.

59. A. Stein, "Wo trugen die korinthischen Christen ihre Rechtshändel aus?" *ZNW* 59 (1968): 86–90, believes that the trials took place before Jewish judges, taking καθίζειν in a juristic sense and noting that in Roman civil suits the judge was not "appointed." But Paul proceeds from the conclusion that the community is fundamentally not subject to any judge. One can then take "appoint" in a wider sense: only by seeking out judges do the Christians make these their judges. For an appearance before a judge it was important for the parties involved to come before the court with as many influential friends as possible (Paoli, *Leben*, 231). Bohatec, "Inhalt und Reihenfolge," believes that the wealthier Christians brought the socially "weaker" before the judges. But we hear nothing about that. Von Dobschütz, *Christian Life*, 19, however, is correct in saying that "lawsuits concerning property were certainly not raised by slaves and poor seamen."

60. Cf. M. Weber, *The Sociology of Religion* (Boston, 1963), 80ff.

61. So Conzelmann, *1 Corinthians*, 15 n. 114. For a review of the places in 1 Corinthians where citations from the community letter have been surmised see J. C. Hurd, *The Origin of 1 Corinthians* (London, 1965), 68.

62. On this *topos* cf. Betz, *Paulus*.

63. Among the Corinthian succession of offices mentioned in n. 35 are also to be found explicitly pagan religious offices: cf. Kent, *Inscriptions*, nos. 152, 154, 156, 158. Whoever aspired in Corinth to a municipal career could hardly have kept public distance from Hellenistic rites and celebrations. F. J. M. de Waele, "Ausgrabungen," 54, even supposes, somewhat fancifully, that Erastus "must have executed his office and his munificence in the time of Nero, perhaps to counter hostility arising from his religious convictions."

64. For a short overview of the history of Corinth on the basis of excavations see de Waele, *Corinthe*. On the political and economic situation of Roman Corinth cf. in detail Kent, *Inscriptions*, 17–31. The economic situation in Corinth is also briefly sketched in U. Kahrstedt, *Das wirtschaftliche Gesicht Griechenlands in der Kaiserzeit: Kleinstadt, Villa und Domäne*, Dissertationes Berneses I, 7 (Bern, 1954), 116–17. [A valuable survey with extensive bibliography is now available in J. Wiseman, "Corinth and Rome I: 228 B.C.–A.D. 267," in H. Temporini and W. Haase, eds., *Aufstieg und Niedergang der römischen Welt: Geschichte und Kultur Roms in Spiegel der neueren Forschung*, II (Principat), 7/1 (Berlin/New York, 1979), pp. 438–548—Trans.] On Roman Corinth also see de Waele, *Corinthe*, 85–103.

65. So Broneer, "Corinth," 78: ". . . the new city could be expected to be more receptive to novel religious beliefs than a place like Athens with unbroken cultural history of several thousand years. Perhaps even more important was the fact that many visitors came to the great cosmopolitan

city on the Isthmus and some of his most faithful followers in his future missionary work were, like the apostle himself, foreigners in the city."

66. The opponents of Paul in 2 Corinthians appear to have had success with similar propaganda. Cf. D. Georgi, *Die Gegner des Paulus im 2. Korintherbrief: Studien zur religiösen Propaganda in der Spätantike,* WMANT 11 (Neukirchen, 1964), 51ff.

67. Contemporary complaints about the decline of the Greek *polis* are certainly not pertinent to Corinth. This is a *topos* which arose from comparing the present situation of Greece with the memory of her great past. So, J. A. D. Larsen, "Roman Greece," in *An Economic Survey of Ancient Rome,* ed. T. Frank (Baltimore, 1938), IV:465.

68. Cf. the list in Kent, *Inscriptions,* 21.

69. The geo-economic situation of Corinth has been illuminated by the discovery of coins (cf. K. N. Edwards, *Coins 1896–1929; Corinth, Results of Excavations Conducted by the American School of Classical Studies at Athens VI* [Cambridge, 1933]; and Kahrstedt, *Gesicht,* 116). Of 892 coins thirty-nine percent are not of local origin: 630 come from the West, 77 from Argolis, 66 from the Peloponnesus, 51 from central and northern Greece, 28 from the Orient. Because of the special political and economic connections of Corinth with the West, this city appeared to be a most appropriate place to prepare for the mission to the West and to initiate a relationship with the Roman community (Rom. 15:24).

70. Cf. Larsen, "Roman Greece," 259–498, 472.

71. Cf. Kahrstedt, *Gesicht,* 116.

72. R. Liechtenhan, "Paulus als Judenmissionar," *Judaica* 2 (1946): 56–70.

73. So, above all, H. Gülzow, *Christentum und Sklaverei in den ersten drei Jahrhunderten* (Bonn, 1969), 12–15, 22–28. Further arguments for the receptivity of the God-fearers to Christianity are found in Filson, "Early House Churches," 112.

74. What follows is based on K.G. Kuhn and H. Stegemann, "Proselyten," PRE. Suppl. IX, 1248–83.

75. It was possible to become a knight only if one had four hundred thousand sesterces. That among the proselytes attested by inscriptions there are more women (namely five) than among the God-fearers (four) fits the picture.

76. Kuhn and Stegemann, "Proselyten," 1266–67.

77. So Filson, "Early House Churches," 112.

78. Cf. Liechtenhan, "Paulus," 64; H. Kasting, *Die Anfänge der urchristlichen Mission* (München, 1969), 26.

79. The βῆμα (*rostra*) of the governor has been uncovered in the Corinthian agora (cf. de Waele, *Corinthe,* 95). In the meantime an inscription has also been discovered (Kent, *Inscriptions,* no. 322) which confirms the interpretation of the archaeological finds as the βῆμα (cf. Acts 18:16).

80. Cf. Gülzow, *Christentum*, 24.

81. Cf. Judge, *Pattern*, 56ff.

82. T. Mommsen, "Die Rechtsverhältnisse des Apostles Paulus," *ZNW* 2 (1901): 81–96; G. Kehnscherper, "Der Apostel Paulus als römischer Bürger," in TU 87 (= *Studia Evangelica* II, Berlin, 1964): 411–40. For a justifiable criticism of Kehnscherper cf. O. Kuss, *Paulus: Die Rolle des Apostels in der theologischen Entwicklung der Urkirche, Auslegung und Verkündigung* III (Regensburg, 1971), 40 n. 2.

83. Cf. Bienert, *Arbeit*, 302ff.

84. Filson particularly stresses this ("Early Houses Churches," 111). In my opinion he draws the correct conclusion: "The apostolic church was more nearly a cross section of society than we have sometimes thought."

85. Judge, *Pattern*, 60, is thus inclined.

86. Ibid.

87. The idea of love-patriarchalism is derived essentially from E. Troeltsch, *The Social Teaching of the Christian Churches* (New York, 1931), I: 69–89, and refers to that Christian patriarchalism which receives its special coloration from the warmth of the ideal of love (78). Troeltsch's concept turns on the "basic idea of the willing acceptance of fixed inequalities and of making them fruitful for the ethical values of personal relationships" (78).

88. H. Bolkestein's book, *Wohltätigkeit und Armenpflege im vorchristlichen Altertum* (Utrecht, 1939 = Groningen, 1967), the importance of which goes far beyond the theme suggested by the title, is very informative about this change. Cf. particularly the sociological interpretation (438–84).

89. On the problem cf. Vittinghoff, *Kolonisation*, passim.

90. On this crisis cf, M. Rostovtzeff, *Social and Economic History of the Roman Empire*, 2d ed. (Oxford, 1957), 393ff., and F. Millar, *The Roman Empire and Its Neighbours* (London, 1967), 239–48.

91. Bolkestein, *Wohltätigkeit*, 483–84, also assigns this transformation of φιλανθρωπία based on the equal rights of all citizens into *caritas* to the historical context of the social and political crisis of the third century. The reduction of φιλανθρωπία to φιλοπτωχία "was an inevitable consequence of the tremendous impoverishment which from the third century engulfed more and more of mankind. In these difficult times the Christian church took over the task, through the preaching of *caritas* and the organization of relief, of providing support for the suffering poor whom the state had abandoned to their fate, thus playing the role of comforter at the deathbed of a perishing world in which for the first time misery had gripped the masses" (484). Cf. further F. G. Maier, *Die Verwandlung der Mittelmeerwelt* (Frankfurt, 1968), 97, who stresses the importance of forced labor in the transformed society which emerged from the third century. "The role of the church in the shaping of social behavior, and thus in the process of social transformation, was essentially passive. . . . Rather,

it contributed decisively to the recognition of the idea of forced labor, so ubiquitous in the new society, thereby indirectly but substantially promoting the existing authorities and patterns of dependence" (97). H. Bolkestein and F. G. Maier are looking at the social attitude characterized here as love-patriarchalism from two different perspectives: on the one hand the idea entails the obligation of the stronger elements of society for the social welfare of the weaker; on the other hand, it entails forced labor for the weaker elements of society.

3

The Strong and the Weak in Corinth: A Sociological Analysis of a Theological Quarrel

Sociological analysis investigates human social behavior with an eye to those characteristics which are typical and those conditions which transcend individuals. It is interested in what is usual and normal, in what applies to many individuals and many situations. By contrast, what has come down from the past focuses primarily on the unusual or unique. For that reason, evaluating such materials sociologically is often difficult if not impossible. Among the unusual and singular events about which we have some knowledge, however, conflicts play a special role. Here the various customs of social groups collide with one another. In such circumstances the unusual actually sheds light on the ordinary, the dramatic conflict reveals the banal. If ever we can derive information about the social background of our historical traditions, it is through the analysis of such conflicts.

The quarrel between "the strong" and "the weak" in the Corinthian congregation is a matter of just such different customs. The weak avoid all meat sacrificed to idols since it could never be known with certainty that ritual actions had not accompanied the slaughter of the meat. The strong, on the other hand, appeal to their "knowledge": there is only one God; there are no idols and hence "no meat sacrificed to idols" (1 Cor. 8:4ff.).

Paul argues differently. He distinguishes cultic meals in an official setting (8:10) from meals in private houses (10:25ff.). To be sure, his opinion about official cultic meals in a temple is not quite uniform, but the intention is clear. Thus in 8:10ff. he urges the general waiver of a right which he himself would not contest, the right to participate in temple meals with the appropriate mental reservations. In 10:1–22 he goes farther and regards such meals as fundamentally incompatible with the Christian Lord's Supper. This shift in accent could be explained by a situation such as this: anyone who only passively participated in such pagan cultic meals, that is, did so as an invited guest, would eventually face the problem of whether or not he was obliged to extend a reciprocal invitation for the same kind of meal. To do so would make him the initiator of "idol worship." Whether this is the problem cannot be settled here.

What is in any event unmistakable in our text is the fact that from 10:23ff. Paul deals with the problem of private meals. These may be meals eaten at home but involving meat bought in the market—a wholly unproblematic case (10:25–26)—or meals by invitation to others' houses where one is served meat (10:27ff.). Paul has reservations about such meat only if its "sacred" character has been specifically pointed out. Since it would be understood that in a temple only consecrated meat would be offered, he must be referring to a meal in a private setting. It could be said that Paul is inconsistent in distinguishing between public and private behavior and that his position is dependent on the social context of the behavior. He is inclined to go along with the weak where the eating of meat takes on an official character (because of the location, or because of the formula "this is sacred meat") and to go along with the strong when the problem is one of a private setting.

Our task is to analyze the reasons for the opposing attitudes of the weak and the strong. It is doubtless proper to look for theological reasons, on the assumption that at the root of different behavior are to be found different convictions about humanity, the world, and God. Yet the truth of that does not preclude a sociological analysis as well. Convictions and concepts are usually effective only if social groups have invested them with the power to shape behavior. In the case of this conflict it is particularly true that social relationships represent a major theme. Since meals are an important form of social communication and the customs surrounding them are often socially determined there can be no argument, in my opinion, about whether one can or ought to interpret this conflict sociologically. The only argument is about how to do so. Which social factors are responsible for the conflict, religious traditions (whether of Jewish or gentile groups) which have shaped behavior, or class-specific customs and attitudes? It goes without saying that apart from all of this there can be divergent opinions about the significance of sociological analysis for throwing light on the meaning of theological texts. The sociological analysis of a theological quarrel does not, in my opinion, mean reducing it to social factors.

SOCIO-CULTURAL FACTORS

To a great extent exegesis has confined itself to these alternatives: either the weak are Jewish Christians or they are gentile Christians.[1] Paul himself, however, seems to have regarded the problem as somewhat more general. He refers to his own behavior as an example of that respect which it is necessary to show the weak, but does so without limiting his behavior to a particular ethnic group: to the Jews he became a Jew, to those outside the Law as one outside the Law, and so forth (9:19–22). This could be a generalization which deliberately goes beyond the concrete context. But at the end of his instructions about meat sacrificed to idols Paul again addresses the strong with these words: "Give no offense to Jews or to Greeks or to the church of God" (10:32). If both Jews and pagans can take offense, then the weak Christians who take offense could themselves have once been either Jews or pagans. Nor do other clues suggest that the weak were an ethnically or socio-culturally homogeneous group. Some of the weak were certainly gentile Christians. It makes no difference whether in 8:7 we read συνηθείᾳ or συνειδήσει, for in either case it is assumed that some eat meat sacrificed to idols "even now." On the other hand, the opposite conclusion follows from 8:10: if there is a danger that the behavior of one of the strong will mislead someone into eating meat sacrificed to idols, then presumably at the moment this person does not eat such meat but is only tempted to do so. In 8:10 it is a matter of being seduced into eating, while in 8:7 the eating is presupposed as taking place. Naturally, there are possible ways of harmonizing these texts. But it is quite possible that there were two different types of weak Corinthians: a gentile Christian type who always used to eat such consecrated meat but developed a guilty conscience after conversion to Christianity, and a Jewish Christian type who had always avoided such ritually slaughtered meat and who, after conversion, could exercise his unaccustomed freedom from restrictive ritual rules only with a bad conscience.

Finally, it should be pointed out that some of the Corinthian Christians cannot be sorted into these alternatives of Jewish or gentile Christians. These are the former "God-fearers," Gentiles who were sympathetic to Judaism well before their conversion to Christianity but never made a complete commitment to Judaism, possibly because of restrictive ritual rules such as the ban on consecrated meat. For these God-fearers Pauline Christianity offered an "accommodated Judaism."[2] In Corinth these people will have been of particular significance for the Christian congregation. The house of one "God-fearer" provides Paul with the base for his successful missionary work (Acts 18:7–8). Perhaps just such people now find themselves among the strong.

Socio-cultural customs, traditions and attitudes of various ethnic groups certainly will have been significant in influencing behavior regarding consecrated meat. At the same time, however, it is also conceivable that divergent cultural traditions led to similar rather than divergent behavior. Therefore, we should look for other factors as well.[3]

SOCIO-ECONOMIC FACTORS

Paul himself suggests that we look for the weak among the lower strata. It is hardly an accident that the first chapters of the Corinthian letter already give voice to the distinction between strong and weak, connecting this with the social structure of the Corinthian congregation. In 1:26ff. Paul states that among the Corinthians are not many who are "wise, influential, of noble birth" (author's trans.)—δυνατοί is the term he uses for the influential, the same term he uses for the strong in Rom. 15:1—and he continues: "God chose what is weak in the world to shame the strong." It appears that already here Paul wants to say that it is precisely the weak, people who admittedly lack wisdom, whom God has chosen. And when in 4:10 he draws the contrast with the Corinthians, "We are weak, but you are strong," we may be hearing reverberations of Paul's solidarity with the weak people of Corinth; for in connection with the question of meat sacrificed to idols he expressly repeats the idea that to the weak he himself became weak (9:22). The first Corinthian letter itself, therefore, suggests the hypothesis that the socially weak of 1:26–27 are identical with those who are weak in the face of consecrated meat. This hypothesis can be tested only by looking for class-specific characteristics in what can still be discerned of the behavior of the weak and the strong, that is, behavioral traits which can be correlated with wealth, occupation, and education and thus to a higher or lower social status.

Class-specific Characteristics in Eating Habits

We can begin with the commonplace assumption that then, as today, wealthy people could eat meat more often than others. We cannot base our judgment of eating habits in the ancient world on the literary depictions of great banquets (Petronius, *Satyricon* 52ff.; Juvenal, *Satura* 5; Martial, *Epigrammata* III, 60), as if these revels were typical for ordinary people.[4] It must be borne in mind that most such testimonies are produced by a narrow upper stratum and its followers, and that even so, meat was not necessarily a part of such festive meals. When his friend Septicius fails to show up at a meal which the younger Pliny had prepared for him, Pliny writes a letter of reproach (*Epistulae* I, 15) cataloguing the delights which his friend has missed, including lettuce, snails, and eggs. Nothing is said about meat. Pliny, as it happens, lived quite modestly, and perhaps that is why he was left in the lurch at his own table, for he discreetly hints that his friend had preferred to dine where he could get better food than this.

From other sources we learn something about the ordinary person's meal habits. Greek cities, like Rome, had a system of public food distribution.[5] This provisioning included grain, but not meat. Such is the case both for the public distribution of foodstuffs in Samos and for the Roman grain distribution which was regulated by law from the time of Gaius Gracchus. Septimius Severus (193–211 C.E.) was the first to add to the grain a daily ration of oil, and Aurelian (270–275 C.E.) subsequently expanded the provisions by allowing the sale of pork and wine at reduced prices. A Roman citizen of lower social status probably had little more available than what he was allowed from the state.

In Greece the great mass of the people were nourished by food made from flour, such as porridge made of barley flour (ἄλφιτα) or bread baked from wheat flour (ἄρτος). That the terms σῖτος and ἄλφιτα could mean simply "sustenance" speaks for itself. In addition, we know from Delos that three stonemasons spent nineteen drachmas and four oboli, or almost two-thirds of their monthly income of thirty drachmas, just for barley flour.[6] Not much was left over for other kinds of food.

The same is true for the Roman situation. From reports that soldiers ate meat only in exceptional circumstances (when no grain was available) it can be concluded that meat did not normally belong to their diet: *ipse exercitusque . . . ita per inopiam et labores fatiscebant, carne pecudum propulsare famem adacti* ("He himself and his army . . . were yet beginning to feel the strain of short rations and hardship—they had been reduced to keeping starvation at bay by a fish diet," Tacitus, *Annales* 14, 24); *usque eo ut complures dies frumento milites caruerint et pecore ex longinquioribus vicis adacto, extremam famem sustentarent* (". . . so much so that for several days the troops were without corn, and staved off the extremity of famine by driving cattle from the more distant hamlets," Caesar, *Bellum Gallicum* 7:17). H. Bolkestein is of the opinion that "the mass of people, in Italy as in Greece, lived primarily on a diet of flour, in earlier times made into porridge (*puls*) and later baked into bread."[7]

On the relationship between social status and meal habits *b. Hullin* 84a is also instructive: "A man having one *maneh* may buy a *litra* of vegetables for his bowl; if ten a *litra* of fish; if fifty *maneh* a *litra* of meat. If someone has a hundred *maneh* he may have a pot cooked for him every day. And how often for the others? From Sabbath eve to Sabbath eve" (that is, once a week).

If in the Corinthian Christian congregation the problem of eating meat became a central point of strife between different groups, that was hardly because of the behavior of Christians of lower social status. Those who scarcely ever eat meat can hardly give offense by eating consecrated meat.[8] For those who lack sufficient money to procure meat in the market, it is a purely theoretical question whether all such meat bought there should be avoided (10:25). To the extent that the conflict originates in the area of private meals it can be explained by the eating habits of various classes. Such instances (10:25ff.), however, do not constitute the real problem. There can be no doubt that Paul is primarily concerned with the problem of cultic meals which take place in an official setting, which means that the matter is more complicated.

From 8:7 it can be inferred that the weak certainly did eat meat, even if they did so with a bad conscience. According to 8:10ff., doing so in a cultic setting is a genuine temptation. In fact, the consumption of meat in a cultic setting is a problem for all citizens and residents of a city, regardless of their social status, since at a celebration open to the public all might participate. Even the lower classes had their chance to eat meat under such circumstances. We can sketch briefly the various kinds of opportunities which might arise.

1. In Greece and Rome meat was publicly distributed to all citizens in connection with extraordinary events[9] such as the celebration of a victory (Plutarch, *Demetrius* 11; Suetonius, *De vita Caesarum* 38) or at a funeral (Livy, VIII, 22, 2, 4; XXXIX 46, 2; XLI 28, 11). More generally, Cicero includes the distribution of meat among the public *beneficientia* by which private individuals seek to win the public's good will (Cicero, *De officiis* II, 52ff.), for example when competing for a municipal office.

2. In addition to such irregular occasions, public sacrificial meals were instituted for particular days. These were sometimes intended for only a limited circle of people, but often they were intended for all the citizens and residents of a city. Xenophon, for example, who instituted a feast at Scillum, expressly states that "all the citizens and men and women of the neighborhood took part in the festival" (πάντες οἱ πολῖται καὶ πρόσχωροι ἄνδρες καὶ γύναικες μετεῖχον τῆς ἑορτῆς, *Anabasis* V, 3, 7ff.). Everyone received flour, bread, wine, and meat. A document for a banquet at Amorgos from the second century C.E. provides that not only all the citi-

zens are to be treated to meat but also all sojourners, strangers, Romans, and women (*IG* XII, 515).[10]

3. More permanent than these bequests were the great religious feasts, frequently involving a distribution of meat to the general populace paid for either by the state or by the contribution of wealthy individual citizens. For example, meat was served in Athens at the Dionysia and Panathenaea. Was there, perhaps, a public sacrificial meal at the international Isthmian games?[11]

4. Further possibilities for the ceremonial or cultic consumption of meat were provided by the many associations whose bylaws provided for specific feasts. It may be questioned whether in these cases the lower classes always got to eat meat, since the *collegium* of Lanuvium (136 C.E.), for example, provided no meat for its feasts, which were celebrated six times a year (*CIL* XIV 2112 = Dessau, 7212), but only wine, bread, and sardines.[12] This *collegium* included slaves.

5. Finally, there were private invitations to a temple. Those found in Oxyrhynchus are well known, as, for example, "Charemon invites you to a meal at the table of the Lord Serapis in the Serapeum tomorrow, the fifteenth, beginning at 9 o'clock" (*P. Oxy*. I, 110). Whether such invitations could be found among the poor may be questionable, however.

To sum up: Members of the lower classes seldom ate meat in their everyday lives.[13] For that they were largely dependent on public distributions of meat which were always organized around a ceremonial occasion. The community meals of the *collegia* were also religious feasts. As a result, those from the lower classes knew meat almost exclusively as an ingredient in pagan religious celebrations, and the acts of eating meat and worshiping idols must have been much more closely connected for them than for members of the higher strata who were more accustomed to consuming meat routinely. For the poorer classes meat was truly something "special." It belonged to a sacred time segregated from the everyday world. It had a "numinous" character.

Conversion to Christianity brought similar difficulties to both Jewish Christians and gentile Christians of the lower classes. Those who had been pagans must have found it difficult to view meat as something perfectly natural and independent of its ritual setting, while at the same time they were sorely tempted not to miss out on what little bit of meat was offered to them by pagan feasts and institutions. Hence they would eat meat, but with a guilty conscience (8:7). Former Jews who had converted to Christianity had been liberated from Judaism's restrictions. Must it not have been tempting finally to be able to participate in public ceremonies involving meat (8:10)? Yet if they had but little opportunity, now as before, to buy meat which had not been ritually slaughtered, they would not have found it easy to break down the old negative taboos surrounding such meat. On the other hand, we can look for the "less biased" position of the strong among members of the higher classes. Someone accustomed to getting around the positive as well as negative taboos of eating meat could shed any anxiety over demonic infection to the very extent that he has survived eating meat without coming to harm.

Signs of Stratification Within Patterns of Sociability

Invitations to sacrificial meals served basically as a means of communication. Families, associations, and cities came together on such occasions and in so doing expressed ceremonially their common membership. This social aspect emerges particularly clearly in Aelius Aristides:

> Moreover, in sacrifices men maintain an especially close fellowship with this god alone. They call him to the sanctuary and install him as both guest of honor and host, so that while some divinities provide portions of their common meals, he is the sole provider of all common meals, holding the rank of symposiarch for those who at anytime are gathered about him. Just as Homer said (*Odyssey* iii, 62) that Athena both poured a libation and completed each request, so he is at one and the same time both participant in libations and the one who receives them, both coming himself to the revelry and inviting to himself the revellers, who because of him dance their dance free from the fear of evil and carry homeward with their crowns a feeling of true well-being, offering a return invitation (*Orationes* 45, 27).

Here we clearly have harmless forms of sociability, the "parties" of the ancient world. The hint about reciprocal invitations at the close marks a connection with the usual obligations of social, and sociable, life.

Restrictions on meat sacrificed to idols were barriers to communication which raised the problem of the relationship of Christians to the society of the ancient world. Originally the debate began over the general problem and only later shifted to the question of eating meat. In 5:9 Paul mentions a lost letter to the Corinthians[14] in which he warned them against contact with the πόρνοις, the greedy, robbers, and idolaters. That must have been interpreted as his wishing to check every contact with non-Christians. In any event, he corrects himself: He is not referring to contact with non-Christians outside the congregation, but to contact with sinners within it. The relationship of Christians to those outside the community is not to be limited. These relationships, however, cannot have been restricted to casual contact. To the prohibition against contact with Christian sinners Paul specifically adds that one should not even eat with them. From this it follows indirectly that common meals are included among the kinds of contact allowed with non-Christians. Thus even here we encounter the problem raised in 1 Cor. 8—10, but in a somewhat different light. The religious aspect of common meals is touched on, certainly, but contact with idolaters is only mentioned fourth in a list as a special instance of social contact with the world in general. If this social aspect has faded in 1 Cor. 8—10 that is because the debate has there been focused on one issue most accessible to theological argument, the problem of meat sacrificed to idols.

It is perfectly clear, I think, on which side of this conflict the wealthier Christians must have stood. Erastus, the "city treasurer" (Rom. 16:23), could have jeopardized his public position had he rejected all invitations where "consecrated meat" might have been expected. If he is identical with the aedile Erastus known from an inscription,[15] and thus somebody who at one time or another wished to be chosen as overseer for those public places and buildings where such meat was sold, he scarcely could have demonstrated an attitude of reserve about "consecrated meat." Such an attitude would have been wholly inappropriate for his office.

The relationship between high social status and "idolatry" is not ignored by early Christian paraenesis. It is not accidental that the specific vice of the rich, πλεονεξία, "wanting to have more," is closely linked with idolatry and even identified with it (Col. 3:6; Eph. 5:5; cf. 1 Cor. 5:10–11). There are also social reasons for this close association of wealth and idolatry. Those who are wealthy, or want to be, must seek and cultivate contact with pagans. That is clearly stated in Polycarp's letter: "Unless one steers clear of greed he will be tainted by idolatry and judged, as it were, with the pagans" (*Phil.* XI, 2). A greedy person belongs with the pagans. He has numerous social contacts with the pagan world. The Shepherd of Hermas says reproachfully of the wealthy that they live together with the pagans (*Similitudines* VIII, 9, 1). There may have been only a few powerful and well-born in Corinth (1:26), but it is among them that we ought to look for those "gnostics" who, in their contacts with the pagan world, neither could nor did take much notice of their poorer Christian brother's scruples.

It could be objected that according to 10:27ff., both the weak and the strong Christians alike appear in social contact with pagan hosts. The information that this is consecrated meat, however, cannot have come from a Christian. Only a pagan could describe ritually slaughtered meat this way. Respect for this pagan's conscience has a quite different motive from the respect for a Christian brother's conscience in 8:10ff. Thus his conscience is never characterized as "weak," a term which would suggest that it lagged behind the norms appropriate for him. Only "conscience" as such is mentioned. And while in 8:11–13 Christ's death serves as the motive for renouncing a right on the basis of love, this specific Christian motivation is completely missing in 10:27–30. Thus the passage does not presuppose that weak and strong Christians find themselves together as guests at the same meal.

Public and professional duties dictated that Christians of high social status were probably integrated into pagan society than the Christians of more modest circumstances. We may question whether those who belonged to the lower classes might not now be motivated to remain in their pagan clubs in order to participate in the feasts. Paul certainly assumes that the weak also ate meat sacrificed to idols. But it must be remembered that many of these clubs did not offer much more than did the Christian Lord's Supper—bread and wine—while Christians shared meals together far more frequently than perhaps did the members of the *collegium* of Lanuvium, mentioned above, which sponsored six modest public banquets in a year. The lower strata of society found in the congregation full compensation for what they gave up elsewhere. Indeed, they found even more. For while the ancient clubs were largely socially homogeneous,[16] these people had access in the congregation to the upper classes who could use their wealth to serve the congregation and thus to serve the socially weaker. There is also another reason why we must look for the weak among the lower strata. Those who do not have much to lose in the way of "worldly" relationships are more inclined to free themselves of these. In the process a certain *ressentiment* may color their negative opinions. Those for whom the world is full of demons and taboos show by their views, which are designed to steer clear of these, how much at heart they are nevertheless attracted to that world.

Class-specific Traits in the Forms of Legitimation

The strong base their position on their "gnosis." Paul seems to take up some of their arguments:[17] "All of us possess knowledge" (8:1); "an idol has no real existence . . . there is no God but one" (8:4); "all things are lawful" (10:23). The idea of the "weak conscience" (8:7, 10, 12) may have come from them, as well as the argument that "food is meant for the stomach and the stomach for food" (6:13). Unmistakable in all these arguments is the determination to surmount obsolete religious restrictions through "knowledge." Even if the speculative fantasies of later Gnostics cannot be imputed to the Corinthian "gnostics," as they certainly cannot, neither can the parallels between the two be ignored. For a comparable "liberal" position on meat sacrificed to idols the only analogies within Christianity come from Gnostic groups, as may be seen in the following:[18]

Justin on Gnostics in general: "But know that there are many who profess their faith in Jesus and are considered Christians, yet claim there is no harm in their eating meat sacrificed to idols" (*Dialogus cum Tryphone* 35, 1). ". . . Of these some are called Marcionites, some Valentinians, some Basilidians and some Saturnilians" (*Dial*. 35, 6).

Irenaeus on the Valentinians: "For this reason the most perfect among them freely practice everything which is forbidden. . . . For they eat food that was offered to idols with indifference, and they are the first to arrive at any festival party of the gentiles that takes place in honor of the idols, while some of them do not even avoid the murderous spectacle of fights with beasts and single combats, which are hateful to God and man. And some, who immoderately indulge the desires of the flesh, say that they are repaying to the flesh what belongs to the flesh and to the spirit what belongs to the spirit" (*Adversus haereses* I, 6, 3).

Irenaeus on the followers of Basilides: "They despise things sacrificed to idols and think nothing of them, but enjoy them without any anxiety at all. They also enjoy the other (pagan) festivals and all that can be called appetite" (*Adv. haer.* I, 24, 5; cf. Eusebius, *Historia ecclesiastica* IV, 7, 7).

Irenaeus on those descended from Basilides and Carpocrates: "Others . . . taught promiscuous sex and many marriages and claimed that God does not care about their participation in pagan cultic meals" (*Adv. haer.* I, 28, 2).

Irenaeus on the Nicolaitans (cf. Rev. 2:14f.; 2:6; Hippolytus, *Adv. haer.* VII, 36): "They live promiscuously. They teach that it is of no significance if one fornicates or eats food sacrificed to pagan gods . . ." (*Adv. haer.* I, 26, 3).

Origen on the Simonians: "Nowhere in the world are Simonians now to be found, although Simon, in order to win a larger following, freed his disciples from the peril of death, which the Christians are taught to prefer, by instructing them to regard pagan worship as a matter of indifference" (*Contra Celsum* VI, 11).

Epiphanius on libertine Gnostics of a much later period: "And whatever we eat, be it meat, vegetables, bread or anything else, we are doing a kindness to created things by collecting the soul from all things and transmitting it with ourselves to the heavenly world. For this reason they eat every kind of meat and say that they do so that we may show mercy to our kind" (*Panarion* XXVI, 9, 2).

It cannot simply be assumed on the basis of these texts that eating meat sacrificed to idols was common to all Gnostic groups. There were also ascetic currents in Gnosticism (cf. Irenaeus, *Adv. haer.* I, 24, 2; Tertullian, *Adv. haer.* I, 14). Eating such meat is not *the* typical, but *one* typical behavior of the Gnostics. Orthodox Christianity rather uniformly forbade eating such consecrated meat.[19] That is confirmed by the one example of doing so which we have from non-Gnostic groups. Lucian reports of Peregrinus that when he was a Christian charismatic he was caught in a lapse from the prohibition: "Then he somehow committed an offense—I believe he was seen eating something which was forbidden . . ." (*De morte Peregrini* 16), following which he lost all influence in the Christian community and became a convert to Cynicism. Thus it seems to be the case that a liberal attitude toward meat sacrificed to idols was to be found only among Gnostic Christians.

The links between the "gnosis" in Corinth and Christian Gnosticism of the second century are a matter of controversy, and with good reason. There is scarcely a direct connection. Yet that simply underlines the problem of how to interpret the obvious analogies. The opinion that in Corinth we are dealing with an incipient Gnosticism is of itself unsatisfactory. Gnosticism's beginnings can be dated much earlier if by that is meant the initial appearance of concepts which play a role in the later Gnostic systems.

What is needed is a sociological-structural perspective to complement the developmental-historical perspective. For example, analogies between Corinthian gnosis and later Gnosticism could be found in the fact that in both instances a typical recasting of Christian faith is evident with its rise into the higher classes. Inferences from Gnosticism to the Corinthian gnosis would then have to be confined to those characteristics which could result from a comparable social situation: intellectual level, soteriology based on knowledge, and elite self-consciousness within the community combined with taking pleasure in contact with the pagan world. Problematic assumptions about the Corinthian gnostics' concepts can thus be left to one side.[20]

a. The Gnostic systems of thought demand a high level of intellect. Their speculations are full of ludicrous systems and logic, and as such were not accessible to simple people. These are set down in numerous books which, in the second century, quite possibly outnumber the writings of orthodox Christians.[21] Basilides will serve as an example of a prolific author. He is said to have written a book of odes (*Muratorian Canon* 83f.), a gospel (Origen, *Homiliae in Lucam 1*), and twenty-four books of gospel commentary (Eusebius, *Hist. eccl.* IV, 7, 7; Clement of Alexandria, *Stromateis* IV, 12, 1). More writings have been preserved from the Valentinians than from all other Gnostic groups. Such an enormous production of books is conceivable only in relatively wealthy circles—and one recalls the wealthy Valentinian Ambrose who could put seven stenographers at Origen's disposal so that his lectures could be copied and published (Eusebius, *Hist. eccl.* VI, 18, 1; 23, 1–2). The Corinthian gnostics, to be sure, did not produce any books, but they did avail themselves of the medium of writing. The community's letter is written entirely from their point of view. Its arguments assume a certain intellectual standard.

b. A soteriology of knowledge, faith in the saving power of discernment, can also be a class-specific factor. Where salvation takes place less through the agency of a deity than through the inner process of "knowledge," the felt need which gives rise to the quest for salvation is also less likely to be rooted in material circumstances. Max Weber has ascribed to the upper classes this kind of hope for salvation: "The success of philosophical salvation doctrines and the propaganda of salvation cults among the lay elite during late Hellenic and Roman times parallels these groups' final turning aside from political participation."[22] When the educated classes no longer can or will shape the world, they frequently transcend it all the more radically by means of ideas. The transition from being lost to being saved is then regarded as one of gaining "true knowledge." On this score there are comparable characteristics in the "knowledge" of Gnosticism and that of the Corinthian gnosis. For the latter, knowledge means recognizing that idols do not really exist, that is, stripping this world's mythically intensified appellate agencies of their demands. This might be called demystifying a portion of the world. In later Gnosticism such knowledge becomes radicalized so that even the Old Testament's creator God is unmasked as a mythical being to whom this world traces back its restrictive commands and prohibitions.

c. People who understand themselves to be elevated above the "world" also understand themselves to be superior in a very concrete way to those who are imprisoned by it. The division of humankind into three classes encountered in so many Gnostic writings, and especially the differentiation of Christians as either pistics or gnostics, betrays a sharply elitist consciousness in Gnostic circles: normal Christians are only second-rate people. Such rankings may reflect the internal stratification of Hellenistic Christian communities in which—as for example in Rome[23]—Christians of the upper classes frequently separated themselves as Gnostics from the common Christian people. In Corinth there were the beginnings of such a differentiation within the community. Here too the strong were distinguished from the weak, and we even find the terminology of *pneumatikoi* and *sarkikoi* (3:1). Here too some Christians seek to distinguish themselves from others of a lower rank on the basis of "wisdom" and "knowledge."

d. Finally, there is the matter of the relative openness of Gnostics to the culture of antiquity. An example is the reception of pagan mythology and literature among the Naasenes (Hippolytus, *Adv. haer.* V, 6, 3–11, 1). Many of the moral objections raised by the church fathers against Gnostics concern what was but ordinary behavior for that time. Gnostics take part in the pleasures of their day, banquets, theatrical performances, and social life. Many of them were no more strict about sexual morality than was the era itself. They cautioned against seeking martyrdom. In the case of Basilides and Valentinus themselves, however, there can be no denying the earnestness and sympathetic differentiation within their ethical views. C. Andresen is right when he says: "These people belonged to social strata which did not usually find their way into the early catholic communities. The aura of a certain liberality, one that spills over the narrow limits of a community piety anxious for its own traditions, suffuses the testimony to Valentinian and Basilidian Gnosis."[24] It is for just such groups that we have evidence of eating meat sacrificed to idols. This fits with their liberal disposition. It is a mark of broader integration within the society of that day which is at the same time thoroughly comfortable with a radical "theoretical" critique of the world. The world is rejected in a theoretical way in order to profit from it in a practical way—the usual verbal radicalism of the affluent.

The Christian Gnosticism of the second century may have been largely a theology of the upper classes. And even if we may not assume that there were Christians of elevated social status in all Gnostic groups, we may assume that such were to be found in those groups said to eat meat sacrificed to idols, for example the Valentinian and Basilidian Gnostics. It is permissible to make a connection with the Corinthian gnosis since doing so rests not on an inference from the realm of mythic concepts but on the four criteria listed above. In the case of the Corinthian gnostics we also find a certain level of education, the significance of knowledge and wisdom for ethics and salvation, and an elitist self-consciousness within the community which goes hand in hand with a considerable liberalism about associating with the pagan world. In both instances these characteristics taken together point to an elevated social status.

What thus seem probable on the basis of analogy is also independently plausible. Is it not likely that in class-specific conflicts those of higher social standing will appeal to their superior insight? In other instances they were certainly accustomed to play their better insight off against the common man. On the other hand, it seems more reasonable to ascribe superstitious notions of a sort which impede contact with outsiders to the perspective of the lower classes, with their limited experience, than to those whose social status gives them a broader perspective.

Class-specific Traits in the Forms of Communication

First Corinthians is itself a social fact, evidence of communication between Paul and the congregation. From it we learn, first of all, something about the position within the community of those involved in the communication. Indirectly, however, we also get some hints about their general position in society. Three matters are particularly instructive: Paul's informants, those whom he addresses, and his critics.

Paul is told of the problems by a congregational letter which clearly is formulated from the standpoint of the strong. Other opinions are not reflected, the catch phrase "all of us possess knowledge" (8:1) leaving little room for that. The authors write in the conviction that they can represent the community. They comprise the leading circles. Paul is thus informed on the basis of a perspective "from above." It is scarcely an accident that in contrast to this he receives oral information (1:11; 11:18) about problems within the Corinthian community which sees things from below (1:26ff.; 11:20ff.). Might these divergent paths by which information travels have a class-specific character?

Interestingly, Paul also addresses his reply almost exclusively to the strong. Almost all passages in which we find the second person used are directed to them, as for example "Only take care lest this liberty of yours somehow become a stumbling block to the weak" (8:9; cf. 8:10, 11; 10:15, 31). On that basis we can conclude with M. Rauer that the weak have no position of leadership within the congregation.[25]

It is also significant that in his statements addressed to the strong Paul includes a long excursus (9:1–27) in which he appears to have two groups in mind. One group consists of some critics who have attacked him because of his renunciation of support (9:3). The other consists of the strong to whom he represents this posture as a model. Is it not likely that the critics and those whom Paul addresses are partly identical? The critics who reproach Paul because he would not accept material support from them are not likely to have belonged to the materially impoverished, since they are at the moment supporting other missionaries. If these critics of Paul are at least in part identical with the strong, that would confirm their sociological orientation, since renunciation of material privileges is a much more effective example in an exhortation directed to those who are materially privileged.

All of our observations, about forms of eating, sociability, legitimation, and communication, point to the fact that the strong probably belong to the few who are "wise . . . powerful . . . and of noble birth" (1:26). Their more liberal attitude belongs primarily in the upper classes. Naturally, this attitude will have been extended beyond those limits. It is just such Christians of higher social status who bring with them a larger household unit. It is just such Christians who have been influential. But they were unable to win all to their position. There were also the weak, for whom pagan or Jewish traditions still had their influence. Such traditions, however, could be effective only because they undergirded a class-specific attitude.

Finally, we must consider Paul's own position in this conflict between the strong and the weak. It has always been something of an offense to modern exegesis that Paul does not consistently champion the enlightened position of the strong, even though he is in basic agreement with it. If we understand his argument—quite possibly in a way which goes beyond the self-understanding inherent in it—as a plea for consideration of the lower strata by the higher strata, then Paul's alleged inconsistency appears to be quite consistent. For the fact is that for Paul the revaluation of all norms of social rank and dominance—including the dominance of a higher "knowledge" and "wisdom"—proceeds directly from the preaching of the cross (1:18ff.). To be sure, seen from today's perspective it must be emphasized that this revaluation has no "revolutionizing" consequences in the social realm. Paul's recommendation, based on love, that the higher classes accommodate their behavior to the lower classes, only mitigates the tension between the two but allows the differing customs to continue to exist. The factual privileges of status enjoyed by the higher strata are preserved. For example, private meals with consecrated meat continue to be allowed in principle (10:23ff.). Nor is participation in cultic meals excluded in principle. All that is prohibited is disturbing a weak person by doing so. In other words, everything must take place in a very "exclusive" circle. But just those possibilities continue to be available which, as it happens, are more accessible to members of the upper classes. To be sure, the norms for the Christian community are advocated with vigor. But without doubt there is the obvious danger that those who are better off have de facto more possibilities of avoiding the restrictive effects of these norms than do those of the lower classes. The latter come up short—as far as the material side of things is concerned. For it is those very cultic feasts of an official nature, where each can monitor the behavior of the other, but which also would have afforded an opportunity for the lower classes to eat some meat, which are covered by the prohibition against pagan worship. Paul's solution is a compromise. The wishes (or prejudices) of the weak are upheld just as is the knowledge (and social privilege) of the strong. For that very reason it is realistic and practicable. Something comparable is to be found in the solution to a conflict referred to in 1 Cor. 11:17ff. There we find that wealthy Christians can eat their "own" meal privately to their heart's content (11:33–34), but in the congregation they are to be satisfied with the Lord's Supper, with the bread and wine of the fellowship.

These are solutions which are characteristic for the love-patriarchalism of the Pauline letters. This love-patriarchalism[26] allows social inequities to continue but transfuses them with a spirit of concern, of respect, and of personal solicitude. Concern for the conscience of the other person, even when it is a "weak" conscience and obedient to norms now superseded, is certainly one of the congenial characteristics of this love-patriarchalism. This should not be overlooked even if Pauline love-patriarchalism cannot be considered the solution to contemporary social problems. It must be asked critically, however, whether love and knowledge can be joined without restricting knowledge. Was it just cynicism if some of the strong in Corinth believed that under the circumstances they could "edify" the weak by their example (1 Cor. 8:10)? Could they not have believed, with a very clear conscience, that the lower classes should not further curtail their already limited possibilities in life with such religious scruples? For the most part we hear only one side of the argument between Paul and the "gnostics." That should be kept in mind by anyone attributing simply unsocial behavior to the "gnostics." We do not know precisely how they argued their case. The gnostic *Gospel of Philip*, which comes from a later time but is close in spirit to these people, proposes a relationship between love and knowledge in which neither is compromised by the other: "Love, however, builds up. But whoever is free because of knowledge is a slave on account of love for those who cannot yet accept the freedom of knowledge. But knowledge makes them suitable by working to make them free" (110). Perhaps in principle Paul felt not much differently. Perhaps the Corinthian gnostics were even his best "pupils." We ought not to blame Paul because he wanders from this principle. It was being played off against the socially weak. In such a context one can insist on one's right in such a way as to wind up in the wrong.

NOTES

1. For an overview of opinions cf. M. Rauer, *Die "Schwachen" in Korinth und Rom nach den Paulusbriefen*, BSt(F) 21, 2–3 (Freiburg, 1923), 36ff.; K. Maly, *Mündige Gemeinde* (Stuttgart, 1967), 96–99. On the basis of 1 Cor. 8:7 the weak are most often identified with gentile Christians. Among those championing an identification with Jewish Christians, however, are L. Batelaan, *De Sterken en Zwakken in de Kerk van Korinthe* (Wageningen, 1942), 21–26; M. Coune, "Le problème des idolothytes et l'éducation de la syneidêsis," *RSR* 51 (1963): 497–534; W. T. Sawyer, "The Problem of Meat Sacrificed to Idols in the Corinthian Church" (diss., Southern Baptist Theological Seminary, 1968, according to

Dissertation Abstracts 29, 1968/69, no. 1285A). H. Conzelmann, *1 Corinthians* (Philadelphia, 1975), 138, is among the few exegetes who have freed themselves from the alternative Jewish *or* Gentile.

2. The idea comes from A. von Harnack, *The Mission and Expansion of Christianity in the First Three Centuries* (New York, 1908), 1ff. On the God-fearers cf. K. G. Kuhn and H. Stegemann, "Proselyten," P.R.E. Suppl. IX, cols. 1248–83. A fair number were of high social status, and this may also be supposed for the strong (see below).

3. It is frequently held that the weak were members of the party of Cephas who wished to make the apostolic decree obligatory in Corinth. So. T. W. Manson, "The Corinthian Correspondence I," in *Studies in the Gospels and Epistles* (Manchester, 1962), 190–209, esp. 200; C. K. Barrett, "Things Sacrificed to Idols," *NTS* 11 (1964/65): 138–53, esp. 146; idem, "Cephas and Corinth," in *Abraham unser Vater, Festschrift für O. Michel* (Leiden, 1963), 1–12, esp. 7–8. The reference to Peter in 1 Cor. 9:5 and the fact that he did not renounce his rights cannot be cited in support of this view. In fact, the strong could well be the very people who have cited his example. If 1 Cor. 8—10 is addressed to the same people in Corinth, then perhaps those circles most closely associated with the strong were playing Peter and other apostles off against Paul. But it is idle to identify the weak with one of the parties named in 1:12. Their anxiety does not fit the self-consciousness of any "party." So also Rauer, "*Schwachen*," 67, and Conzelmann, *1 Corinthians*, 175.

4. M. Rostovtzeff, *The Social and Economic History of the Hellenistic World* (Oxford, 1941), II: 1177: "Bread and fish, with the addition of olive-oil and wine, formed in ancient times the most substantial parts of the diet of the people, rich and poor." But see H. Blümer, "Die römischen Privataltertümer," in HAW VI, 2, 2 (1911): 173.

5. Cf. on that H. Bolkestein, *Wohltätigkeit und Armenpflege im vorchristlichen Altertum* (Utrecht, 1939 = Gröningen, 1967), 251–67, 364–78; F. Millar, *The Roman Empire and Its Neighbours* (New York, 1967), 26.

6. *BCH* (1890):481, cited according to Bolkestein, *Wohltätigkeit*, 251–52. On the price of food at Delos cf. J. A. O. Larsen, "Roman Greece," in T. Frank, ed., *An Economic Survey of Ancient Rome* (Baltimore, 1938), IV: 259–498, esp. 379ff.

7. Bolkestein, *Wohltätigkeit*, 365. Barrett, "Things Sacrificed," 145, refers to Caesar, *Bellum Civile* III, 47, according to which meat was much in demand among soldiers.

8. The class-specific nature of the problem of meat in the Corinthian congregation is also seen by Barrett, "Things Sacrificed," 146, and A. Ehrhardt, "Social Problems in the Early Church," in *The Framework of the New Testament Stories* (Manchester, 1964), 275–312, esp. 280–81. To be sure, both presume that the Corinthian community was socially homo-

geneous. For a contrary view cf. "Social Stratification in the Corinthian Community," above, pp. 69–119.

9. Cf. W. Eisenhut, s. v. "visceratio," *PRE* II, 17, cols. 351–53; P. Stengel, "Die griechischen Kultusaltertümer," in HAW V, 3 (1920[3]), 106ff. On *beneficientia* in Cicero cf. Bolkestein, *Wohltätigkeit*, 314ff.

10. Cf. B. Laum, *Stiftungen in der griechischen und römischen Antike*, 2 vols. (Aalen, 1964). The document from Amorgos is found in vol. II, no. 50. Its detailed account of the course of a feast is very instructive. On charitable endowments cf. further Bolkestein, *Wohltätigkeit*, 233–34.

11. Cf. O. Broneer, "The Apostle Paul and the Isthmian Games," *BA* 25 (1962): 1–31; idem, "Paul and the Pagan cults at Isthmia," *HThR* 64 (1971): 169–84. Unfortunately, no distribution of meat can be documented.

12. The association laws are reprinted in H. Lietzmann, *An die Korinther I/II*, HNT 9 (Tübingen, 1949[4]), 91–93. Cf. also J. Carcopino, *Daily Life in Ancient Rome* (New Haven, 1940), 275.

13. From Pliny (*Epistulae* X, 96, 10) it could be concluded that Christians from the lower classes also bought meat, for he says that with the spread of Christianity there was no market for sacrificial meat. But it is to be observed that (1) Pliny explicitly states that Christians embraced all social classes (*Epistulae* X, 96, 9), and only those Christians with purchasing power could possibly have endangered the market for meat; (2) the native priestly aristocracy will have exaggerated the problems of the market, in accordance with their own personal interests. Pliny himself can no longer determine that this is a problem. Ehrhardt's assumption ("Social Problems," 282ff.) that the Christians seriously endangered the meat market of the ancient world is improbable.

14. On that cf. N. A. Dahl, "Der Epheserbrief und der verlorene erste Brief des Paulus an die Korinther," in *Abraham unser Vater*, 65–77; J. C. Hurd, *The Origin of I Corinthians* (London, 1965), 213–39.

15. Cf. H. J. Cadbury, "Erastus of Corinth," *JBL* 50 (1931): 42–58. In my opinion, his objections to an identification can be refuted [cf. above on Erastus, pp. 75–83, Trans.]. For the identification see J. H. Kent, *The Inscriptions 1926–1950: Corinth, Results of Excavations Conducted by the American School of Classical Studies at Athens VIII*, 3 (Princeton, 1966), 27, 99–100.

16. Cf. E. A. Judge, *The Social Pattern of Christian Groups in the First Century* (London, 1960), 44; F. Bömer, *Untersuchungen über die Religion der Sklaven in Griechenland und Rom. IV*, AAWLM.G 10 (Mainz, 1963), 236–41.

17. Hurd, *Origin*, 68, offers an overview of the passages which exegetes have supposed are citations from the congregational letter.

18. Cf W. Schmithals, *Gnosticism in Corinth* (Nashville, 1971), 224–29, 372–73. Ehrhardt, "Social Problems," 278–79, cites as evidence *Gospel of*

Thomas 14 and a fragment of Mani. *Gospel of Thomas* 14, however, contains no reference to meat.

19. Cf. Acts 15:20, 29; 21:25; *Did.* 6:3ff.; Minucius Felix, *Octavius* 30; Tertullian, *Apologeticum* 9; Eusebius, *Hist. eccl.* V, 1, 26; Pseudo-Clementine *Recognitiones* 4:36; *Homiliae* 7:4, 8; *Homiliae* 8:19, 23.

20. On the problematic nature of Corinthian gnosis, cf. most recently R. McL. Wilson, "How Gnostic were the Corinthians?" *NTS* 19 (1972): 65–74. H. G. Kippenberg, "Versuch einer soziologischen Verortung des antiken Gnostizismus," *Numen* 17 (1970): 211–31, rests on inference from mythical ideas. For criticism see P. Munz, "The Problem of 'Die soziologische Verortung des antiken Gnostizismus,'" *Numen* 19 (1972): 41–51. In any case, Kippenberg is correct in observing that the Gnostics belonged to the upper classes.

21. Cf. W. Bauer, *Rechtgläubigkeit und Ketzerei im ältesten Christentum*, BHTh 10 (Tübingen, 1964[2]), 150–97; Eng. trans., *Orthodoxy and Heresy in Earliest Christianity*, ed. R. A. Kraft and G. Krodel (Philadelphia, 1971), 147–94.

22. M. Weber, *The Sociology of Religion* (Boston, 1963), 124, who also mentions the "Gnostic mysteries."

23. Cf. K. Langerbeck, "Zur Auseinandersetzung von Theologie und Gemeindeglauben in der römischen Gemeinde in den Jahren 135–165," in *Aufsätze zur Gnosis*, AAWG.PH 3, 96 (Göttingen, 1967), 167–79. The Valentinians, who only later separated from the community (Irenaeus, *Adv. haer.* I, 6, 3), testify that sacrificial meat was eaten in the Roman community. The polemic of Hermas against the rich may also refer to them. Thus, for the first half of the second century the problems are like those in Corinth. May not the conflict there between the weak and the strong in the first century also have had a similar background as in Corinth—despite different arguments?

24. C. Andresen, *Die Kirchen der alten Christenheit* (Stuttgart, 1971), 103–4.

25. Rauer, "*Schwachen*," 67.

26. In my opinion, the characterization of this love-patriarchalism by E. Troeltsch, *The Social Teaching of the Christian Churches* (New York, 1931), 69–89, is still pertinent. To be sure, the term "love-patriarchalism" is not found there but is implicit in what is said.

4

Social Integration and Sacramental Activity: An Analysis of 1 Cor. 11:17–34

From time to time in recent years a certain uneasiness with the humanistic interpretation of "traditional" texts has become evident. This dissatisfaction is aimed not at specific results but at the basic hermeneutical stance of interpreting the past as it understood itself. In various ways a demand has been expressed not only that the meaning of what has been transmitted be developed, but that this also be confronted with its own empirical realities—in other words, that the conflict between the past's interpretation of itself and a critical analysis of that interpretation be made clear.[1] Not least of all it is hoped that we might thereby achieve a greater freedom from the self-interpretations of the present.

Contemporary interest about the place of sociological questions in interpreting such traditional texts should be seen in this light. In New Testament exegesis this interest can be connected with the central insight of classical form criticism, that texts have a "setting in life" *(Sitz im Leben)*, that their forms have been shaped by social relations. That insight can be further elaborated. At the outset it must be kept in mind that the social relations which have shaped transmitted texts have only in a fragmentary way made their mark on what we understand the text to mean, and that these relations may have been different from the way they are interpreted within the texts themselves. With this possibility in mind we will analyze the controversy surrounding the Lord's Supper, about which Paul expresses his opinion in 1 Cor. 11:17ff.

Exegetical attention has largely concentrated on the theological dimensions of the dissension in Corinth. Concerning a number of issues there is no agreement. Was the Lord's Supper profaned by being allowed to become an ordinary meal?[2] Did spiritualizing gnostics wish to demonstrate their independence from external forms?[3] Did crude sacramentalists suspend its obligatory character?[4] It remains to be explained why Paul is silent about these theological motives and leaves exegesis groping in the dark on this matter. Only the social causes of the conflict emerge more clearly. Therefore it may be suggestive to put forward the thesis that this conflict has a social background and becomes more comprehensible when we correlate its social conditions with the theological arguments of 1 Cor. 11:17ff.

Early Hellenistic Christian congregations were not only of a different legal structure than the associations of the surrounding world;[5] they also differed in regard to their social composition. These associations of the ancient world were, to a great extent, socially homogeneous. Religious associations give evidence of expressing class-specific forms of sociability to an even greater degree than do professional groups of persons bound together by common occupation, where members of different social strata, such as more and less wealthy merchants,[6] could meet. By contrast, the Hellenistic congregations of early Christianity, as we find them in Corinth and Rome, display a marked internal stratification.[7] In Corinth only a few are "wise," "powerful," and "of noble birth" (1 Cor. 1:26), but they seem to dominate and stand in contrast with the majority of members who come from the lower strata. A congregation so structured faces a difficult task in balancing differing expectations, interests, and self-understandings that are class-specific.

Therefore, the possibility cannot be excluded that in theological quarrels as well this inner social stratification is a factor which needs to be taken into consideration, that various conflicts within the congregation also have been socially conditioned. By the same token it is to be expected that many of the theological ideas of those who are party to these conflicts express an interest in shaping social relationships or have social functions extending beyond their more immediate intention. Thus we may approach our analysis of 1 Cor. 11:17ff. from two directions: first, from that of the social conditions which can still be discerned; and second, from that of social intentions. Both perspectives are legitimate; even when taken together they analyze the text from only one particular perspective and do not make a claim to definitive interpretation.

THE SOCIAL CONDITIONS OF THE CONFLICT IN 1 COR. 11:17–34

Analysis of the social conditions surrounding human behavior presupposes that this behavior will be described with the greatest precision, but in our case a great deal remains unclear. Four questions require an answer: (1) Were there different groupings at the celebration of the Lord's Supper, or is it a matter of a conflict between the congregation and some of its individual members? (2) Were there various points at which the meal began, and what is the sequence of the various actions mentioned in 1 Cor. 11:17ff.? (3) Were there quantitative differences in the portions served at the meal, or (4) qualitatively different meals for different groups? To answer these questions we must also draw on other contemporary texts to understand better what kinds of behavior were possible at this time.

Different Groups at the Lord's Supper

The conflict at the Lord's Supper is revealed in the fact that "it is not the Lord's supper that you eat. For in eating, each one goes ahead with his own meal" (1 Cor. 11:20–21). That statement could be taken to mean that an exaggerated individualism is the cause of the strife, as if each person had eaten independently of the others. Paul, however, speaks not only of individual Christians but also of divisions (σχίσματα) and factions (αἱρέσεις), which sounds as if he thinks not in terms of a string of individuals but of groups. He has already used the same term σχίσμα in 1 Cor. 1:10 to refer to such groups. The plural form, σχίσματα, however, leaves open the question of how many groups are involved in the contention surrounding the Lord's Supper. It is only from 1 Cor. 11:22 that we learn that there are two groups opposed to one another, those who have no food, the μὴ ἔχοντες, and those who can avail themselves of their own meal, ἴδιον δεῖπνον. This does not, however, absolutely exclude a more "individualistic" interpretation[8] which might find support in the words ἕκαστος and ἴδιον.

The idea that every person (ἕκαστος) individually has his own meal should not be pressed. Apparently this does not mean "every" one, for there are some who "have nothing." Similarly, 1 Cor. 14:26 does not mean that each (ἕκαστος) individual member of the congregation contributes a hymn, a lesson, a revelation, or a tongue, or it would be superfluous to include a word for those who possess no such manifest pneumatic gift (1 Cor. 12:4ff.).[9] Nevertheless, Paul speaks about "every" Christian. The same is true in 1 Cor. 1:12, where it is by no means certain that every member (ἕκαστος) of the Corinthian congregation is to be considered a member of one of the parties mentioned there. Thus, even if the phrase ἕκαστος γὰρ τὸ ἴδιον δεῖπνον προλαμβάνει ἐν τῷ φαγεῖν ("for in eating each one goes ahead with his own meal") leads to the conclusion that Paul is describing individual behavior, it is a behavior which in the circumstances is confined to a certain group.

The idea of ἴδιον δεῖπνον can first of all be defined in contrast with its opposite, κυριακὸν δεῖπνον ("the Lord's supper"). ἴδιος and κυριακός refer to questions of ownership, as in the phrases κυριακὸς λόγος and ἴδιος λόγος specifying, respectively, imperial and private treasuries (*OGIS* 669).[10] ἴδιον recalls in particular the stereotyped inscriptional phrase ἐκ τῶν ἰδίων (cf. Frey, *CIJ*, nos. 548, 766), indicating that the object furnished with this inscription was paid for by a donor. Thus the ἴδιον δεῖπνον is most likely the meal which individual Christians bring with them. If some Christians have no ἴδιον δεῖπνον, that suggests that not all contributed to the Lord's Supper but that the wealthier Christians provided for all ἐκ τῶν ἰδίων.[11] In this connection the words of institution have the added function of converting a private contribution into community property. For the words "this is my body for you," spoken over the contribution of bread, have the practical meaning: This bread is here for all of you. Bread which has its origin ἐκ τῶν ἰδίων is thus publicly declared to be the Lord's own, to be κυριακὸν δεῖπνον.[12] It would thus be understandable that Paul here once again expressly quotes the Lord's words.

The adjective ἴδιος carries a second nuance as well. Not only does it characterize the food as a private possession; it also suggests something about the way it is consumed. Eratosthenes (*FGH* 241, fgm. 16) criticizes a public feast (συνοίκια) because each participant drank privately, from his own cup brought along for that purpose, what had been provided for all: καὶ ἐξ ἰδίας ἕκαστος λαγύνου παρ' αὐτῶν φέροντες πίνουσιν ("each one drinks from his own flask which he has brought along"). Plutarch takes up the same problem in his table talk: Should each person be given an individual portion, or should all drink from one cup and eat from one joint of meat?

> When I was holding the eponymous archonship at home, most of the dinners (τῶν δείπνων) were portion-banquets, and each man at the sacrifices was allotted his share of the meal. This was wonderfully pleasing to some, but others blamed the practice as unsociable (ἀκοινώνητων) and vulgar and thought the dinners ought to be restored again to the customary style when my term as archon was over. "For in my opinion," said Hagias, "we invite each other not for the sake of eating and drinking, but for drinking together and eating together, and this division of meat into shares kills sociability (κοινωνία) and makes many dinners and many diners with nobody anybody's dinner-companion when each takes his share by weight as from a butcher's counter and puts it before himself. Again, how does placing a cup before each guest and a pitcher full of wine and his own (ἰδίαν) table (as the Demophontidae are said to have done for Orestes) and bidding him drink without heed to the others, differ from entertaining him in the manner which now prevails, serving him meat and bread as though from his individual manger, except that no compulsion to silence lies upon us as upon those who entertained Orestes?" [*Quaestiones Convivales* II, 10, 1]

Hagias's point of view is summed up later in one sentence (II, 10, 2): Ἀλλ' ὅπου τὸ ἴδιον ἐστιν, ἀπόλλυται τὸ κοινόν ("But where each guest has his own private portion, companionship fails").

We find that the relationship between ἴδιον δεῖπνον and κοινὸν δεῖπνον is also discussed in other places. It would fit with good Greek tradition to put the idea of community at the head of the list of debatable issues. Plato's phrase κοινὰ τὰ τῶν φίλων ("friends have all things in common," Plato, *Phaedrus*, 279c) comes to mind. But Greek banquets presuppose a certain homogeneity—not to mention the fact that the Roman colony of Corinth had been culturally very much influenced by non-Greek traditions. The problems of Greek dinner parties, as discussed by Plutarch, are at heart problems in the relationship of the individual to a community. What is problematic is thus the conduct of the individual, not the relationship of groups. In Corinth it is otherwise.

The two nuances of ἴδιον should be taken together: a portion of the Corinthian community brings food ἐκ τῶν ἰδίων for the congregational gathering and eats it, at least in part, as ἴδιον δεῖπνον. If this behavior has certain "individualistic" traits it is nonetheless the individualistic behavior of a particular group which as such, under some circumstances, is class-specific. Those Christians who eat a private meal probably have a high social status not only because they, in contrast with other Christians, can bring food both for themselves and for others. Their social position also is apparent in Paul's question "Do you not have houses to eat and drink in?" That certainly sounds as though some Christians in Corinth owned houses. Had Paul merely wished to say that each should eat alone, a phrase like ἐν οἴκῳ (1 Cor. 11:34; 14:35) or παρ' ἑαυτοῦ (16:2) would be more likely. As it stands his question can be addressed to only a certain portion of the Christian community, and his advice to eat and drink at home (11:34) applies only to those who have something to eat and drink. It would be cynicism of scarcely imaginable proportions to advise those who have nothing to eat at home. One might as well Hunger at home.[13] If when they read the letter it is supposed to be clear to the Corinthians to whom the question in v. 22 is addressed, then the question itself must entail a characteristic of the group for which it is intended, namely that the group is at least to some degree well-off. Only the phrase οἰκίας ἔχειν answers to that. Thus it is probable, if not entirely certain, that in this phrase there echoes the notion of house ownership. Apart from this we know that some Corinthians had houses at their disposal. Gaius is ξένος μου καὶ ὅλης τῆς ἐκκλησίας ("host to me and to the whole church," Rom. 16:23), and Titius Justus entertained Paul as a guest (Acts 18:7).

It can be assumed that the conflict over the Lord's Supper is a conflict between poor and rich Christians. The cause of this conflict was a particular habit of the rich. They took part in the congregational meal which they themselves had made possible, but they did so by themselves—possibly physically separated from the others and at their own table.[14] Yet we learn but little about the ways and means of their "private meal."

Variable Beginnings for the Meal

Apparently there were problems with the inception of the meal. Paul admonishes them to wait for one another (1 Cor. 11:33). Moreover, v. 21 could be taken to mean that each begins to eat "right away" (προλαμβάνειν). However, these two passages cannot immediately be squared with each other. While according to v. 33 it seems as if the corporate meal has begun prematurely so that those who come later get less than their fair share,[15] v. 21 strongly hints that some Christians had already begun earlier with their private meal, the congregational meal then following later. In this case, those who came later would be less disadvantaged. We notice that 1 Cor. 11:21 is a statement, v. 33 an exhortation. For that reason, in the case of a conflict v. 21 gets the nod for reconstructing the situation, especially as v. 33 would then become a meaningful warning if addressed to those who went ahead first with their private meal. In any case, the inception of the Lord's Supper was not "regulated."

The Lord's Supper begins with the word spoken over the bread, by means of which "private" contributions were extended to the group. So long as the words of institution were not spoken the food which was brought remained a "private possession." Up to this point there could be only private meals. An external reason for the conflict over the Lord's Supper could also be the absence of any fixed order in the Corinthian service of worship, or the fact that nobody was able to impose an order.[16] There was too much ἀκαταστασία (1 Cor. 14:33).

It is frequently assumed that in Corinth a regular meal, designed to satisfy hunger, was eaten prior to the cultic meal. The fixed sequence in the words of institution (the word over the bread, the δεῖπνον, the word over the cup) would then recall a practice no longer in use.[17] According to this view, quarrels resulted from the fact that some Christians came too late for the regular meal so that nothing was left for them. But the presumed sequence, a real meal followed by the Lord's Supper, is improbable.

In my opinion it is unthinkable that Paul would quote a sacred, cultic formula, expressly state that he received it in just this and no other form, yet at the same time tacitly suppose that its order is not to be followed. The formula presumes that there is a meal *between* the word over the bread and that spoken over the cup. One gets to the cup μετά τὸ δειπνῆσαι (1 Cor. 11:25). If there were already disorder in the Corinthian worship, Paul would simply be abetting it. If he wants to bring about some order, he cannot possibly repeat obsolete instructions lest the ἀκαταστασία (1 Cor. 14:33) be complete.

The arguments assembled by P. Neuenzeit for a regular meal prior to the Eucharist in Corinth are scarcely persuasive:[18]

1. Although the cup and bread are closely linked in 1 Cor. 10:16, it by no means follows that they were administered together after the meal. Moreover, in 1 Cor. 10:16 Paul reverses the customary order (bread/cup) so that we can hardly learn from this passage anything about the sequence used in actual practice.

2. Nor does anything in 1 Cor. 11:21 suggest a communal meal prior to the Lord's Supper. Only anticipatory ἴδια δεῖπνα are mentioned, not a κοινὸν δεῖπνον. Neuenzeit argues: "If breaking the bread had taken place at the beginning of the celebration, then those who came later could have shared in only the Eucharist of the cup. Paul would have severely criticized any such exclusion of the poor from the Eucharist of the bread."[19] This argument is correct. This bread-Eucharist did not come at the beginning of the ceremony. However, neither did it come after some ordinary, general meal of which Paul approved. It came after the private meal of which he did not approve.

3. Neuenzeit further argues that 1 Cor. 11:34 "smooths the way for a

complete separation of the regular meal from the Eucharist." But only the private meals have been separated off from the community's meals.

4. Conclusions about the sequence of the supper celebration in Corinth cannot be drawn from Acts 20:7ff.; Mk. 14:17–21; and John 6:52, even if one could find in these passages a sequence which goes from an ordinary community meal to a cultic Eucharist.

The wealthy Christians not only ate separately that food which they themselves had provided, but it appears that they began doing so before the commencement of the congregational meal.[20] But that alone does not adequately describe their odd behavior. The private meal seems not to be just a preliminary meal, which leads to the next point.

Different Amounts of Food and Drink

There are some indications that the ἴδια δεῖπνα extended into the Lord's Supper itself. Paul says, "For in *eating*, each one goes ahead with his own meal" (emphasis added). The word προλαμβάνειν need not mean "anticipate" but can simply mean "eat."[21] The doubling of the terms "meals" and "eating," δεῖπνον and φαγεῖν, is hardly mere pleonasm. Rather, φαγεῖν refers back to the phrase κυριακὸν δεῖπνον φαγεῖν of the preceding clause, while corresponding to the phrase εἰς τὸ φαγεῖν in v. 33. In both instances it is the Lord's Supper to which the verb refers. The proper meal occurs ἐν τῷ φαγεῖν, "during the Lord's Supper," and not only prior to its inception. At the very least v. 21 does not exclude that possibility.

So it may be that with the words of institution, not all the food on hand was shared with the congregation, but a certain portion was claimed as "private." Under such circumstances, those who are wealthier would get larger portions than the others. Paul's warning in 1 Cor. 11:29 also points to such a "supplementary" meal in addition to the Lord's Supper: "For any one who eats and drinks without discerning the body (μὴ διακρίνων τὸ σῶμα) eats and drinks judgment upon himself." In all probability this should be interpreted to mean that some do not distinguish in the Lord's Supper between the food which belongs to the supper and their ἴδιον δεῖπνον. Some have more than others.

It is not inconceivable that there was a larger portion of food for those whose contribution made the meal possible in the first place. Various associations or clubs in antiquity observed such distinctions in allotment and officially recognized "material gifts to certain members, primarily in the form of larger shares in feasts for officials and staff members. These shares ranged from between one and one-half to two and three times the normal, giving rise to the terms *sesquiplicarii, duplicarii, triplicarii* for the various categories of officials."[22] The *collegium* in Lanuvium (136 C.E.),[23] which included slaves, might be cited as an example since it had an established rule (*CIL* XIV 2112 = Dessau 7212) that read "*ut quisquis quinquennalitatem gesserit integre, ei ob honorem partes sesquiplas ex omni re dari,*" that is, "any member who has administered the office of the *quinquennalis* honestly shall receive a share and a half of everything as a mark of honor." There were also special allotments, for example, for those officials who rendered lifelong service in some capacity such as secretary or messenger. A normal portion at feasts consisted of some bread, four small sardines, and an amphora of wine.

We certainly should not think that in the Corinthian congregation there was a similar rule. On the contrary, in distinction from other kinds of associations in antiquity, there were in this case apparently no formal regulations, no bylaws or procedure by means of which conflicts could be avoided. It had never been determined who might merit special consideration. The existence of such regulations within other associations is significant here only in this one respect: apparently nobody was in the least offended if certain deserving members of the community received larger allotments than others. Such discrepancies were, in fact, considered fair and proper.

Had not the wealthy Christians in Corinth rendered incontrovertible service to the congregation?[24] They made rooms available for the common meal. Only through their contribution was the common meal available to everybody. If they had their own ἴδιον δεῖπνον in addition to the general meal, perhaps they simply adopted a pattern of behavior customary at that time. The regulations characteristic of other associations at least enjoyed this advantage over the "charismatic," unregulated life of the Corinthian congregation—that it gave even those who performed only service chores the opportunity to distinguish themselves by rendering special assistance. When, by contrast, everything is left to the free sway of the "Spirit," those who are of privileged status are much more likely to have things their way.

Thus the wealthy Christians not only ate by themselves and began before the regular Lord's Supper, but also had more to eat. Paul alludes to the greater quantity of the ἴδιον δεῖπνον when he writes, "one is hungry and another is drunk" (1 Cor. 11:21). Yet even this assumption, that there were unequal portions of food and drink, does not make wholly comprehensible the conflict connected with the Lord's Supper. For in that case Paul would only have to admonish all to share equally. But in fact he recommends that they celebrate the "private meal" at home. One ought not to be too hasty in imputing sarcasm to Paul, as if he were saying that those who have enough to eat should eat at home; that it is not so bad if at the Lord's Supper some are hungry so long as these people are not made inordinately conscious of how much better off other members are. Yet as long as it is assumed that it is a matter merely of different quantities of food for the rich and the poor Christians, Paul's suggested solution must seem odd.

Meals of Different Quality

Paul's instruction to eat the "private meal" (ἴδιον δεῖπνον) at home becomes more readily comprehensible if it is assumed that something better than mere bread and wine was involved, some further delicacy as was sometimes customary: ἐσθίουσι μὲν γὰρ δὴ πάντες ἐπὶ τῳ σίτῳ ὄψον, ὅταν παρῇ ("for all, I presume, eat meat with their bread when they get the chance," Xenophon, *Memorabilia* III, 14, 2). Even the modest collegium of Lanuvium, comprised of members from the lower classes, provided fish in addition to bread and wine. It seems reasonable that in the Corinthian congregation some Christians were not satisfied with just bread and wine. If this were the case, however, Paul could not simply demand that this additional dish also be shared, for the very good reason that nothing was said about it in the words of institution. These words of institution are for him without doubt holy and irrevocable. But they provide only for bread and wine.

These words were also holy and irrevocable for the Corinthian congregation. In their letter they expressly declare that they have followed the traditions received from Paul. Paul takes note of this in 1 Cor. 11:2 and praises the congregation for doing so. Later, in the passage we are examining, he returns to this idea and asks ironically: "Shall I commend you in this [scilicet, that you distinguish a private meal from the Lord's Supper]? No, I will not" (11:22). From this it might be inferred that even in the matter of the Lord's Supper the Corinthians could maintain that they had remained true to the Pauline traditions. One could even argue that since the words of institution provide only for the distribution of bread and wine, everything else can be regarded as a "private meal." Thus the tradition is being strictly adhered to. Should Paul have praised them for that?

Such an "ingenious" interpretation of the tradition of the Lord's Supper is not at all ingenious when seen in the framework of what was widespread and customary at that time. For some Corinthians it would not be at all strange to think that common meals, involving people of varied social status, should include food of varying quality. Such practice is well attested for the period.[25] If in our sources we hear only criticism of this custom, that is not surprising. Those who were in agreement with a practice had little reason to express themselves on the subject. More interesting for our purposes is the fact that the criticism comes from different perspectives. The humane tactfulness of a member of the upper classes leads Pliny the Younger to criticize the practice, while Martial and Juvenal, by contrast, express the wounded self-esteem of those who have been snubbed at such a meal. Pliny writes:

> It would be a long story, and of no importance, were I to recount too particularly by what accident I (who am not at all fond of society) supped lately with a person, who in his own opinion lives in splendour combined with economy; but according to mine, in a sordid but expensive manner. Some very elegant dishes were served up to himself and few more of the company; while those which were placed before the rest were cheap and paltry. He had apportioned in small flagons three different sorts of wine; but you are not to suppose it was

that the guests might take their choice: on the contrary, that they might not choose at all. One was for himself and me; the next for his friends of a lower order (for, you must know, he measures out his friendship according to the degrees of quality); and the third for his own freed-men and mine. One who sat next to me took notice of this, and asked me if I approved of it. "Not at all," I told him. "Pray, then," said he, "what is your method on such occasions?" "Mine," I returned, "is to give all my company the same fare; for when I make an invitation, it is to sup, not to be censoring. Every man whom I have placed on an equality with myself by admitting him to my table, I treat as an equal in all particulars." "Even freed-men?" he asked. "Even them," I said; "for on these occasions I regard them not as freed-men, but boon companions." "This must put you to great expense," says he. I assured him not at all; and on his asking how that could be, I said, "Why you must know my freed-men don't drink the same wine I do—but *I* drink what *they* do" (*Epistulae* II, 6).

It is interesting to notice that in one matter Pliny's suggested solution is comparable to Paul's: In a common meal, one of higher social status should adjust his eating habits to those appropriate to one of a lower social class. On the other hand, when we read the criticism "from below" in Martial and Juvenal, it is obvious that here the intention, understandably, is to put those of a lower station on the same plane as those of higher status:

Since I am asked to dinner, no longer, as before, a purchased guest, why is not the same dinner served to me as to you? You take oysters fattened in the Lucrine lake, I suck a mussel through a hole in the shell; you get mushrooms, I take hog funguses; you tackle turbot, but I brill. Golden with fat, a turtledove gorges you with its bloated rump; there is set before me a magpie that has died in its cage. Why do I dine without you although, Ponticus, I am dining with you? The dole has gone: let us have the benefit of that; let us eat the same fare. [Martial, *Epigrammata*, III, 60]

In another passage Martial can express himself even more bitterly and curse his "host," who is demonstrating before all eyes his social superiority:

Tell me, what madness is this? While the throng of invited guests looks on, you, Caecilianus, alone devour the mushrooms! What prayer shall I make suitable to such a belly and gorge? May you eat such a mushroom as Claudius ate! (*Epigrammata* I, 20; cf. further IV, 85; VI, 11; X, 49).

Juvenal has described in detail Virro's banquet (*Satura* V). While the host helps himself to good and old wine, fresh bread, plump liver, and all kinds of delicacies, the guests must be content with bitter wine, moldy bread, cabbage which smells like lamp oil, suspicious-looking mushrooms, an old hen, and rotten apples. The result is a violent squabble among those invited.

The most detailed evidence all comes from Latin authors, but for that very reason it is valuable for throwing light on the Corinthian situation. For Corinth of the first century C.E. was a new Roman foundation. The official language was Latin, and most of the inscriptions from this period are written in Latin. Even if in many instances contact was sought with the older Greek tradition—the resumption of the Isthmian games, for example—the construction of an amphitheater nevertheless demonstrates how strong was the Roman, non-Greek influence.[26] Furthermore, the Corinthian congregation in all likelihood included people of Latin origin. Among the seventeen names of Corinthian Christians recorded, eight are Latin: Aquila Fortunatus, Gaius, Lucius, Priscilla, Quartus, Titius Iustus, Tertius. One of them, Gaius, is the host of the entire congregation according to Rom. 16:23, suggesting, among other things, that the communal meal took place in his house.

Again, it should not be supposed that the Roman (bad) manners just described were widespread in the Corinthian congregation. The passages only provide evidence for contemporary patterns of behavior allowing a host at a common meal to treat his guests differently depending upon their social status. Freedmen and clients served as the background against which he could demonstrate his power as patron. Of course the banquets described by Pliny, Marital, and Juvenal are private banquets, but so may have appeared the common meals of the Corinthian congregation. Gaius would serve as host to the congregation, as if, so the speak, he had invited them to his house. Those who through their contribution made the common meal possible were in fact acting like private hosts, like patrons, supporting their dependent clients.

Thus we may conclude with some confidence that when the community in Corinth came together for the common κυριακὸν δεῖπνον there was for some, in addition, an ἴδιον δεῖπνον containing something in addition to bread and wine. Baked goods, fish, and meat would be candidates for such a supplementary dish. In my opinion it is quite possible that among other things meat was also eaten. Meat was apparently a food served to invited guests in Corinth, as we learn from 1 Corinthians itself. One accepts an invitation assuming that the host will serve meat (1 Cor. 10:28). Plutarch also assumed that in communal meals meat is eaten (*Quaest. conv.* II, 10, 1). From 1 Cor. 11:17ff. only this much is clear, that the ἴδιον δεῖπνον is solid food. "For any one who eats and drinks [scilicet, bread and wine] without discerning the body eats and drinks judgment upon himself" (1 Cor. 11:29). Interestingly, Paul does not say "without discerning the body and blood," but only μὴ διακρίνων τὸ σῶμα, indicating that the problem is with the "body of Jesus," the bread, that is, with solid food.[27] The danger is that this food will not be distinguished from another kind of σῶμα. It does not seem to me impossible that we have here an allusion to the σώματα of animals (cf. James 3:3).

If it be conceded that some Corinthians now and then also ate meat as their ἴδον δεῖπνον, then a further hypothesis seems probable, one that can only be briefly sketched here. It is possible that 1 Cor. 10:14–22 and 11:17ff. deal with the same problem—the problem of eating meat in the congregational gatherings—from different perspectives.[28] In both passages the issue is whether the Lord's Supper is incompatible with any additional meal. There it is a matter of εἰδωλόθυτον (10:19), here of ἴδιον δεῖπνον. It is possible that the two issues are in part identical, that in Corinth one could never absolutely exclude the possibility that a piece of meat was already ritually "implicated." Every piece of meat purchased could be meat sacrificed to idols, possibly even that which was consumed by some Christians at the Lord's Supper. The plausibility of this hypothesis depends on the exegesis of 1 Cor. 8—10, which would exceed the boundaries of this essay. Accordingly, the hypothesis can only be noted as a possibility but will not be presupposed in what follows.

It is worth summarizing once again our reconstruction of the behavior of those Christians who consume their "own meal" in the congregational gathering. Some wealthier Christians have made the meal itself possible through their generosity, providing bread and wine for all. What was distributed is declared by means of the words of institution to be the Lord's and given to the congregation. Thus, in conjunction with this common meal there could take place a private meal because the starting point of the Lord's Supper was not regulated, and up to this starting point (that is, until the words of institution) what had been brought and provided was private property. More importantly, this distinction was possible because the wealthier Christians ate other food in addition to the bread and wine, and the words of institution made no provision for sharing this with the fellowship.

This behavior elicited criticism. The core of the problem was that the wealthier Christians made it plain to all just how much the rest were dependent on them, dependent on the generosity of those who were better off. Differences in menu are a relatively timeless symbol of status and wealth, and those not so well off came face to face with their own social inferiority at a most basic level. It is made plain to them that they stand on the lower rungs of the social ladder. This in turn elicits a feeling of rejection which threatens the sense of community. One need only think of the verbal aggressiveness of Martial who, as his host's client, was only a second-class guest. Paul rightly raises his voice in protest against the wealthy Christians: "You despise the church of God and humiliate those who have nothing" (1 Cor. 11:22). Thus the bases for the conflict at the Lord's Supper are neither purely material nor purely theological. Above all, they are social, the problems of a socially stratified community in which the community's κυριακὸν δεῖπνον threatens to become an ἴδιον δεῖπνον betokening social standing, and the Lord's Supper, instead of providing a basis for the unity of the body of Christ, is in danger of becoming the occasion for demonstrating social differences.

We ought not to make the mistake of raising moralistic objections against the wealthy, as historical and sociological analysis makes possible a more measured evaluation. Before sweeping judgment is rendered on the wealthy Christians, several things should be remembered:

a. Congregational meetings probably took place in the private homes of the wealthier Christians[29] and were made possible by their contributions. Under these circumstances such people would demonstrate their social status even if they had not wished to, and this quite independently of the specific content of the Lord's Supper.

b. The wealthier Christians were not simply inviting the whole congregation, but in doing so were also at the same time inviting some of their peers who belonged to it. Within the framework of social intercourse among Christians of equal standing, those ordinary standards for solicitousness and hospitality, which applied socially apart from the congregational life, could not suddenly be suspended. It was part of such expectations, for example, that there would be meat to eat (1 Cor. 10:27–28). Expectations closely linked to social status have their own force, regardless of personal attitudes. When Gaius, to fashion an example, plays host to the congregation at his house, he is also playing host at the same time to those who belong to the few Corinthians who are "wise," "powerful," and "of noble birth" (1 Cor. 1:26). It is natural that such people would extend special privileges to one another.

c. To justify the exclusion of other Christians from their "own meal," the wealthier Christians could formally appeal to the *paradosis* of the Lord's Supper itself, which applied only to bread and wine. Whatever went beyond that could be declared part of a "private meal."

d. Furthermore, the behavior of such people could take its orientation from the surrounding culture, where a lack of regard for others of those invited to the common meal was not simply outrageous. We have seen that some associations built into their regulations preferential treatment at festival meals for those who had rendered particular service, while influential Roman patrons treated clients and freedmen at their banquets as second-class guests.

In all likelihood wealthy Christians probably did not suffer from a guilty conscience in this entire matter. It is more likely that they thought of themselves as having supported the poorer Christians in generous fashion by providing a meal. The conflict thus has its roots in the collision between a consistent theory of community on the one hand and, on the other, behavior produced by social differences, something which existed not only in the Christian tradition but in Greek traditions as well. One thinks of Plutarch's discussion about the nature of community in the meal (*Quaest. conv.* II, 10); of Pliny's criticism of the way in which guests are snubbed, a criticism argued on the basis of a certain ideal of community (*Epist.* II, 6); of the κοινὰ τὰ τῶν φίλων (Plato, *Phaedrus*, 279c; cf. *Diodorus Siculus* 5, 9, 4; Iamblichus, *Vita Pythagorae* 30, 168; Porphyry, *Vita Pythagorae* 20). The close link between early Christian and Greek tradition on this point is demonstrated by the idealized representation of the primitive community in Luke (Acts 2:44). Thus the conflict is to be understood as a conflict between two different patterns of conduct, both of which could be expressed by the wealthier Christians as an expectation rooted in social reality. The conflict is one between class-specific expectations on the one hand and on the other the norms of a community of love which encompasses men of different social strata. Even if we cannot reconstruct in every detail the form which this role-conflict assumed, at least this much is clear: the conflict itself is rooted in the structure of the Christian congregation. In a group showing internal stratification, which supports itself through mutual generosity, those who are able to contribute the most come to achieve a certain position of superiority—even if that does not correspond to the group's self-understanding.

One final observation helps to illuminate the social side of this conflict. Those members of the congregation who come from the upper strata appear in a less advantageous light in Paul's statements. The conflict is not seen from their perspective. It is instructive, then, that Paul does not derive his information from the congregational letter.[30] It can be assumed that this letter was written by those from the upper strata. Some *topoi* of popular philosophy, which in all probability had their origin in that letter, so indicate.[31] One would hardly expect that the authors divulged anything unfavorable about themselves. Others must have done that. Paul has heard by word of mouth about "divisions" at the Lord's Supper (1 Cor. 11:18). He carefully puts some distance between himself and his informants, as if only partly willing to credit what he has heard, but perhaps that is mere diplomacy.[32] It is consistent with this that he immediately goes on to emphasize the basic legitimacy of divisions, as if he would believe these reports only to the extent that they tell of legitimate conflicts, and those of a sort unavoidable if the congregation is to be tested (11:19).

In fact Paul must have been fairly clear about the matter. Naturally, we do not know who informed him. Possibly it was Chloe's people, who perhaps were "dependent" persons bearing their mistress's name.[33] These could then have reported not only about the partisan strife among followers of different apostles but also about the conflicts at the Lord's Supper. The repetition of the term σχίσμα in both contexts would thus be understandable. So too would be the fact that Paul takes a perspective "from below" on the Corinthian problems in both 1 Cor. 1:18ff. and 11:17ff. Stephanus is less likely to have been the informant. One cannot recommend somebody wholeheartedly (1 Cor. 16:15ff.) and at the same time suggest that one only "partly" believes his reports. And of course there could have been others to whom Paul was indebted for his information. In any event, the problems were described to him from the perspective of those "below." And quite possibly the letter from the congregation touches on the same problems when it comes to the meat sacrificed to idols—now, however, from a quite different perspective.[34]

THE SOCIAL INTENTIONS OF 1 COR. 11:17–34

Paul's ideas in 1 Cor. 11:17ff. do not simply presuppose certain social relationships within the Corinthian community. Above all they express social intentions, the desire to influence interpersonal relationships in a certain direction. It is not accidental that Paul's statements issue in a very concrete suggestion for the Corinthian congregation's behavior. Paul wants to settle the problem of the "private meal" by confining it to private homes. At home everybody may eat and drink in whatever way seems proper. The final result would be a lessening of the role conflict in which the wealthier Christians find themselves. Within their own four walls they are to behave according to the norms of their social class, while at the Lord's Supper the norms of the congregation have absolute priority. Clearly this is a compromise. It would be much more consistent with the idea of community to demand that this "private meal" be shared. Paul's compromise, which simply acknowledges the class-specific differences within the community while minimizing their manifestations, corresponds to the realities of a socially stratified congregation which must yield a certain preeminence to the rich—even contrary to their own intentions. Within such a community the compromise suggested by Paul is realistic and practical. It offers a good example of the ethos of early Christian love-patriarchalism which arose in the Pauline communities and which we encounter most clearly in the household codes (*Haustafeln*) of the deutero-Pauline letters (Col. 3:18ff.; Eph. 5:22ff.).

This compromise, however, is the result of ideas which come from two quite different spheres.[35] Paul's own analysis of the conflict is informed by "sociological" perceptions, but at heart is derived from the *theological* sphere. For him, the Corinthian conflicts are part of the eschatological testing of the congregation (11:19). The social tensions between rich and poor Christians have been transposed to a symbolic world transcending the everyday reality. They become part of an eschatological drama and belong to the separation of the righteous from the unrighteous in a world which is coming to its end. By the same token, what stands at the heart of Paul's suggested solution is not simply a pragmatic suggestion to eat at home but an appeal to the real meaning of the Lord's Supper: the covenantal sacrificial victim *(Bundesopfer)* of the community is here proclaimed as the future ruler of the world. Behavior at the meal commemorating his death becomes the basis for a future judgment. Whoever partakes of the meal in an unworthy manner risks death. The sacrament is treated as being in a taboo zone, where violating the norm brings with it incalculable disaster. Paul cites as proof the incidence of sickness and death in the congregation. The sociological analysis of the circumstances of the conflict as these are presupposed in 1 Cor. 11:17ff., and his interpretation of the conflict within the self-understanding of those directly or indirectly involved, contradict each other.

We have here a hermeneutical conflict. And it is better to make this clear than to mask it. Otherwise one would fail to recognize that Paul's intention in no way (or at best only marginally) lay in regulating social conflicts. His intentions are to be found on another level. Social realities are interpretively transformed into a symbolic world[36] in which rich and poor Christians play a role, but within the framework of a drama whose *chief* actors are God, the cultic sacrifice, the sacrament, and a world which is passing away. The social realities are interpreted, intensified, transcended. Nevertheless, all these interpretations and intensifications stand—even beyond their own intentions—in a functional relationship with this social reality. That is made clear by the example of the Lord's Supper which is at the heart of Paul's remarks.

The meaning of the Lord's Supper cannot be reduced to a single formula, but discrete sectors of meaning can nonetheless be distinguished from one another: the idea of the elements, of sacrifice, and of judgment. Each of these has a social function.

The elements are, for Paul, more than graphic representations. Bread and wine become something special in the Lord's Supper. They must be distinguished from other food. They have a numinous quality. If this is ignored, illness and death threaten.[37] In 1 Cor. 10:17 Paul links a social goal with this notion of numinously charged elements: "Because there is one bread, we who are many are one body." That means, quite realistically: Because all have eaten portions of the same element, they have become a unity in which they have come as close to one another as members of the same body, as if the bodily boundaries between and among people had been transcended. Dogmatically one may speculate in various ways about how bread and wine are transformed into the designated elements, but in any case a transformation of social relationships takes place. From a plurality of people emerges a unity. This transformation is also represented at the level of the elements: bread becomes the body of Christ, wine the blood of the new covenant.

The idea of sacrifice also represents a social dynamic. It does so, however, not on the level of inert elements but of a living being. The propitiatory sacrifice surmounts social tensions; the scapegoat takes away unresolved conflicts. There is scarcely a community that does not exist at the expense of some scapegoat. The union of human beings is strengthened when their aggressions can be focused on a common external object. It is not otherwise with the "new covenant in my blood" (1 Cor. 11:25). The sins of all are transferred to one. The latent human desire to murder is actualized in one person—representative for others. What is new in the Christian idea of sacrifice is that the scapegoat is not driven from the community and sent off into the desert but instead is made the Lord of the world and recognized as its ultimate ruler.[38]

At the heart of the idea of judgment[39] is to be found neither the "elemental" nor the "organic" metaphor, but a social metaphor. The one sacrificed becomes the judge, the powerless one the ruler of the world. Here too one could ponder endlessly what is really meant by the expectation of the eschatological judge, but independently of that it is easy to see that a posture of obligation appropriate for the new social relationships is being inculcated. Eschatological punishments correspond to violation of the norm. In the symbolically interpreted and transformed social world, the sanctions also appear in intensified form. Even incidences of death and illness which have already occurred are integrated into this interpreted world.

These different "images" (the elements, sacrifice, judgment) cannot be rigorously separated from one another. They overlap, giving expression to a social dynamic which they represent on an empirical, "organic," or social plane. For Paul, of course, these are more than images. They are realities. We must free ourselves from that "philological cultural Protestantism" which finds Paul's weighty sacramentalism too "primitive." If something primitive is at work here, it is less Paul's weighty sacramentalism than the even weightier human tendency for individuals to find within the community an outlet for their need to dominate. Sacramental actions are dramatic representations of social processes, whatever else they may be. "The bread which we break, is it not the fellowship of Christ's body [RSV "a participation in the body of Christ]?" The sacramental act of the Lord's Supper is a symbolic accomplishment of social integration. From many people emerges a single entity. Interpersonal tensions are represented, and overcome, in the sacrifice. Sanctions are inculcated. This social dynamic is expressed in palpably perceptible actions. The fellowship here achieves embodiment (*Aussenhalt*).

It is not our task to evaluate the socio-historical significance of sacramental integration. According to W. E. Mühlmann, it was an important element in the rise of a sense of solidarity which transcends social stratification.

> In Europe the bourgeoisie arose from the tradition of the ancient polis, combined with the Christian sense of communal religiousness, which, in turn, had its roots in the idea of the community of the Eucharist. Such a concept, for example, is wholly foreign to a true Hindu, because to him the idea of meal fellowship with someone of a different caste is abhorrent. Even a man as enlightened as Ghandi declared that free opportunities for association in matters of table fellowship and in institutions like marriage were not essential for the furtherance of the democratic spirit; that eating and drinking had no social significance whatsoever but were simply physical matters. Ghandi thereby proved that he did not understand the historical significance of the Lord's Supper for integrating in Western culture a sense of community which transcends every boundary established by caste and ritual.[40]

Whether or not this far-reaching thesis is correct cannot be decided here, but it fits the Corinthian congregation. In the face of class-specific social conflicts, Paul moves the sacrament to the center to achieve a greater social integration. Even if the meanings bound up with the Lord's Supper transcend that social reality, they are nonetheless functionally embedded in such reality. Thus the sacrament appears in a different light from that appropriate to a theological self-understanding. But of course that is just the goal of a sociological viewpoint. E. Troeltsch wrote with some justification:

"Whoever busies himself with sociological studies and the literature of sociology will doubtless achieve a new attitude to all historical matters and to the objective cultural values which arise in historical life. Everything about causal understanding as well as about the establishment of norms and values is bathed in a new light."[41] Of what does this new light consist? There is nothing new in understanding that texts which have been handed down to us deal with social situations, and certainly a sociological point of view helps us better understand these situations. In the final analysis, however, it is not just a matter of the social factors by which people at that time were confronted. It is rather a matter of those factors by which they were shaped while pursuing their goals. The sociology of literature is exegesis κατὰ σάρκα. What Paul finds objectionable, that the Corinthians are humans (1 Cor. 3:4), that they are σαρκικοὶ (3:4), is the starting point which they take for granted. And indeed it was a very human situation.

There is an obvious contradiction between an early Christian congregation's quarrels and its understanding of itself as an eschatological community of love. Playing the reality off against the self-understanding reveals an unrealistic excess. Or one can adopt the radical self-understanding of early Christianity and from that standpoint criticize the realities. We are, however, more likely to be cautious in moving either way once we become aware that the Corinthian conflicts between rich and poor were built into the very structure of things. A community of love would certainly be more easily and consistently achieved within a socially homogeneous group than in groups having internal social stratifications. Anyone wishing to see "brotherhood"[42] penetrate every social stratum must make allowances for conflicts which arise from the merging of class-specific self-understandings, expectations, norms, and interests. Factions are necessary (δεῖ αἱρέσεις εἶναι), Paul says, but the sociological δεῖ is of a different order from the eschatological δεῖ in 1 Cor. 11:19, and the factual reality of this statement should be distinguished from its theological intent. Nevertheless, factual reality and theological intent cannot be sundered. They are bound together in the functional context of social action.

NOTES

1. P. Ricoeur, *Freud and Philosophy: An Essay on Interpretation* (New Haven, 1970), has pointed out this "hermeneutical conflict" through the example of the psychoanalytical interpretation of traditional religious texts. Sociological analysis leads to a comparable hermeneutical conflict.

2. So, for example, J. Weiss, *Der erste Korintherbrief* (Göttingen, 1910), 283: the Corinthians were indifferent "toward the religious character of the meal." E. von Dobschütz, *Christian Life in the Primitive Church* (New York, 1904), 21: "The Corinthians treated the Supper as a common meal."

3. W. Schmithals, *Gnosticism in Corinth* (Nashville, 1971), 250–56, esp. 257.

4. H. von Soden, "Sakrament und Ethik bei Paulus," *Urchristentum und Geschichte* (Tübingen, 1951), 239–75 = *Das Paulusbild in der neueren deutschen Forschung,* ed. K. H. Rengstorf (Darmstadt, 1969), 338–79, esp. 364ff.; abridged Eng. trans. in *The Writings of St. Paul,* ed. W. A. Meeks (New York, 1972) 257–68; G. Bornkamm, "Lord's Supper and Church in Paul," *Early Christian Experience* (New York, 1969), 123–60.

5. This question was raised in the previous century above all by G. Heinrici, "Die Christengemeinde Korinths und die religiösen Genossenschaften der Griechen," *ZWTh* 19 (1876): 465–562; idem, "Zum genossenschaftlichen Charakter der paulinischen Christengemeinden," *ThStKr* 54 (1881): 505–24. J. Weiss, *Korintherbrief,* xx–xxix, summed up the discussion with the conclusion "that the Christian community in Corinth in this early time may well have given to outsiders the impression of being a θίασος; on the other hand, however, it would also have appeared similar to the Jewish communities in the Diaspora" (xxiv–xxv). How influential the Hellenistic idea of the association (*Verein*) could be, however, even in the Jewish tradition, can be seen in the analogies between the Qumran community and these ancient associations; cf. H. Bardtke, "Der gegenwärtige Stand der Erforschung der in Palästina neu gefundenen hebräischen Handschriften: Die Rechtsstellung der Qumran-Gemeinde," *ThLZ* 86 (1961): esp. 93–104.

6. Cf. F. Bömer, *Untersuchungen über die Religion der Sklaven in Griechenland und Rom. IV,* AAWLM.G,10 (Mainz, 1963), 236–41: "Especially in commercially organized groups advancement as a result of economic success was frequently easier than in religious groups, which in their very nature were more rooted in tradition and where—in antiquity—the pattern of state cults also exercised a conservative effect" (240).

7. E. A. Judge, *The Social Pattern of Christian Groups in the First Century* (London, 1960), 60: "The interests brought together in this way

probably marked the Christians off from the other unofficial associations, which were generally socially and economically as homogeneous as possible. Certainly the phenomenon led to constant differences among the Christians themselves . . ." On the social stratification of the communities, cf. further R. Knopf, "Über die soziale Zusammensetzung der ältesten heidenchristlichen Gemeinden," *ZThK* 10 (1900): 325–47; H. Gülzow, *Christentum und Sklaverei in den ersten drei Jahrhunderten* (Bonn, 1960). I have analyzed the social structure of the Corinthian community above, pp. 69–119.

8. Cf. for example, H. Conzelmann, *1 Corinthians* (Philadelphia, 1975), 194: Behind the various groups there is a "theological attitude . . . an individual pneumatism, which leads to rallying around party leaders."

9. Similarly, πάντες in 1 Cor. 14:23 may not be taken literally. Cf. H. Greeven, "Propheten, Lehrer, Vorsteher bei Paulus: Zur Frage der 'Ämter' im Urchristentum," *ZNW* 44 (1952/53): 6.

10. Cf. A Deissmann, *Light from the Ancient East* (New York, 1927) 357ff. In Ptolemaic Egypt there was a special office of the *idiologos* who administered the private royal funds. The Roman administration took over this office. Cf. J. Marquardt, *Römische Staatsverwaltung II* (Leipzig 1884², 311 n. 1, and the inscriptional evidence adduced there).

11. E. von Dobschütz, *Christian Life*, 61–62: "Every man brought his own portion—in distinction from the custom of the Greek guilds, where the cost of the meal was defrayed out of the guild's treasury or by individual members—but the idea was that all the contributions should be put together and then equally divided. In this way the Lord Himself, to whom the gifts were brought, was made to appear the host (κυριακὸν δεῖπνον, I, 11:20)." But certainly not all were able to contribute to the meal, as J. Weiss, *Korintherbrief*, 293, emphasizes: "Well-to-do members brought along more ample provisions, intended as a contribution so that also the poor who had nothing could take part."

12. In Hellenistic sacrificial meals, too, a transfer of the offering takes place; cf. Aelius Aristides' hymn to Sarapis, 45, 27: "They call him [Sarapis] to the sanctuary and install him as both guest of honor and host . . . So he is at once both sharer of the offering and the one who receives the offering." On that A. Höfler, *Der Sarapishymnus des Aelios Aristeides*, Tübinger Beiträge zur Altertumswissenschaft 27 (Stuttgart/Berlin, 1935), 96 writes: "The devotee of Sarapis invites his friends to the meal. He brings the food as a sacrifice to the temple, dedicates it to the god, and receives it back again as a gift from the god, perhaps after a portion has been allotted to Sarapis and his priest. Then the meal takes place, and Sarapis is thus both the guest and host in one."

13. A low social status has often been inferred for the μὴ ἔχοντες from 1 Cor. 11:33: Because they come late to the meal, they cannot have had much control over their own time. So H. Lietzmann, *An die Korinther*

I/II, HNT 9 (Tübingen, 1949[4]), 59; Bornkamm, "Lord's Supper," 126; and Conzelmann, *1 Corinthians*, 195 n. 26.

14. Cf. J. Weiss, *Korintherbrief*, 293: "That members sat in groups, some together at separate tables, would have been unavoidable. Any injurious separation, however, into cliques or between well-off and poor, was to be avoided." Any such division according to groups can, naturally, only be surmised. Two things speak for it: (1) The Corinthian community was very large (Acts 18:10). (2) We have a picture of the celebration of the Lord's Supper from the ancient church according to which various groups eat together. Cf. plate 9 in H. Lietzmann, *Petrus und Paulus in Rom* (Berlin/Leipzig, 1927[2]). It is not certain, however, that the picture does not actually depict a miraculous feeding.

15. A. Ehrhardt, "Sakrament und Leiden," *EvTh* 7 (1947/48): 99–115, and H. W. Bartsch, "Der korinthische Missbrauch des Abendmahls: Zur Situation and Struktur von I Korinther 8–11," *Entmythologisierende Auslegung*: *Aufsätze aus den Jahren 1940–1960* (Hamburg, 1962), 169–83, esp. 182, offer a quite different interpretation of 1 Cor. 11:33–34, according to which v. 33 does not concern congregational gatherings but individuals' private meals to which the poorer Christians will have been invited. The advice, then, is to wait for these people. But it is quite improbable that "coming together" and "eating" in vv. 20 and 33 have different meanings. Meals in private houses are mentioned for the first time in the following verse (34).

16. E. von Dobschütz, *Christian Life*, 61–62, traces the problem of the Lord's Supper back to the fact that in the gathering of the congregation there is no figure of authority in charge. Paul and Apollos, each of whom could have exercised such authority, were absent.

17. Bornkamm, "Lord's Supper," 142, believes that μετὰ τὸ δειπνῆσαι was for Paul "only an ancient oral liturgical formula." So also P. Neuenzeit, *Das Herrenmahl. Studien zur Paulinischen Eucharistieauffassung*, StANT 1 (München, 1960), 71–72, and Conzelmann, *1 Corinthians*, 199.

18. Neuenzeit, *Herrenmahl*, 71–72.

19. Ibid., 71.

20. Bornkamm, "Lord's Supper," 128, very clearly describes the possible grounds for going ahead with the meal. Until the poor came, "they could confidently spend the time eating and drinking in table fellowship with family, friends, and peers. Everyone can imagine the very understandable reasons which may have played a role there: the very human tendency to a sociability among one's own; antipathy for the embarrassment that comes when rich and poor, free and slave, sit bodily at one table—real table fellowship is something quite different from charity at a distance; the worry that the 'atmosphere' for receiving the sacrament may be spoiled by such an embarrassing rubbing of elbows with the poor. All that had led to the 'taking beforehand' of their own meal."

21. προλαμβάνειν occurs on the stele of Apellas (ca. 160 C.E.) without a discernible temporal sense (*IG* IV² 126, *SIG*³ 1170). Cf. J. H. Moulton and G. Milligan, *The Vocabulary of the Greek Testament* (London, 1963²), 542. On the stele cf. further R. Herzog, *Die Wunderheilungen von Epidauros, Ph.S* XXII, 3 (Leipzig, 1931), 43ff. He finds here a medical expression.

22. E. Kornemann, s.v. "Collegium," PRE 7, 380–480, esp. 441.

23. The text of this bylaw is reproduced in the appendix to Lietzmann, *Korinther*, 91–93.

24. That service for the community led to some people's having special authority in early Christianity as well is shown by Paul's recommendation of Stephen in 1 Cor. 16:15–16: "We observe here a frequent phenomenon of life, that people who do something for the community thereby naturally come into a position of authority" (Weiss, *Korintherbrief*, xxvi). The idea that holders of Christian offices enjoy even material privileges is also present in primitive Christianity: 1 Cor. 9; 1 Tim. 5:17; *Did*. 13:3.

25. Cf. J. Carcopino, *Daily Life in Ancient Rome* (New Haven, 1940), 270–71.

26. On the cultural situation cf. J. H. Kent, *The Inscriptions 1926–1950: Corinth, Results of Excavations Conducted by the American School of Classical Studies at Athens VIII*, 3 (Princeton, 1966), 17–31; F. J. de Waele, *Corinthe et Saint Paul* (Paris, 1961), and O. Broneer, "Corinth: Center of St. Paul's Missionary Work in Greece," *BA* 14 (1951): 78–96.

27. A concrete interpretation based on distinguishing among foods is still the most probable. So also Lietzmann, *Korinther*, 59. Differently, J. Moffatt, "Discerning the Body," *ET* 30 (1918/19): 19–23; W. G. Kümmel, in the supplement to Lietzmann, *Korinther*, 186; and A. Ehrhardt, "Sakrament." Certainly Paul also associates with σῶμα the meaning "Body of Christ," but since the sentence speaks of "eating and drinking," the object of eating is most likely what is meant. Ehrhardt's translation is improbable: "Whoever eats and drinks, eats and drinks condemnation for himself, since for his own person he makes no exception."

28. H. W. Bartsch, "Missbrauch," is perhaps correct when he sees the same problem in 1 Cor. 8–10 and 11:17ff. The common element, however, is scarcely the idea of abstinence.

29. Cf. F. V. Filson, "The Significance of the Early House Churches," *JBL* 58 (1939): 105–12.

30. The relation between oral and written information is rightly accounted as being of fundamental importance for exegesis by J. C. Hurd, *The Origin of I Corinthians* (London, 1965), and N. A. Dahl, "Paul and the Church at Corinth according to I Corinthians 1:10—4:21," in *Christian History and Interpretation: Studies presented to J. Knox*, W. Farmer et al, eds. (Cambridge, 1967), 313–35, esp. 323ff. = *Studies in Paul* (Minneapolis, 1977), 40–61, esp. 50ff. They argue that the letter contained favor-

able news concerning the Corinthian community while the oral reports put the Corinthians in a much worse light.

31. Hurd, *Origin*, 65–74, gives a detailed account of the community letter. A table showing all passages containing what are generally assumed to be citations or *topoi* of the lost community letter is found on pp. 67–68. Conzelmann, *1 Corinthians*, 15, accepts the following as community *topoi:* "The wise man is king"; "To the wise man all things belong"; and "Knowledge makes free."

32. Differently, Lietzmann, *Korinther*, 56: "Thus Paul considers much of the report to be an exaggeration."

33. Family members would retain the name of their father even after he had died. Quite improbable, in my opinion, is F. R. Hitchcock's interpretation, "Who are 'the people of Chloe' in I Cor. 1:11?" *JThS* 25 (1923): 163–67, that we are dealing with devotees of Demeter, who was also sometimes known as "Chloe." [Cf. above, 92–95, Trans.]

34. There is in my opinion no compelling argument on literary–critical grounds for removing 1 Cor. 11:2–34 from its present context and assigning it to Paul's letter mentioned in 1 Cor. 5:9. On the contrary: (1) 1 Cor. 11:1 and 2 are closely linked. The admonition to pursue the imitation of Paul and the praise of the community for following all the traditions received from Paul can hardly be separated from each other. (2) 1 Cor. 11:34 presupposes the same situation as 1 Cor. 4:19, namely that Paul will soon come to Corinth, so that one can hardly assign 1 Cor. 1—4 and 11 to different letters. For further discussion of the literary-critical problem see W. G. Kümmel, *Introduction to the New Testament*, rev. ed. (Nashville, 1975), 275ff.

35. J. Weiss, *The History of Primitive Christianity* (New York, 1937), II: 648–89, correctly sees in the relation of sacramental and social ideas the main problem of the passage: "The entire discussion in I Cor. 11:20–34, seen from without, is dominated by two different aims: vss. 20–22 and 33–34 by the social, and vss. 23–32 by the sacramental. As a result the critic who is looking for interpolations might hit upon the idea of excluding this latter group of verses (23–32). And in fact it is not entirely clearly stated how far the appeal to the Lord's sayings and the exposition of the meaning of the celebration are to serve the purpose of combating Corinthian abuses. This question constitutes the peculiar problem of the passage."

36. On the idea of "symbolic world" cf. W. E. Mühlmann, "Umrisse und Probleme einer Kulturanthropologie," in W. E. Mühlmann, *Homo Creator* (Wiesbaden, 1962), 107–29, reprinted in W. E. Mühlmann and E. W. Müller, *Kulturanthropologie* (Köln/Berlin, 1966), 15–49. See further P. Berger and T. Luckmann, *The Social Construction of Reality* (Garden City, N.Y., 1967).

37. Catholic exegesis can—for understandable reasons—render far less

prejudiced opinions about the sacramental thought of Paul than can Protestant exegesis. Cf. O. Kuss, *Paulus: Die Rolle des Apostels in der theologischen Entwicklung der Urkirche, Auslegung und Verkundigung* III (Regensburg, 1971), 416: "The food—eating and drinking—is a miraculous food, a food charged with power and having its effect everywhere in this concrete life. And over against the salvation, won by whoever eats 'worthily,' stands the threatening destruction (*Unheil*) which unfailingly overtakes whoever eats 'unworthily.' "

38. This has obviously not prevented the church from searching again and again for scapegoats. Nevertheless, the possibility should not be ruled out that early Christian thought concerning sacrifice implies an effort to overcome the "scapegoat complex." The meaning of the New Testament transcends what was made of it.

39. This idea has been particularly explored by E. Käsemann, "The Pauline Doctrine of the Lord's Supper," *Essays on New Testament Themes*, SBT 41 (London, 1964), 108–35.

40. W. E. Mühlmann, "Okzident und Orient," *Homo Creator*, 411.

41. E. Troeltsch, *Gesammelte Schriften*, Bd. IV, ed. H. Baron, *Aufsätze zur Geistesgeschichte und Religionssoziologie*, (Tübingen, 1925), 705.

42. Cf. F. Bömer, *Sklaven*, 178–79: "Apparently Christianity alone consistently championed in the religious realm the idea of religious brotherhood. The precedents for this were not to be found in the spiritual possession of antiquity but were brought along from Judaism. In the New Testament this idea is already the common possession of the new world religion, and there was no other ancient community of belief in which the equality and brotherhood of all people was set forth so early and consistently as here."

5

The Sociological Interpretation of Religious Traditions: Its Methodological Problems as Exemplified in Early Christianity

Every age has its preferred intellectual procedures for grappling with the irritating and fascinating phenomenon of religion. It may do so systematically or normatively through philosophy of religion and criticism of religion, historically through analysis of the multiplicity of religions, or phenomenologically through the isolation of that which is most "essential" from the ebb and flow of the history of religions.

By all indications, questions from the sociology of religion are in the forefront today. This is certainly true for inquiry into contemporary religious phenomenon; but it is also increasingly, if hesitantly, the case in connection with specific topics of historical research.[1] Hesitation on the part of historical research is understandable and justified. Contemporary sociology of religion which conducts empirical research can avail itself of the methods of interview, questionnaire, observation, field investigation, and sometimes even laboratory investigation in order to arrange its material from the outset with an eye to statistical evaluation. The historian, however, is entirely dependent on chance sources which have survived. Moreover, these have been shaped by interests quite different from that of providing information about their social background.[2] In fact, it is a characteristic trait of religious tradition that it masks its mooring in human activity, preferring to speak of the gods' activity or to testify to an experienced reality lying beyond the world of human sense perception. The problematic nature of sociological research in the field of the history of religion is, therefore, problematic first of all in terms of methodology. To phrase this as a question, How does one obtain information about sociological circumstances from religious expressions in our sources? In what follows this question is discussed with reference to early Christianity. But first the material problem of a sociology of early Christianity should be sketched out at least in brief. Methodological reflections without application to a concrete case are fruitless.

The sociology of primitive Christianity is the sociology of an emerging ancient Christianity and its radical transformation. It began as a renewal movement within Judaism and became an independent religion. It took root in rural areas but spread primarily through the cities of the Hellenistic Mediterranean. It was at first a movement of those who were socially unintegrated; but it soon developed a new pattern of integration which later could be taken over by the larger society. The basic problem in a sociology of primitive Christianity is this: How could this marginal, subcultural current conquer and transform an entire culture? A sociology of *primitive* Christianity investigates only a part of this process, namely the period prior to the institutional consolidation of ancient Christianity by means of canon, episcopal office, and *regula fidei* and before the transformation of Hellenistic-Roman culture through the crisis of the third century C.E., that is, the period up to the close of the enlightened monarchy of the Antonines in the second century C.E.

Primitive Christian sources contain no sociological statements and only a few prescientific sociological references, but do contain historical, paraenetic, poetic, ecclesiological, and mythical statements. We thus face a methodological problem. How does one derive sociological statements from these nonsociological forms of expression? What, indeed, *is* a sociological statement? The following working definition may suffice for our investigation: A sociological statement seeks to describe and explain interpersonal behavior with reference to those characteristics which transcend the personal. First of all, then, a sociological question is less concerned with what is individual than with what is typical, recurrent, general. Second, it is less concerned with the singular conditions of a specific situation than with structural relationships which apply to several situations.[3] Therefore, a sociology of primitive Christianity has the task of describing and analyzing the interpersonal behavior of members of primitive Christian groups.

A discussion of available procedures can begin with the form-critical analysis of texts, which construes a text's *Sitz im Leben* in three ways: constructively, analytically, and comparatively.[4] In form criticism the "constructive" approach is that which rests on direct disclosure of the *Sitz im Leben*, that is, on expressions which intend to describe the social situation to which we owe the transmission and formulation of the texts. We can generalize by saying that "constructive" refers to the interpretation of all texts with (prescientific) sociological elements. The "analytic" approach infers from the form of a text the underlying *Sitz im Leben*. Here too it is possible to generalize. Analytic refers to every inference *from* poetic, ethical, ecclesiological, and historical expressions *to* the underlying social reality. It is characteristic of this process of inference that it puts to the texts questions which are independent of the intention which originally shaped those texts. Finally, "comparative" refers to that procedure which considers texts which neither deal with, nor come from, early Christian groups. These must in turn be investigated constructively and analytically in their own right, while their use for shedding light on primitive Christianity raises special methodological problems.

CONSTRUCTIVE METHODS

Constructive methods can be applied to sociographic or prosopographic statements. All descriptions of groups, institutions, organizations, and so forth, may be termed "sociographic," while all statements about individuals, their background, status, and roles are prosopographic. Unfortunately, there are but few statements with sociographic intent about early Christian groups. In Acts 4:32ff. Luke depicts a communism and fellowship of the primitive community which is based on agape. From a Roman official in Bithynia we learn that Christianity there has spread through all levels of society, both in the cities and in the countryside (Pliny, *Epistulae*

X, 96). For the milieu of primitive Christianity we have Josephus's descriptions of the Pharisees, Essenes, and Zealots (*Bellum Judaicum* II, 18; *Antiquitates Judaicae* XVIII, 1:1–6). It goes without saying that these sociographic sketches are to be read critically. Luke and Josephus both write for the Hellenistic reader. Josephus portrays the religious currents of Judaism as philosophical schools; Luke sees the ancient ideal of πάντα κοινά "everything in common" realized in the primitive community. Both idealize or negatively distort, as Josephus does in the case of the Zealots—he makes them responsible for the Jewish War—or as Christian authors do in the case of the Pharisees.

Prosopographic statements about individuals are more numerous. We learn, for example, that the first disciples were fishermen (Mk. 1:16ff.); that fishermen could recruit day laborers (Mk. 1:20); that some of the first Christians owned houses (Peter, Mt. 8:14; Mary, Acts 12:12ff.); and that others owned land (Barnabas, Acts 4:36–37; Ananias and Sapphira, Acts 5:1ff.). The sociological assessment of these bits of information presents the same basic problems to be found in any social-scientific assessment of empirical data: problems of reliability, validity, and representativeness. This can be illustrated by the example of Manaen in Acts 13:1, a *syntrophos* [foster brother; RSV "member of the court"] of the Roman client prince Herod Antipas.

The Problem of Reliability

The first question is whether this note is historical. Does every investigator, after repeated examination of the same sources, conclude that according to everything we can know, Manaen was actually raised as a youth with the young prince Herod? We must be clear about whether the text is reliably transmitted—this piece of information is missing, for example, in St. Gall Codex 133, but that is easily explained[5]—or whether anything points to a legendary tradition. Luke is happy to report on Herod Antipas and his circle in order to bring Christianity into contact with the larger world and to synchronize the two. But even if this note were unhistorical and an unwarranted supposition, sociologically it would not be without value inasmuch as it gives information about what a later generation thought possible with reference to earliest Christianity or what seemed plausible within the frame of reference of its own experience: that members of the higher classes also belonged to the primitive Christian fellowship. Thus, while it is the case that within historical research the question of reliability is identical with that of historicity, the concept of historicity can also be taken in a wider sense. From historical sources we get insight not only about what is reported but also about those who report it and hand it on. Since those who hand on such material do so within a framework of social groups, even the "unhistorical" is relevant for a sociological analysis of primitive Christian sources, so long as it originates from these groups and permits inferences about them.

The Problem of Validity

Validity presupposes or implies reliability. Here the specific question is, Can an elevated social standing be inferred from the status of *syntrophos?* We know from contemporary witnesses about *syntrophoi*[6] that the term refers not just to childhood "playmates" but also to confidants who often exercised influence as mature adults. Nevertheless, it cannot simply be concluded that Manaen belonged to the upper circles in Antioch. Herod Antipas had in the meantime lost his holdings and principality and been exiled to Lyons (*AJ* XVIII, 7, 2). Manaen could have become entangled in this fate, so that with equal justification we might look on him as a failure who now found in a position of control and influence within the Christian community a substitute for what he had lost. We don't know which was the case. It is only certain that at one time he belonged to the upper classes. This conclusion is valid, but not the unqualified conclusion of current elevated social status based on wealth and influence.

The Problem of Representativeness

For sociological analysis what is interesting is not the biography of Manaen but the question of whether or not, on the basis of these statements, we can learn something about the class membership of Christians. This can never be done directly. It can be assumed that the (possibly former) status of Manaen is emphasized precisely because it represents something unusual. We must utilize further clues. In that regard, it is scarcely accidental that an elevated social status seems probable for three of the five "prophets and teachers" of the Antioch community (Acts 13:1). Barnabas is known for his gift to the Jerusalem community (Acts 4:36f.). Later he also organized relief efforts for it (Acts 11:30). Paul was only a cloth worker, but he possessed Tarsian and Roman citizenship (Acts 21:39; 22:25ff.). Since we know from Dio Chrysostom (*Orationes* 30, 21–23) that at a later time the civil rights of cloth workers were in some dispute, we must accord Paul a particularly privileged status. We learn nothing further about the other two members of this "leadership" group in Antioch. In any event, people with a relatively elevated social status .predominate in this group. Further, it is interesting that almost all come from outside: Barnabas from Cyprus (Acts 4:36), Paul from Tarsus, Lucius from Cyrenaica. Furthermore, Manaen probably was not raised in Antioch, and Simeon's epithet "Niger," while it certainly could refer to his Negroid appearance, also might serve as a designation of origin. Therefore Manaen, while certainly not representative of all Christians, does represent the leadership group in the community in Antioch. It is also true of other Hellenistic Christian communities that they display an internal social stratification (cf. 1 Cor. 1:26ff.; Pliny, *Epistulae* X, 96) and that the higher strata dominate, not in numbers, but in influence.

In any event, discrete statements must be evaluated very cautiously. For example, it is not permissible to assume, on the basis of the few Christians who are specifically named and their often rather high social status, to have refuted the view that the rise of primitive Christianity had something to do with social contradictions.[7] The very assumption that those few who are specifically named are typical of early Christianity is itself problematic, not to mention the fact that whether early Christianity is class-specific or not says little about whether its origins are linked with social tensions. It is well known that most lower-class movements articulating protest had leaders from the upper classes.

ANALYTIC METHODS

Since there is available but a limited number of statements containing express sociographic elements, we usually rely on analytic methods, that is, inferences drawn from historical events, social norms, or religious symbols.

Inferences from Events

Above all, historiographic texts from the past preserve for posterity that which is unusual. The normal situation is not worth mentioning. Sociological interest, however, is geared to the normal case, that which is typical and recurrent. For that reason we learn from historiographic traditions—it makes no difference whether we are speaking about the popular religious traditions of the New Testament or the literary traditions of Josephus—only incidentally about the social relationships which interest us. Nevertheless, we do learn something. Focusing attention on that which is unusual often allows us to look more carefully as well at the background, that is, the usual. For example, the unusual fact is that Christians were given the name "Christians" in Antioch (Acts 11:26); it follows, therefore, that they were not ordinarily distinguished from Jews by a special designation (or set apart within Judaism). The execution of James by the high priest Ananus II was exceptional, arousing indignation (*AJ* XX, 9, 1). Thus the normal relationship between Jewish Christians and Jews was scarcely characterized by routine persecution. A second way of deducing the typical from discrete historical events is to search for events which reoccur in relation to a particular feature. For example, Jesus frequently touches on the territory belonging to cities without entering the cities themselves (Mk. 5:1; 7:24, 31; 8:27). From this it may be concluded that his movement was at home in the rural districts. Initially, it had no success in cities (Mt. 11:20–24).

What is most instructive, however, is the analysis of conflicts. To be sure, conflicts are also atypical events, but in most cases they expose to view the structures which transcend individuals. Personal animosities are more likely to be their occasion than their real cause. In most cases entire groups are partners to the conflicts, individual protagonists serving as representatives of institutions and authorities. Their cause often lies in various, but typical, behavior of social groups, in differing attitudes, customs, and social assumptions. In such cases the extraordinary makes directly visible the ordinary; beyond the dramatic we can see the banal. Such is the case in the conflict between the weak and the strong in Corinth (1 Cor. 8:1—11:1) where the different customs of eating emerge, customs probably determined by class attitudes.[8] The problem of the ritual character of meat purchased in the market (1 Cor. 10:25) is no problem for those who have little money with which to buy meat. Other conflicts are similarly illuminating, such as those between Christians and Pharisees, between Hellenistic and "Hebraic" Christians in Jerusalem (Acts 6:1ff.), between Jewish and Gentile Christianity (Gal. 2:1ff.), between Paul and his Corinthian opponents (2 Cor. 10—13). Conflicts also characterize the transition from primitive Christianity to the established, institutionalized church, as in the case of Gnosticism or Montanism. The analysis of such conflicts is one of the most fruitful analytic approaches of a sociology of primitive Christianity. Conversely, every sociology of primitive Christianity must seek to determine to what extent it can make such conflicts comprehensible.

Inferences from Norms

Norms are social regulations and as such are social facts regardless of the extent to which they are observed. Primitive Christian norms (in the broadest sense) come to us in two ways. Either they are explicit (that is, ethical norms) or can be inferred from the regularity of some well-attested behavior, as in the case of norms governing speaking and literary activity.

An initial group of explicitly formulated norms are practical norms, general rules by means of which every social world orders and governs the impressions, experiences, and certitudes of its members.[9] One such practical norm is the (very pessimistic) recognition that those who have will receive more while from those who have not even what they have will be taken (Mk. 4:25). One can scarcely imagine such a piece of wisdom at home in the social circles of those in society who earn a profit. Numerous such "insights" are transmitted in the New Testament through aphorisms, wisdom sayings, and maxims. In them we have fragments from that world of certitudes and truisms by which any group or society orders the experience of its members.

Such practical norms are not expressly sanctioned. They belong to the everyday certitudes which suggest themselves automatically. Nobody commands that the world must be seen as it is seen in them, but anyone entertaining other opinions will soon feel the pressure of social control. With ethical and juridical norms it is quite different. Here nonobservance will be deliberately punished. These norms appear as commands, which is particularly clear in the case of legal norms. Usually these are formulated in some express statute, while sanctions are provided and institutional mechanisms are devised to govern the interpretation, application, and sanctioning of the norms. It is precisely these institutional regulations which make legal norms so very instructive.[10] In early Christianity, however, we have only a few legal norms with such regulating devices. Perhaps one such is the excommunication procedure in Mt. 18:15–17 in which the *ecclesia* as institution comes to the fore. Further instances are perhaps to be found in other community rules and ordinances with legal characteristics (for example, *Didache*). Many community rules, however, are instances of sacred law (*heiliges Recht*), which means that the sanctioning of the norm rests with God, so that it is often difficult to say whether there as yet stands behind these an earthly court. For example, was an affront to a member of the community punished by an assembly (*synhedrion*, Mt. 5:22), or did one leave the punishment to God (Rom. 12:19)?

The majority of norms coming down to us are doubtless of the ethical sort. Here too institutional features of life are involved insofar as these build up a framework within which such social regulations become meaningful and practicable.[11] The precept that wives, children, and slaves should respect the head of the household, *paterfamilias*, as well as his obligation to be concerned for those who are dependent on him (Col. 3:18—4:1), presupposes the setting of the Christian house. By contrast, the precept that to follow Jesus requires hating one's relatives, including wife and children (Lk. 14:26ff.), has a quite different social mooring. This is a norm at home among itinerant charismatics, a standard for those apostles and prophets and missionaries who are without home, family, or possessions.

When inferring from prosopographic and historical statements to typical social behavior and its conditions, the methodological problem consists in deriving a generalization from the singular instance. What is given is a statement about an individual social action; the typical is then reached by inference, making problematical the representativeness of the singular. When we infer from explicitly formulated norms, however, the very opposite holds true. What is asserted is a generalization, even if it is asserted as an imperative rather than an indicative. By paying attention to the practical norms, we learn what kind of general behavior is wanted. Here the question becomes how far the norms are really followed and whether discrepancies between reality and norm can be determined retrospectively with any methodological reliability. Some typical discrepancies can doubtless still be recognized. First, it must be determined whether a norm is considered of general applicability and whether it is possibly meant allegorically. For example, the dictum that one should, if the occasion arises, part with a hand or foot or eye in order to enter the kingdom of God (Mk. 9:42ff.) is prescribed in a qualified form with reference to scandal, and is scarcely to be taken literally. Nevertheless, it points without question to an extreme ascetic disposition in early Christianity. Therefore, it is not beyond the realm of possibility that some "disciples," like Origen at a later time, had themselves castrated in literal obedience to Matt. 19:11–12.[12] In general we ought not to be too hasty to relativize a norm as allegorical or of limited application.

Even when it has been determined that we are dealing with a norm which is designed to be taken literally and applied generally, it must be kept in mind that commands are always more radical than actual behavior. For example, the disciples are enjoined to break with their families (Lk. 14:26). We learn from 1 Cor. 9:4–5, however, that some traveled with their wives. The commandment indicates only a certain trend in behavior. In particular instances we must even assume that a command—for example when formulated negatively—runs *counter* to the trend of behavior. Whatever must be forbidden is usually being done somewhere. Thus from the prohibition of a mission among the Samaritans and Gentiles (Mt. 10:5–6) we can infer the existence of such a mission (cf. Acts 8:1ff.). Different forms of discrepancy between actual behavior and the norm can certainly still be recognized, especially when historiographic and sociographic data yield more direct information about actual behavior.

With regard to norms disclosed by linguistic and literary behavior, the methodological procedure is rather different. Here the norm itself is derived from concrete behavior as evidenced in many examples. Because the examples are numerous, decisions about their representativeness are easier. In this case what interests us are language, style, arrangement of material, and genre (*Gattung*) as norms of social interaction. From these we learn something of the educational level of the authors or the brokers of the tradition. To be sure, here too we must have reservations about the representativeness and validity of our inferences. What has been retained for us is only the written form of linguistic behavior. Whoever expresses himself primarily in writing, or puts into writing what was once oral tradition, must possess a certain minimum of education, to wit, at least a familiarity with the written medium. The New Testament authors certainly belong to those of above average education within Christian groups, so that from them we do not learn the daily speech habits of the lower class. To be sure, in antiquity even ordinary people could write, as papyri and ostraca show. Nevertheless, we have only a very limited insight into the speech conventions of lower classes. A. Deissmann's confidence in uncovering these with the help of epigraphy, papyrus discoveries, and ostraca, and in using the results to assess the New Testament sociologically, requires some correction.[13] Thus we cannot simply identify the literary language of poetry and philosophy with the speech habits of the upper class; and many alleged vulgarisms or Semitisms of the New Testament can be demonstrated to be at home in the less pretentious technical prose of medicine.[14] Nevertheless, it is instructive that within the New Testament we can observe various levels of language. The authors of Luke's Gospel and Hebrews are examples of two who can be considered relatively educated people on the basis of their good Greek. Unfortunately, poor Greek does not necessarily indicate lower social status, as is indicated by Josephus, who belongs to the upper strata of Aramaic-speaking Palestinian society but confesses to be not the best master of Greek (*AJ* XX, 12, 1). Semitizing Greek is not in itself vulgar Greek, however attractive the idea might be that the author of the Apocalypse, with its aggressive imagery, came from the lower classes since he writes the worst Greek in the New Testament. Beyond that it must be kept in mind that education is not an absolutely certain criterion of elevated social status. Wealth and ignorance sometimes go beautifully hand in hand.

The idea that literary forms, as genre-specific norms for the shaping of texts, express social relationships is one of the basic perceptions of classical form criticism. Hymns, for example, serve to confirm collectively a mythically interpreted world which was created and inhabited by early Christian groups. Letters provide communication for those who are separated. If the letter was capable of becoming one of the most important "literary" forms of early Hellenistic Christianity, it did so because this form corresponded to the diaspora setting of a small group with a great cohesive strength. Thus from literary forms we learn something basic about the forms of interaction among the individuals involved in the literature, whether it is a matter of polemic, consensus, apologetic, instruction, or whatever. The boundaries of literary forms are the boundaries of social communication. Only in the second half of the second century, for example, did Christianity begin to use the "elevated" literary forms of antiquity (apology, protreptic writing, and so forth), at which point primitive Christian literature came to an end and patristic literature began.[15] Thus even a history of its literature shows that primitive Christianity was a subcultural current at some remove from the general culture. This "general" culture, however, is predominantly a culture of the upper class.

While ethical and juridical norms (often practical norms also) directly express typical social behavior, the social background of linguistic and literary norms must be traced more patiently. The starting point is relatively broad, to be sure, but what can be determined is also relatively general, at least insofar as it is *not* the case with a particular literary genre—as it is the case with the parables—that themes specific to a genre themselves reveal something more precise about the social milieu of that genre.

Inferences from Symbols

Symbols are the result of a metaphorical process: images from life are transferred to other themes. In such instances it is usually no longer possible to decide if the image has attracted the object, the object the image, or if both were originally yoked.[16] Since the concept *metaphor* could involve a prior judgment, we use the term *symbol*.

In the case of ecclesiological symbols we are interested in the image and what it expresses. Descriptions and requirements are here inextricably intertwined. The image of the body of Christ says something about the great cohesion of Christian groups which understood themselves to be bound together as closely as members of a body, as if the personal boundaries of human individuality had been left behind (1 Cor. 12:12ff.). At the same time this image contains an unmistakable demand for the realization of its content. The wish and the reality cannot be separated; the imperative is concealed within the indicative. The same thing is true of other ecclesiological symbols. Now and then Paul refers to the Jerusalem Christians as the "poor" (Gal. 2:10; Rom. 15:26). Later Jewish Christian groups call themselves Ebionites, a self-description used by the Qumran community as well. The "poor" certainly are poor in a literal sense. It is real need which leads to the support of the Jerusalem community (Acts 11:27ff.; Gal. 2:10; 2 Cor. 8:9). Nonetheless, this is not a purely sociographic characterization. The poor, as for example in the Psalms, have a claim on divine help of a very particular sort, so that the term is also a self-description within the framework of a "piety of poverty" widespread in the Orient.[17]

Next to the ecclesiastical, the poetic symbols of the parables are the most instructive. To be sure, they do not express a social condition. The theme of the parables is the kingdom of God, his grace, responsibility before him, and so forth. The images of the parables, however, convey to us a great deal about the social milieu of the Jesus movement: kings, landowners, and moneylenders make their appearance here alongside farmers, workers, and slaves. We learn something of the rebellious cry of tenant farmers against absentee landowners (Mk. 12:1ff.), or the problem of indebtedness (Mt.

5:25f.; 18:23ff). Precisely because the parables are not narratives of real events they are particularly rich for sociological interpretation.[18] They compress normal experience into penetrating scenes of social life. They have a way of distilling that which is typical, even if at times they heighten this beyond the bounds of probability. For example, the situation of being in debt may be typical, but the size of the debt is doubtlessly exaggerated in Mt. 18:23ff.

It is more difficult to get beyond this general social milieu and determine the specific social location of the authors, the brokers of the tradition, and those who are being addressed. For example, a certain identification of the narrator with the socially powerful is unmistakable in many (not all) of the parables: the decent vineyard owner rather than the dissatisfied laborers (Mt. 20:1ff.); the unloved nobleman about to receive kingly power rather than his refractory subjects (Lk. 19:12ff.); the great landholder rather than the rebellious tenant farmers (Mk. 12:1ff.). At the very least, whoever wishes to reconstruct the Jesus movement as a social revolutionary movement ought not to overlook such things. But is it therefore justified to conclude from this, among other things, that those who heard Jesus, and possibly he himself, belonged to the upper social strata?[19] In assessing the parables we must first of all pay attention to the logic imminent in the genre itself. They have as their theme God's surprising, gracious, and challenging activity. To that extent they must emphasize in their imagery the socially powerful. Only a relationship to something superior can serve to make transparent the relationship to God. It could further be argued that in the parables the socially powerful by no means always support the socially weak. In the case of the parable of the unjust judge (Lk. 18:1ff), that is expressly related to the conclusion *a minori ad maius:* If the unjust judge helps, how much more will God help? In this case the sociological interpretation of social symbols in poetic creations poses a fundamental problem endemic to the interpretation of symbols itself: Is the relationship between symbol and social reality symmetrical or asymmetrical? When the poetic fantasy turns to kings, landowners, and the rich, is that the fantasy of kings, landowners, and the rich, or of those who are excluded from these upper social brackets? Fairy tales and the sensational press in our own day show that the latter is also a possibility.

The same problem is encountered with mythical symbols. Unlike poetic images, these do not offer a social reality which then as a whole stands transparently for something else. Instead, they more directly make something "other" their theme, such as the actions of gods, angels, and demons. To be sure, they do this by using images from the familiar social world: God may be represented as a king, the angels as his court; the less comprehensible the old king's actions, the more will hopes focus on his son; rebels, such as Satan and his troops, are made responsible for evil. Whereas in poetic symbols earthly reality is focused in compressed and concentrated form, in mythical symbols it is expanded to the point of transcending reality as experienced.[20] Thus, for example, the mythic symbolism of the domination of demons can be the symbolic intensification of the negative experience of earthly rule, including political rule, as a New Testament demon naively indicates when it calls itself "legion" and expresses the wish to remain in the territory (Mk. 5:9–10)—which was precisely what the Romans wanted too.

Experienced reality, however, is not merely interpreted in symbolic intensification. This intensification is also set over *against* the experienced reality. Without question the expectation of a new world and a divine kingdom is a rejection of this world and its kingdoms.[21] Two possibilities exist in the concept of "symbolic intensification." Reality can be heightened, *via eminentiae,* or denied, *via negativa*. Thus is demonstrated the problem of symmetry versus asymmetry between symbol and reality.

Apart from that, the sociological interpretation of mythical symbolism can choose from among various perspectives: the semantic, the syntagmatic, and the paradigmatic view of myth. The semantic perspective starts with the metaphorical image which is the content of the myth. E. Topitsch has drawn the distinction between biomorphic, sociomorphic, and technomorphic interpretations of the world, depending on which model of the known and familiar is projected onto the unknown and unfamiliar.[22] All these models reveal something about the familiar social world. Nevertheless, it should be noted that mythical symbolism is frequently "residual," that is, that it reflects relationships of earlier times. Thus God is still a king even after monarchy ceases to exist. The Son of God is sacrificed even after human sacrifice has long since been forbidden. Heavenly gods indulge in polygamy long after it has been abandoned in human affairs. Such historical relics are eagerly construed by the psychoanalytic interpretation of myth as psychic regression.[23] Once a polygamous divine family has been established, however, it is scarcely necessary to assume that all members of a society continue to use it to control their polygamous tendencies through projection. Once they have arisen, images quickly attain their own independent value and become available for new uses and interpretations, something which also argues for a certain skepticism in the face of any overly hasty inferences from mythical images to their social basis.[24]

A second mode of interpretation turns less on a correspondence of content than on structural homologies between social reality and religious imagery, frequently observable even when content differs. Here the syntagm of the myth, the relationships among the sequential units, may stand in the foreground. A myth does not consist of static symbols but is based on dramatic events.[25] To the syntagm of the myth, for example, would belong any reference back to prototypic origins.[26] A frequently repeated syntagmatic scheme is the genealogy, by means of which rival primal powers are "reconciled" in a kinship system while at the same time their conflict is understood as a degeneration contrasting with the origin itself.[27] It is sociologically significant that primitive Christianity, as it entered the Hellenistic world of socio-cultural pluralism, did not travel this path of integrating competing cosmic-numinous powers even in the defense against Christian Gnosticism (cf. 1 Tim. 1:4). The integration of numinous powers takes place in primitive Christianity in the form of a suffering *pantokrator* in a much more radical fashion than in any such genealogical system (Col. 1:15ff.). Correspondingly, the social integration of various socio-cultural and ethnic groups moved forward much more decisively in primitive Christianity than elsewhere (Gal. 3:28; Eph. 2:11ff.).[28]

Alternatively one can start with the paradigmatic quality of the myth, that is, from the actual relationships and oppositions between its elements independent of their syntagmatic sequence. God and the devil, heaven and hell are such "oppositions." C. Lévi-Strauss has put forward the thesis that in the paradigmatic structure of the myth can be seen the basic conflicts of a society.[29]

On balance, drawing inferences from mythical symbols must be considered the most problematic way to attain a sociological analysis of religious traditions. Every other means should be attempted first.[30] On the other hand, it is precisely this investigation of the relationship between mythical symbols and social situations which is one of the most interesting tasks on the agenda of research in the sociology of religion.[31]

In the case of all analytic procedures, drawing inferences from historical, normative, and symbolic statements about sociologically relevant matters runs counter to the intention of religious texts, which speak about something else. Such inferences, although contrary to the intention of the texts, are neither illegitimate nor impossible. Every historian works with them. He proceeds not only to "understand," if by that is meant the disclosure of the intentions immanent in the text's expressions, but also puts these intentions into contexts of which the original authors and subsequent conveyors were not conscious. He is always uncovering processes which were operative behind their intentions. At its heart, the procedure of drawing sociological inferences cannot be distinguished from historical source analysis. Nor is there anything novel in the observation that the results of a critical analysis diverge significantly from a text's self-understanding, that there exists a "hermeneutical conflict" (P. Ricoeur).[32] Furthermore, this hermeneutical conflict, which arises from dealing with texts in a scientific and methodical fashion, has nothing to do with a history-of-religions reductionism which regards religious intentions as masking some kind of nonreligious (socio-economic or psychic) reality. Such a reductionism, instead of explaining the conflict, would only unilaterally dissolve it. This kind of interpretation, however, no longer belongs to the methodology proper.

COMPARATIVE PROCEDURES

It is true that in order to describe an individual instance of social behavior a scant single source may suffice, while that which is typical only becomes apparent when social behavior is attested in several circumstances by several sources. This raises an evident query about the methodological feasibility of any sociology of primitive Christianity, since the earliest Christian sources are too fragmentary to offer a satisfactory basis for sociological conclusions. Many of the phenomena of primitive Christianity, however, we find reflected in non-Christian sources, and broadening our analysis to include these non-Christian sources is as essential for a sociology of primitive Christianity as it is for any other scholarly, scientific investigation of primitive Christianity. On the basis of the evidence in the New Testament, for example, one can assume with good reason that the synagogue ruler Crispus, mentioned in Acts 18:8, was a man of some standing. This assumption becomes all the more probable, however, when the inscriptions are studied in which such synagogue rulers boast of their expenditures for synagogue buildings,[33] for these indicate beyond doubt that prudence suggested seeking out wealthy men for that office.

Comparative procedures can take one of two directions. Either we can use them to help establish what is typical for primitive Christianity by analyzing the differences in comparison with the surrounding culture, or we can look for those characteristics which early Christianity shares with comparable movements, groups, or phenomena of whatever era. In the first instance the procedure turns primarily on contrast, in the second on analogy—but only *primarily* in either case, for a comparison marked by absolute divergence or identity would make no sense. It follows that procedures which turn on contrast and analogy themselves presuppose analogies and differences. But the distinction is a significant one. In the one case the analogous factors are less problematic, and methodological interest concentrates on the contrasts, while in the other it is the differences which are obvious and the analogies which must be drawn out.

Common elements shared among different religious groups or movements which are rooted in the same historical and social situation present no problem. One need not analyze these in detail but can start from the heuristic assumption that different religious movements offer different answers to a comparable social situation—for example, Pharisees, Essenes, and Zealots to the social situation of Palestine at that time. In this case the social situation is constant while the corresponding religious movements are variable. Then the task becomes one of correlating the differences among the independently emerging religious movements with the differences within the common social situation.

In this fashion P. Alfaric analyzes the religious movements in Palestinian society in the first century after Christ.[34] Sadduceeism is an association of the privileged strata with religious and political conservatism. Pharisaism represents the aspiring, achievement-oriented middle class. Zealots articulate the protest of the middle and lower strata while Essenes are viewed as a quietistic reaction from the same groups. It would be methodologically consistent to ask also about specific social and religious factors within the Jesus movement. The wish, however, to deny insofar as possible anything unique to the status of early Christianity leads Alfaric to view the Jesus movement as an insignificant variant of the Essene community. Since, however, there can be no doubt that this movement emerged independently of the Essenes, as it clearly distinguished itself from the latter in social behavior—for example, in its attitude toward "sinners," toward "the people," toward the law—this is methodologically inconsistent.

The comparative procedure moves in a different direction when substantively related religious movements in differing historical situations are chosen for comparison. In the case of primitive Christianity the point of comparison would be all messianic-chiliastic movements, where again and again we find comparable characteristics: the expectation of the near end of the world, messianic prophets and leaders, miraculous and ecstatic phenomena (for example, exorcisms), and unfulfilled hopes of a Parousia.[35] Granted the assumption that such movements can, within limits, be compared, sociology of religion's chief comparative task is to inquire into corresponding related structures in the underlying social situation. Thus, messianic-chiliastic movements are frequently reactions of an oppressed people to a politically imposed foreign culture in which the injured sense of self-esteem within the dominated culture seeks to assert itself. No doubt these are structural features which are relevant for the messianic movements in Roman-occupied Palestine including, among others, the primitive Christian movement.

The disadvantage of any such procedure relying on analogies is its relative lack of precision. No phenomenon corresponds entirely to another. It would be a gross contradiction of historical sensibility, for example, to reduce all too quickly to a common denominator the Mau Mau movement in Kenya and early Christianity. On the other hand, the advantage is that we are relatively well informed about some of these messianic-chiliastic movements, particularly through investigations which have been methodically carried out. Thus at the very least we have access to a series of interesting hypotheses worthy of investigation.

Above all, contrasting and analogizing comparisons are distinguished only by a matter of accent. In the one case historical proximity provides the background for the emergence of differences; in the other, historical distance provides the background for structurally related characteristics. The background, and the configuration (*Gestalt*) which stands out in relief from it, can obviously alternate. Methodologically, both procedures are complementary. In a contrasting comparison the overall social situation is perceived as relatively constant, the corresponding religious movements seen as the variable. In an analogizing comparison the structural marks of religious movements are held as relatively constant, the corresponding social situations as variable. In the first example sociology of religion's analysis must look above all for further variables within the static social situation; in the second example, for possible constants within the fluctuating social situation. It is true that historical sociology of religion is not able to collect quantities of empirical data; but when it investigates the material provided by history it proceeds in a fashion which logically speaking is not fundamentally different from the way sociology works when dealing with the present.

Using the example of primitive Christianity, we have looked at various methodological approaches for securing sociologically relevant data from religious traditions. It is not necessary to emphasize that the prospect of achieving an approximate comprehension of the matter to be investigated, by means of adequate statements about it, depends on the plurality, and methodological independence, of various procedures for drawing inferences. Only competing methods offer the possibility of reciprocal control and correction. That is no less true for the methods of sociology of religion than it is with reference to the study of religion (*Religionswissenschaft*) in general, where by necessity different perspectives must compete. The sociological perspective itself is but one among others.[36]

NOTES

1. Still unexcelled in the historical sphere are Max Weber's works in the sociology of religion. Cf. his *Gesammelte Aufsätze zur Religionssoziologie*, 3 vols. (Tübingen, 1963[5]), and *The Sociology of Religion* (New York, 1963).

2. E. von Dobschütz, *Christian Life in the Primitive Church* (New York, 1904), xxxiv: "How, too, were the communities composed? From what social strata did they acquire members? We have nothing but indications and unsafe conjectures. According to modern views, housing arrangements, rate of wages, and other questions of the same kind are of great significance for the development of morality. In that period which resembles our own so much, this must also have been the case to some extent. No such question is ever once touched upon in our Christian sources; even secular works give us no adequate account of these circumstances."

3. Establishing what is typical and what is determined is also considered a specific characteristic of the sociological point of view by M. Scheler, *Die Wissensformen und die Gesellschaft* (Bern/München 1960[2]), 17.

4. Cf. R. Bultmann, *The History of the Synoptic Tradition* (New York, 1963), 2–7.

5. Cf. E. Haenchen, *The Acts of the Apostles: A Commentary* (Philadelphia, 1971), 394 n. 5.

6. Cf. J. Jeremias, *Jerusalem in the Time of Jesus* (Philadelphia, 1969), 88, and the evidence cited in *A Greek-English Lexicon of the New Testament and Other Early Christian Literature*, 2d ed., Eng. trans. W. F. Arndt

and F. W. Gingrich, rev. and augmented by F. W. Gingrich and F. W. Danker from Walter Bauer's 5th ed. (Chicago/London, 1979), 793.

7. Against R. Schumacher, *Die soziale Lage der Christen im apostolischen Zeitalter* (Paderborn, 1924), 40.

8. Cf. C. K. Barrett, "Things Sacrificed to Idols," *NTS* 11 (1964/65): 138–53, esp. 146.

9. Cf. P. Berger and T. Luckmann, *The Social Construction of Reality* (Garden City, N.Y., 1966); and P. Berger, *The Sacred Canopy* (Garden City, N.Y., 1967).

10. Roman law is certainly one of the most important sources for the sociology of the Roman Empire. A. N. Sherwin-White, *Roman Society and Roman Law in the New Testament* (Oxford, 1963), has utilized it in the sociological analysis of early Christianity.

11. E. A. Judge, in the German edition of his book *The Social Pattern of Christian Groups in the First Century* (= *Christliche Gruppen in nichtchristlicher Gesellschaft* [Wuppertal, 1964]), takes ethical (and other) norms as his point of departure: "I try . . . to describe a range of social forms of the age to which Christians, as members of earthly society, would consider themselves obligated." In addition, many ethical norms refer so directly to typical social behavior that their analysis can also be considered at least in part to belong to the constructive method.

12. A different interpretation can be found in J. Blinzler, "εἰσὶν εὐνοῦχοι: Zur Auslegung von Mt 19, 12," *ZNW* 48 (1957): 254–70. That the New Testament norms were not intended to be situationally conditioned (whether de facto they are is another matter) has been demonstrated by W. Schrage, *Die konkreten Einzelgebote in der paulinischen Paränese* (Gütersloh, 1961).

13. A. Deissmann, *Das Urchristentum und die untern Schichten* (Göttingen, 1908[2]); idem, *Light from the Ancient East* (London, 1927). [Cf. above, 147–63, Trans.]

14. L. Rydbeck, *Fachprosa, vermeintliche Volkssprache und Neues Testament* (Uppsala, 1967).

15. F. Overbeck, "Über die Anfänge der patristischen Literatur," *HZ* 48 (1882): 417–72 = Darmstadt, 1966.

16. On the problem of the concept of "metaphor" cf. P. Wheelwright, "The Semantic Approach to Myth," in *Myth: A Symposium,* ed. T. A. Seboek (Bloomington, 1958), 95–103.

17. On the self-designation "poor" cf. L. E. Keck, "The Poor Among the Saints in the New Testament," *ZNW* 56 (1965): 100–137; idem, "The Poor Among the Saints in Jewish Christianity and Qumran," *ZNW* 57 (1966): 54–78. On the oriental piety of poverty cf. H. Bolkestein, *Wohltätigkeit und Armenpflege im vorchristlichen Altertum* (Utrecht, 1939). An interesting contribution to the sociological analysis of religious symbolism inspired

by the sociology of knowledge is W. A. Meeks, "The Image of the Androgyne: Some Uses of a Symbol in Earliest Christianity," *HR* 13 (1974): 165–208.

18. On the legal background of the parables cf. J. D. M. Derrett, *Law in the New Testament* (Leiden, 1971). An evaluation of socio-ecological data can be found in M. D. Goulder, "Characteristics of the Parables in Several Gospels," *JThS* 19 (1968): 51–59. M. Hengel, "Das Gleichnis von den Weingärtnern Mc 12, 1–12 im Lichte der Zenon-papyri und der rabbinischen Gleichnisse," *ZNW* 59 (1968): 1–39, illuminates in exemplary fashion the socio-economic background of this parable.

19. So G. W. Buchanan, "Jesus and the Upper Class," *NT* 7 (1964/65): 195–209.

20. On the symbolic intensification of reality cf. W. E. Mühlmann, "Umrisse und Probleme einer Kulturanthropologie," in W. E. Mühlmann and E. W. Müller, *Kulturanthropologie* (Köln, 1966), 15–49.

21. That eschatology in every form was rejected by the Sadducees, the rich Jewish aristocracy (Josephus, *BJ* II, 8, 14), is understandable. Those who profit from the status quo have no reason to look forward to a day when it will be changed. There is a certain affinity between specific mythical symbols and social agents. It is not permissible, however, to infer elevated social status solely on the basis of the denial of eschatology; this must also be independently confirmed. On the Sadducees cf. Josephus, *AJ* XVIII, 8, 14.

22. Cf. E. Topitsch, *Vom Ursprung und Ende der Metaphysik* (Wien, 1958).

23. From the wealth of literature I cite only W. Schmidbauer, *Mythos und Psychologie. Methodische Probleme, aufgezeigt un der Ödipus-Sage* (München/Basel, 1970).

24. This holds for all inferential methods. Texts are determined as much by the past as by the present; tradition-history and sociological analysis supplement each other. Social situations are repeatedly interpreted in the light of certain traditions, while the traditions are handed on if they illuminate social situations. *Topoi* cast in historical-traditional modes make possible inferences back to a social situation in various ways: (1) The recurrence of the *topoi* can point to the recurrence of underlying experiences. The traditions about the persecuting of the newborn king (Mt. 2:16) would not have survived in early Christianity but for the extirpative policy of Herod over against all rival competitors for the throne, including his own children. (2) Traditions become modified in actual practice. Both the Old and the New Testaments speak of someone's being called at the work place (1 Kings 19:19ff.; Amos 7:15; Mk. 1:16ff.). That in the New Testament fishermen and tax collectors take the place of farmers corresponds to new circumstances. (3) Tradition and situation appear to be incongruent. Con-

trary to the *topos* of creation *ex nihilo*, Paul writes in 1 Cor. 1:26ff. of "not many" wise, powerful, and wellborn. These people must have been very important, therefore, for the social structure of the Corinthian community.

25. Cf. S. Holm, "Mythos und Symbol," *ThLZ* 93 (1968): 561–72, and P. Ricoeur, *The Symbolism of Evil* (New York, 1967), 191ff.

26. So M. Eliade in several publications, among which one in particular might be mentioned: "Significations du Mythe," in *Le Langage II*, Actes du XIIIe Congrès de Philosophie de Langage Française (Neuchâtel, 1967), 165–79, where he distinguishes between two stages of origin.

27. Cf. K. Heinrich, "Die Funktion der Genealogie im Mythos," in *Parmenides und Jona* (Frankfurt, 1966), 9–28.

28. There is in Colossians and Ephesians a structural homologue between the integration of (pagan) powers in the cosmic body of Christ and the integration of Gentiles and Jews in his ecclesiastical body. The alien character of the Logos in this world is structurally homologous to the alien character of the Johannine community in this world (cf. the important essay for the sociology of New Testament literature by W. A. Meeks, "The Man from Heaven in Johannine Sectarianism," *JBL* 91 [1972]: 44–72). Structural homologies between "foundation" and "superstructure" have become the occasion for research into the sociology of literature, especially within "genetic structuralism." Cf. L. Goldmann, "Die Soziologie der Literatur, Stand und Methodenprobleme," in *Literatursoziologie* I, ed. J. Bark (Stuttgart, 1974), 85–113. There are here points of contact with E. Köhler, "Über die Möglichkeiten historisch-soziologischer Interpretation," in idem, *Espirit und arkadische Freiheit* (Frankfurt, 1966), 83–103 (also in *Methoden der deutschen Literaturwissenschaft*, ed. V. Zmegac [Frankfurt, 1972], 227–48). The materialistic point of departure for Goldmann and Köhler, so far as they themselves do not already modify it, need not be appropriated uncritically. The phenomenology of religion also regards the homologous correspondence between man and the universe to be a basic characteristic of religion; cf. M. Eliade, *The Sacred and the Profane* (New York, 1959), 165ff.

29. C. Lévi-Strauss, "The Story of Asdiwal," in *The Structural Study of Myth and Totemism*, ed. E. Leach (London, 1967), 1–47; idem, "The Structural Study of Myth," in *Structural Anthropology* (Garden City, N.Y., 1967), 206–31. For a critique cf. E. Leach, ed., *The Structural Study of Myth and Totemism* (London, 1967), especially the essay of M. Douglas, "The Meaning of Myth," 49–69.

30. This is missing, for example, in the very interesting essay of H. G. Kippenberg, "Versuch einer soziologischen Verortung des antiken Gnostizismus," *Numen* 17 (1970): 211–31. He relies too one-sidedly upon an inference drawn from mythical symbols, regarding the rebellion against the ruler of creation, visible in the devaluation of the monotheistic creator-god to the status of satanic demiurge, as secretly a rebellion against the

world's political ruler. For the correspondence between mythical projections and social reality he appeals especially to E. Topitsch's theory of myth, which is criticized by P. Munz, "The Problem of 'Die soziologische Verortung des antiken Gnostizismus,' " *Numen* 19 (1972): 41–51—although, to be sure, Kippenberg's theses are not thereby refuted. In particular, it remains true that Gnosticism had its social location in the higher strata of society; cf. A. von Harnack, *The Mission and Expansion of Christianity* (London, 1904), II: 36; C. Andresen, *Die Kirchen der alten Christenheit* (Stuttgart/Berlin, 1971),103–04; P. Alfaric, *Die sozialen Ursprünge des Christentums* (Darmstadt, 1963), 363ff.; A. B. Ranowitsch, "Das Urchristentum und seine historische Rolle," in *Aufsätze zur Alten Geschichte* (Berlin, 1961), 135–65; M. Robbe, *Der Ursprung des Christentums* (Leipzig, 1967), 202ff. Proof for this assumption, which is usually simply stated in passing, would have to be based on as many modes of inference as possible, including: (1) Sociographic data. A Valentinian can place seven stenographers at Origen's disposal (Eusebius, *Historia ecclesiastica* VI, 18, 1; 23, lf.). (2) Conflicts. For example, those in the Roman community; cf. H. Langerbeck, "Zur Auseinandersetzung von Theologie und Gemeindeglauben in der römischen Gemeinde in den Jahren 135–65," in *Aufsätze zur Gnosis*, AAWG.PH 3, 96 (Göttingen, 1967), 167–79. (3) The linguistic and literary level of gnostic writings must be evaluated. The astounding production of books by the Gnostics presupposes a certain prosperity. (4) The Gnostic ethos is frequently "liberal." Things like meat sacrificed to idols, entertainment, and sexuality are not denigrated. (5) Ecclesiological symbols, in particular the distinction between *gnostikoi* and *pistikoi*, betray an elitist self-understanding. (6) A soteriology of knowledge may be a characteristic of higher social circles. Where an interior process yields salvation, the fundamental need underlying the quest for salvation is less likely to be grounded in external, material circumstances. (7) By way of analogy, other radical and mystical currents in the history of religions must be canvassed. By way of contrast, other formulations of Christian faith within the upper social strata at that time must be investigated, for we also find members of the upper strata as leaders of the orthodox communities.

31. That would constitute a new stage of investigation. Basic sociological data must first be in hand before social situations and texts can be correlated. There are three possibilities for doing this: (1) Chronological correlation. Most apocalyptic texts come from the period between 200 B.C.E. and 100 C.E., in the very time when Judaism strove for political independence without any lasting success. Chronological relationships of that sort point to substantive relationships. (2) Quantitative correlation. The higher Christianity climbed into the upper classes, the more it took over "elevated" literary forms. For the most part, the realm of history allows only relative assessments ("more/less"), since precise statistics are

usually missing. In every case it should be noted that not everything which can be quantitatively correlated actually belongs together. (3) The material correlation, which is the stipulation of every chronological and quantitative correlation. As an example may be mentioned the sketch of structural homologues in n. 28, *supra*.

32. P. Ricoeur, *The Conflict of Interpretations* (Evanston, 1974), 27ff., 62ff.

33. Cf. J. B. Frey, *CIJ* (Rome, 1936), nos. 265, 548, 722, 766, 781, 1404.

34. Alfaric, *Ursprünge* (Darmstadt, 1963), 43–75. The same methodological objections can be raised against attempts to reduce Jesus and the Zealots to a common denominator—and against the more discriminating essay by S. G. F. Brandon, *Jesus and the Zealots* (Manchester, 1967).

35. Cf., among others, W. E. Mühlmann, *Chiliasmus und Nativismus* (Berlin, 1961); R. F. Wallace, "Revitalization Movements," *American Anthropologist* 58 (1956): 264–81. On early Christianity see esp. C. Colpe, "Der Begriff 'Menschensohn' und die Methode der Erforschung messianischer Prototypen," *Kairos* 14 (1972): 241–57.

36. This essay has concerned itself only with the question of how sociologically relevant data can be derived from our texts. Only when this data is in hand does the further question arise of just how far historical-sociological study is hermeneutically relevant for the interpretation of early Christian texts. The sociology of religion is hermeneutically relevant at least to the extent (1) that the texts from time to time express the theme of social conditions, even if only in this manner, that such themes appear as the imaginative realities of religious parabolic discourse and metaphor; (2) that the form and content of texts stand in a materially illuminating correlation to social conditions; (3) that all texts are forms of social interaction between their authors, those who convey them, and their recipients.

This essay was the theme of a discussion in a seminar of my colleague Dr. K. Berger in Heidelberg on May 30, 1975. I would like to thank my discussion partners, particularly Dr. Berger, for numerous suggestions and arguments which have left their mark especially in notes 24 and 36. I have discussed the question of the integration of data from the sociology of religion within a sociology of early Christianity in my 1974 essay (= Theissen, 1974b).

Bibliography

FRAGMENTS, INSCRIPTIONS, AND PAPYRI

The Collection of Ancient Greek Inscriptions in the British Museum. London 1974ff. = *BrM*.

Corpus inscriptionum Graecarum. Berlin 1828–77. = *CIG*.

Corpus inscriptionum Latinarum. Berlin 1862ff. = *CIL*.

Diehl, E. *Inscriptiones latinae christianae veteres*. Berlin 1924ff.

Edwards, K. N. *Coins 1896-1929*. *Corinth, Results of Excavations VI*. Cambridge 1933.

Frey, J. B. *Corpus inscriptionum Iudaicarum*. Rome 1936ff. = *CIJ*

Grenfell, B. P. and A. S. Hunt. *The Oxyrhynchus Papyri*. London 1898ff.

Inscriptiones Graece. Berlin 1873ff. = *IG*.

Inscriptiones Graece ad Res Romanas pertinentes. Edited by Cagnat, R. Paris 1911ff. = *IGRR*.

Inscriptiones Latinae selectae. Edited by Dassau, H. Berlin 1892ff. = *ILS*.

Jacoby, F. *Fragmente der griechischen Historiker*. Berlin 1923ff. = *FGH*

Judeich, W. *Altertümer von Hierapolis*. München 1898.

Kent, J. H. *The Inscriptions 1926–1950: Corinth, Results of Excavations Conducted by the American School of Classical Studies at Athens VIII*, 3. Princeton 1966.

Kern, O. *Inschriften von Magnesia*. Berlin 1900 = Berlin 1967.

Meritt, B. D. *Greek Inscriptions: Corinth, Results of Excavations VIII*, 1. Cambridge 1931.

Monumenta Asiae minoris antiqua. London 1928ff. = MAMA.

Orientis Graeci inscriptiones selectae. Edited by Dittenberger, W. Leipzig 1903–5.

Patton, W. R., and Hicks, E. L. *The Inscriptions of Cos*. 1891.

Sylloge Inscriptionum Graecorum. Edited by Dittenberger, W. Leipzig 1898ff. 2nd ed. = *SIG*^{2}.

West, A. B. *Latin Inscriptions: Corinth, Results of Excavations VIII*, 2. Cambridge 1931.

CRITICAL LITERATURE

Aland, K. *Die Säuglingstaufe im NT und in der Alten Kirche*. TEH 85. München 1963^3.

Alfaric, P. *Die sozialen Ursprünge des Christentums*. Edited by G. Pätsch and M. Robbe. Darmstadt/Berlin 1963.

Alt, A. "Hellenistische Städte und Domänen in Galiläa." In *Kleine Schriften zur Geschichte des Volkes Israel*, II: 384–95. München 1953.

Andresen, C. *Die Kirchen der alten Christenheit*. Stuttgart/Berlin 1971.

Bardtke, J. "Der gegenwärtige Stand der Erforschung der in Palästina neu gefundenen hebräischen Handschriften: Die Rechtsstellung der Qumran-Gemeinde." *ThLZ* 86 (1961): 93–104.

Baron, S. W. *A Social and Religious History of the Jews*. 16 vols. Philadelphia 1952ff.

Barrett, C. K. "Cephas and Corinth." In *Abraham unser Vater: Festschrift für O. Michel*, edited by Betz, O.; Hengel, M.; and Schmidt, P. Leiden/Köln 1963, 1–12.

______. "Christianity at Corinth." *BJRL* 46 (1963/64): 269–97.

______. "Paul's Opponents in II Corinthians." *NTS* 17 (1971): 233–54.

______. "Things Sacrificed to Idols." *NTS* 11 (1964/65): 138–53.

Bartsch, H. W. "Der korinthische Missbrauch des Abendmahls: Zur Situation und Struktur von I Korinther 8—11." In *Entmythologisierende Auslegung: Aufsätze aus den Jahren 1940–1960*. Hamburg 1962, 169–83.

Batelaan, B. *De Sterken en Zwakken in de Kerk van Korinthe*. Wageningen 1942.

Bauer, W. *A Greek-English Lexicon of the New Testament and Other Early Christian Literature*. 5th ed. Eng. trans. W. F. Arndt and F. W. Gingrich, revised and augmented by F. W. Gingrich and F. W. Danker, 2nd ed. Chicago/London 1979.

______. "Jesus der Galiläer." In *Aufsätze und kleine Schriften*, 91–108, edited by Strecker, G. Tübingen 1967.

______. *Rechtgläubigkeit und Ketzerei im ältesten Christentum*. BHTh 10. Tübingen 1964^2. *Orthodoxy and Heresy in Earliest Christianity*. Edited and translated by Kraft, R. A., and Krodel, G. Philadelphia 1971.

Bibliography

Berger, P. *The Sacred Canopy: Elements of a Sociology of Religion*. Garden City, N.Y., 1967.

Berger, P., and Luckmann, T. *The Social Construction of Reality*. Garden City, N.Y., 1967.

Betz, H. D. *Der Apostel Paulus und die sokratische Tradition*. BHTh 45. Tübingen 1972.

Bienert, W. *Die Arbeit nach der Lehre der Bibel: Ein Beitrag zur evangelischen Sozialethik*. Stuttgart 1956².

Blinzler, J. "εἰσὶν εὐνοῦχοι: Zur Auslegung von Mt 9, 12." *ZNW* 48 (1957): 254–70.

Blümer, H. "Die römischen Privataltertümer." HAW VI, 2, 2 (1911).

Bömer, F. *Untersuchungen über die Religion der Sklaven in Griechenland und Rom*. 4 vols. AAWLM.G, 10. Mainz 1957ff.

Bohatec, J. "Inhalt und Reihenfolge der 'Schlagworte der Erlösungsreligion in 1 Kor 1:26–31." *ThZ* 4 (1948): 252–71.

Bolkestein, H. *Wohltätigkeit und Armenpflege im vorchristlichen Altertum*. Utrecht 1939 = Gröningen 1967.

Bornkamm, G. "Die Vorgeschichte des sogenannten zweiten Korintherbriefes." In SHAW.PH (1961), Klasse 2. Résumé in English: "The History of the Origin of the So-called Second Letter to the Corinthians." *NTS* 8 (1962): 258–64.

———. "Lord's Supper and Church in Paul." In *Early Christian Experience*, 123–60. New York 1969.

Brandon, S. G. F. *Jesus and the Zealots*. Manchester 1967.

Braun, H. *Spätjüdisch-häretischer und frühchristlicher Radikalismus*. BHTh 24. Tübingen 1957.

Brockmeyer, N. *Sozialgeschichte der Antike*. Stuttgart 1972.

Broneer, O. "The Apostle Paul and the Isthmian Games." *BA* 25 (1962): 1–31.

———. "Corinth. Center of Saint Paul's Missionary Work in Greece." *BA* 14 (1951): 78–96.

———. "Paul and the Pagan Cults at Isthmia." *HThR* 64 (1971): 169–84.

Buchanan, G. W. "Jesus and the Upper Class." *NT* 7 (1964/65): 195–209.

Bultmann, R. *Exegetische Probleme des zweiten Korintherbriefes*. Darmstadt 1963.

———. *History of the Synoptic Tradition*. New York 1963.

Cadbury, H. J. "Erastus of Corinth." *JBL* 50 (1931): 42–58.

Carcopino, J. *Daily Life in Ancient Rome*. New Haven 1940.

Colpe, C. "Der Begriff 'Menschensohn' und die Methode der Erforschung messianischer Prototypen." *Kairos* 14 (1972): 241–57.

Conzelmann, H. *A Commentary on the First Epistle to the Corinthians* (Hermeneia—A Critical and Historical Commentary on the Bible). Philadelphia 1975.

———. *The History of Primitive Christianity*. Nashville 1973.

Coune, M. "Le problème des idolothytes et l'éducation de la syneidêsis." *RSR* 51 (1963): 497–534.

Dahl, N. A. "Der Epheserbrief und der verlorene erste Brief des Paulus an die Korinther." In *Abraham unser Vater: Festschrift für O. Michel*. Edited by Betz, O.; Hengel, M.; and Schmidt, P. Leiden/Köln 1963, 65–77.

———. "Paul and the Church at Corinth According to 1 Corinthians i 10—iv 21." In *Christian History and Interpretation: Studies Presented to J. Knox*, edited by Farmer, W., et al., Cambridge 1967, 313–35 = Dahl, N. A., *Studies in Paul*, Minneapolis 1977, 40–61.

Dautzenberg, G. "Der Verzicht auf das apostolische Unterhaltsrecht: Eine exegetische Untersuchung zu I Kor. 9." *Bib*. 50 (1969): 212–32.

Deissmann, A. *Light from the Ancient East*. London 1927.

———. *Das Urchristentum und die unteren Schichten*. Göttingen 1908².

Delling, G. "Zur Taufe von 'Häusern' im Urchristentum." *NT* 7 (1965): 285–311.

Derrett, J. D. M. *Law in the New Testament*. Leiden 1971.

Dinkler, E. s.v. "Dura-Europas." *RGG*³, II, 290–92.

Dobschütz, E. von. *Christian Life in the Primitive Church*. New York 1904.

Ehrhardt, A. "Sakrament und Leiden." *EvTh* 7 (1947/48): 99–115.

———. "Social Problems of the Early Church." In *The Framework of the New Testament Stories*, 275–312. Manchester 1964.

Eisenhut, W. s.v. "Visceratio." PRE II 17, 351–53.

Eliade, M. *The Sacred and the Profane*. New York 1959.

———. "Significations du Mythe." In *Le Langage II*, Actes du XIIIe Congrès de Philosophie de Langage Française. Neuchâtel 1967, 165–79.

Farmer, W. R. "The Economic Basis of the Qumran Community." *ThZ* 11 (1955): 295–308; 12 (1956): 56–58.

Filson, R. V. "The Significance of the Early House Churches." *JBL* 58 (1939): 105–12.

Friedrich, G. "Die Gegner des Paulus im 2. Korintherbrief." In *Abraham unser Vater: Festschrift für O. Michel*, edited by Betz, O.; Hengel, M.; and Schmidt, P. Leiden/Köln 1963, 181–215.

Georgi, D. *Die Gegner des Paulus im 2. Korintherbrief: Studien zur religiösen Propaganda in der Spätantike*. WMANT 11. Neukirchen 1964.

Goldmann, L. "Die Soziologie der Literatur, Stand und Methodenprobleme." In *Literatursoziologie*, 85–113. Edited by Bark, J. Stuttgart 1974.

Goulder, M.D. "Characteristics of the Parables in the Several Gospels." *JThS* 19 (1968): 51–69.

Grant, F. C. *The Economic Background of the Gospels*. Oxford 1926.

Greeven, H. "Propheten, Lehrer, Vorsteher bei Paulus: Zur Frage der 'Ämter' im Urchristentum." *ZNW* 44 (1952/53): 1–43.

Gülzow, H. *Christentum und Sklaverei in den ersten drei Jahrhunderten*. Bonn 1969.

Güttgemanns, E. *Offene Fragen zur Formgeschichte des Evangeliums*. München 1971. Eng. trans. William G. Doty, *Candid Questions Concerning Gospel Form Criticism*. Pittsburgh 1979.

Haenchen, E. *The Acts of the Apostles*. Philadelphia/Oxford 1971.

Harnack, A. von. *The Mission and Expansion of Christianity in the First Three Centuries*. 2 vols. New York 1905, 1908[2].

Heinrich, K. "Die Funktion der Genealogie im Mythos." In *Parmenides und Jona*. Frankfurt 1966, 9–28.

Heinrici, G. "Zum genossenschaftlichen Charakter der paulinischen Christengemeinden." *ThStKr* 54 (1881): 505–24.

———. "Die Christengemeinde Korinths und die religiösen Genossenschaften der Griechen." *ZWTh* 19 (1876): 465–562.

Hengel, M. "Das Gleichnis von den Weingärtnern Mc 12, 1–12 im Lichte der Zenopapyri und der rabbinischen Gleichnisse." *ZNW* 59 (1968): 1–39.

———. *Judaism and Hellenism*. 2 vols. Philadelphia/London 1974.

———. "Maria Magdalena und die Frauen als Zeugen." In *Abraham unser Vater: Festschrift für O. Michel*, edited by Betz, O.; Hengel, M.; and Schmidt, P. Leiden/Köln 1963, 243–56.

———. *Die Zeloten: Untersuchungen zur jüdischen Freiheitsbewegung in der Zeit von Herodes I bis 70 n. Chr.* Leiden 1961.

Herzog, R. *Die Wunderheilungen von Epidauras*. *Ph.S* XXII, 3. Leipzig 1931.

Hitchcock, F. R. "Who are 'the people of Chloe' in I Cor. 1:11?" *JThS* 25 (1923): 163–67.

Höfler, A. *Der Saraphishymnus des Aelios Aristeides*. Tübinger Beiträge zur Altertumswissenschaft 27. Stuttgart/Berlin 1935.

Holl, K. "Das Fortleben der Volkssprachen in Kleinasien in nachchristlicher Zeit." In *Gesammelte Aufsätze* II. Tübingen 1928, 238–48.

———. "Der Kirchenbegriff des Paulus im seinem Verhältnis zu dem der Urgemeinde." In *Gesammelte Aufsätze* II. Tübingen 1928, 44–67.

Holm, S. "Mythos und Symbol." *ThLZ* 93 (1968): 561–72.

Hurd, J. C. *The Origin of I Corinthians*. London 1965.

Jeremias, J. *Jerusalem in the Time of Jesus*. Philadelphia/London 1969.

———. *The Origins of Infant Baptism*. SHT 1. London 1963.

Jones, A. H. M. *The Cities of the Eastern Roman Provinces*. Oxford 1937.

———. *The Greek City from Alexander to Justinian*. Oxford 1940.

———. "The Urbanization of Palestine." *JRS* 21 (1931): 78–85.

Judge, E. A. *The Social Pattern of Christian Groups in the First Century: Some Prolegomena to the Study of New Testament Ideas of Social Obligation*. London 1960.

Käsemann, E. "Die Legitimität des Apostels." *ZNW* 41 (1942): 33–71.

———. "The Pauline Doctrine of the Lord's Supper." In *Essays on New Testament Themes*, SBT 41. London 1964, 108–35.

———. "A Pauline Version of the 'Amor Fati.'" In *New Testament Questions of Today*. Philadelphia/London 1969, 217–35.

Kahrstedt, U. *Das wirtschaftliche Gesicht Griechenlands in der Kaiserzeit: Kleinstadt, Villa und Domäne*. Dissertationes Berneses I, 7. Bern 1954.

Kasting, H. *Die Anfänge der urchristlichen Mission*. München 1969.

Keck, L. "The Poor Among the Saints in Jewish Christianity and Qumran." *ZNW* 57 (1966): 54–68.

———. "The Poor Among the Saints in the New Testament." *ZNW* 56 (1965): 100–137.

Kehnscherper, G. "Der Apostel Paulus als römischer Bürger." In TU = *Studia Evangelia* II. Berlin 1964, 411–40.

Kippenberg, H. G. "Versuch einer soziologischen Verortung des antiken Gnostizismus." *Numen* 17 (1970): 211–31.

Klausner, J. *Jesus of Nazareth: His Life, Times and Teaching*. New York 1929.

Knopf. R. "Über die soziale Zusammensetzung der ältesten heidenschristlichen Gemeinde." *ZThK* 10 (1900): 325–47.

Köhler, E. "Über die Möglichkeiten historisch-soziologischer Interpretation." In *Espirit und arkadische Freiheit*. Frankfurt 1966, 83–103 = *Methoden der deutschen Literaturwissenschaft*, edited by Zmegac, V. Frankfurt 1972, 227–48.

König, R. s.v. "Anomie." In *Fischer-Lexikon Soziologie*. Frankfurt 1958, 17–25.

Kornemann, E. s.v. "Collegium." PRE 7, 380–480.

Kubitschek, J. s.v. "Aedilis." PRE 1, 448–68.

Kümmel, W. G. *Introduction to the New Testament*. Rev. ed. Nashville 1975.

Küss, O. *Paulus: Die Rolle des Apostels in der theologischen Entwicklung der Urkirche*. In *Auslegung und Verkundigung*, III. Regensburg 1971.

Kuhn, K. G., and Stegemann, H. s.v. "Proselyten." PRE.Suppl. 9, 1248–83.

Landvogt, P. "Epigraphische Untersuchungen über den οἰκονόμος: Ein Beitrag zum hellenistischen Beamtenwesen." Diss. Strasbourg 1908.

Langerbeck, K. "Zur Auseinandersetzung von Theologie und Gemeindeglauben in der römischen Gemeinde in den Jahren 135–165." In *Aufsätze zur Gnosis*, AAWG.PH 3, 96. Göttingen 1967, 167–79.

Larsen, J. A. O. "Roman Greece." In *An Economic Survey of Ancient Rome IV*, edited by Frank, T. Baltimore 1938, 259–498.

Laum, B. *Stiftungen in der griechischen und römischen Antike*. 2 vols. Aalen 1964.

Leach, E., ed. *The Structural Study of Myth and Totemism*. London 1967.

Lévi-Strauss, C. "The Story of Asdiwal," in Leach, *Structural Study* (above), 1–47.

———. "The Structural Study of Myth." In *Structural Anthropology*, Garden City, N.Y., 1967, 206–31.

Liebenam, W. *Städteverwaltung im römischen Kaiserreich*. Leipzig 1900.

Liechtenhan, R. "Paulus als Judenmissionar." *Jud*. 2 (1949): 56–70.

Lietzmann, H. *An die Korinther I/II*. HNT 9. Tübingen 1949^4.

———. *Petrus und Paulus in Rom*. Berlin/Leipzig 1927^2.

Linton, R. "Nativistic Movements," *American Anthropologist* 45 (1943): 230–40.

McDonald, W. A. "Archaeology and Saint Paul's Journey in Greek Lands. Part III: Corinth." *BA* 4 (1942): 36–48.

Maier, F. G. *Die Verwandlung der Mittelmeerwelt*. Fischer Weltgeschichte 9. Frankfurt 1968.

Maly, K. *Mündige Gemeinde*. Stuttgart 1967.

Manson, T. W. "The Corinthian Correspondence I." In *Studies in the Gospels and Epistles*. Manchester 1962, 190–209.

Marquardt, J. "Das Privatleben der Römer." In *Handbuch der römischen Altertümer*, edited by Marquardt, J., and Momsen, T. Leipzig 1886. = Marquardt, J. "La Vie privée des Romains." In *Manuel des antiquités romaines*, Eng. trans. M. G. Humbert. Paris 1888–1907.

Marx, K. "Introduction to the Critique of Hegel's Philosophy of Right." In *Early Writings*, Eng. trans. T. B. Bottomore. New York 1963, 41–59.

Mauer, Ch. "Grund und Grenze apostolischer Freiheit: Exegetisch-theologische Studie zu I. Korinther 9." In *Antwort: K. Barth zum 70 Geburtstag*. Zurich 1956, 630–41.

Meeks, W. A. "The Image of the Androgyne: Some Uses of a Symbol in Earliest Christianity." *HR* 13 (1974): 165–208.

———. "The Man from Heaven in Johannine Sectarianism." *JBL* 91 (1972): 44–72.

Meyer, R. *Der Prophet aus Galiläa*. Leipzig 1940 = Darmstadt 1970.

Miller, F. *The Roman Empire and Its Neighbors*. New York 1967.

Moffatt, J. "Discerning the Body." *ET* 30 (1918/19): 19–23.

Mommsen, T. "Die Rechtsverhältnisse des Apostels Paulus." *ZNW* 2 (1901): 81–96.

Moulton, J. H., and Milligan, G. *The Vocabulary of the Greek Testament*. London 1963².

Mühlmann, W. E. *Chiliasmus und Nativismus*. Berlin 1961.

———. "Okzident und Orient." In *Homo Creator*. Wiesbaden 1962, 409–48.

———. "Umrisse und Probleme einer Kulturanthropologie." In *Homo Creator*, 107–29. = *Kulturanthropologie*. Edited by Mühlmann, W. E., and Müller, E. W. Köln/Berlin 1966, 15–49.

Munz, P. "The Problem of 'Die soziologische Verortung des antiken Gnostizismus.'" *Numen* 19 (1972): 44–51.

Neuenzeit, P. *Das Herrenmahl. Studien zur Paulinischen Eucharistieauffassung*. StANT 1. München 1960.

Oehler, J. s.v. "'Αργυροταμίας." PRE 2, 802. Stuttgart 1896ff.

Overbeck, F. Über die Anfänge der Patristischen Literatur," *HZ* 48 (1892) 417–72. = Darmstadt 1966.

Paoli, U. E. *Das Leben im alten Rom*. Bern/München 1961².

Pakozdy, L. M. "Die wirtschaftliche Hintergrund der Gemeinschaft von Qumran." In *Qumran-Probleme*, edited by Bardtke, H. Berlin 1963, 167–91.

Preisigke, F. *Wörterbuch der griechischen Papyrusurkunden*. Berlin 1925.

Ranowitsch, A. B. "Das Urchristentum und seine historische Rolle." In *Aufsätze zur Alten Geschichte*. Berlin 1961, 135–65.

Rauer, M. *Die "Schwachen" in Korinth und Rom nach den Paulusbriefen*. BSt(F) 21, 2–3. Freiburg 1923.

Reitzenstein R. *The Hellenistic Mystery-Religions*. Pittsburgh 1978.

Ricoeur, P. *The Conflict of Interpretations*. Evanston 1974.

———. *Freud and Philosophy: An Essay on Interpretation*. New Haven 1970.

———. *The Symbolism of Evil*. New York 1967.

Robbe, M. *Der Ursprung des Christentums*. Leipzig/Jena 1967.

Roos, A. G. "De titulo quodam latino nuper reperto." *Mn.* 58 (1930): 160–65.

Rostovtzeff, M. *Social and Economic History of the Roman Empire.* 2 vols. Oxford 1957².

Rydbeck, L. *Fachprosa, vermeintliche Volkssprache und Neues Testament.* Uppsala 1967.

Sawyer, W. T. "The Problem of Meat Sacrificed to Idols in the Corinthian Church." Dissertation, The Southern Baptist Theological Seminary 1968.

Schalit, A. "Herodes und seine Nachfolger." *Kont.* 3 (1966): 34–42.

———. *König Herodes.* SJ 4. Berlin 1969.

Scheler, M. *Die Wissensformen und die Gesellschaft.* Bern/München 1960².

Schmidbauer, W. *Mythose und Psychologie. Methodische Probleme, aufgezeigt an der Ödipus-Sage.* München/Basel 1970.

Schmithals, W. *Gnosticism in Corinth.* Nashville 1971.

———. "Paulus und der historische Jesus." *ZNW* 53 (1962): 145–60.

Schrage, W. *Die konkreten Einzelgebote in der paulinischen Paränese.* Gütersloh 1961.

Schürer, E. *Geschichte des jüdischen Volkes.* Leipzig 1907⁴. = *The History of the Jewish People in the Age of Jesus Christ (175 B.C.–A.D. 135).* Edinburgh 1886–90. New Eng. version, revised and edited by Vermes, G., and Millar, F. Edinburgh 1973–1979.

Schumacher, R. *Die soziale Lage der Christen im apostolischen Zeitalter.* Paderborn 1924.

Sherwin-White, A. N. *Roman Society and Roman Law in the New Testament.* Oxford 1963. = Grand Rapids 1976.

Smith, M. "Prolegomena to a Discussion of Aretalogies, Divine Men, the Gospels and Jesus." *JBL* 90 (1971): 174–99.

Soden, H. von. "Sakrament und Ethik bei Paulus." In *Urchristentum und Geschichte.* Tübingen 1951, 239–75. = *Das Paulusbild in der neueren deutschen Forschung.* Edited by Rengstorf, K. H. Darmstadt 1969, 339–79. Abridged Eng. trans. in *The Writings of St. Paul.* Edited by Meeks, W. A. New York 1972, 257–68.

Stein, A. "Wo trugen die korinthischen Christen ihre Rechtshändel aus?" *ZNW* 59 (1968): 86–90.

Stengel, P. "Die griechischen Kultusaltertümer." HAW V, 3 (1920³)., 106ff.

Strobel, A. "Der Begriff des 'Hauses' im griechischen und römischen Privatrecht." *ZNW* 56 (1965): 91–100.

Tcherikover, V. A. "Was Jerusalem a 'Polis'?" *IEJ* 14 (1964): 61–78.

Theissen, G. "Theoretische Probleme religionssoziologischer Forschung und die Analyse des Urchristentums." *NZSTh* 16 (1974): 35–56.

Topitsch, E. *Vom Ursprung und Ende der Metaphysik*. Wien 1958.

Troeltsch, E. *Aufsätze zur Geistesgeschichte und Religionssoziologie*. *Gesammelte Schriften* 4. Edited by Baron, H. Tübingen 1925.

———. *The Social Teaching of the Christian Churches*. New York 1931.

Ven. F. v. d. *Sozialgeschichte der Arbeit*. Bd. I, *Antike und Frühmittelalter*. München 1971.

Vittinghoff, F. *Römische Kolonisation und Bürgerrechtspolitik unter Caesar und Augustus*. AAWLM.G 14. Mainz 1951.

Waele, F. J. de. *Corinthe et Saint Paul*. Les antiquités de la Grèce. Paris 1961.

———. "Die korinthischen Ausgrabungen 1928–1929." *Gn*. 6 (1930): 52–7.

———. *Mededeelingen v.h. Nederland. histor. Institut de Rom* 9 (1929): 40–48.

———. Review of R. Carpenter, *Ancient Corinth*. In *Gn*. 10 (1934): 223–30.

Wallace, R. F. "Revitalization Movements," *American Anthropologist* 58 (1956): 264–81.

Weber, M. *Gesammelte Aufsätze zur Religionssoziologie*. 3 vols. Tübingen 1963[5].

———. *The Sociology of Religion*. Boston 1963.

Weigand, P. "Zur sogenannten 'Oikosformel.' " *NT* 6 (1963): 49–74.

Weiss, J. *Der erste Korintherbrief*. Göttingen 1910.

———. *The History of Primitive Christianity*. 2 vols. New York 1937 = *Earliest Christianity: A History of the Period A.D. 30–150*. 2 vols. New York 1959.

Wheelwright, P. "The Semantic Approach to Myth." In *Myth: A Symposium*, 95–103, edited by Seboek, T. A. Bloomington 1958.

Wilcken, U. *Griechische Ostraka aus Aegypten und Nubien: Ein Beitrag zur antiken Wirtschaftsgeschichte*. München 1899 = Amsterdam 1970.

Wilckens, U. *Weisheit and Torheit*. Tübingen 1959.

Wilson, R. McL. "How Gnostic were the Corinthians?" *NTS* 19 (1972); 65–74.

Windisch, H. *Der zweite Korintherbrief*. Göttingen 1924.